大学高级英语系列教材
英语专业研究型系列教材
总主编　武光军

新编汉英翻译教程

A New Coursebook on Chinese-English Translation

武光军　编　著

中国人民大学出版社
·北京·

编写说明

根据编者观察，当前大学汉英翻译教材存在如下问题：1）在编写思路方面，目前的大学汉英翻译教材大都没有按照实际的翻译过程编写，而是按词—句—篇的思路编写；2）版式不够生动，没有做到用户友好（user-friendly）；3）翻译练习多以文学翻译为主，而不是真实的翻译任务，实际上，学生本科毕业后从事的翻译主要是非文学类的；4）集中主要篇幅讲解翻译技巧，忽视了翻译策略层面的教学；5）忽视汉译英作为译入二语的过程及标准的讲述；6）未跟上翻译职业的时代发展，如新题材、网页的翻译及翻译学科的发展（如英国翻译名家Mora Baker的翻译教程*In Other Words*第2版添加了"搭配"与"伦理"两章）；7）大多数教材的写作方法是规定性的，而不是描写性的。

基于以上观察，本教材采取了创新的编写理念与编写思路，主要有以下两大特点：1）在教学内容上，增加了翻译的基本理论和基本知识模块，并基于最新的翻译研究成果，做到科研反哺于教学，使翻译教学与翻译科研相融。翻译研究是日新月异的，每过一段时间我们的研究就会加深对翻译现象的认识。没有翻译科研支撑的翻译教学是无源之水，流淌不远；不能反哺于教学的翻译科研也是无本之木，难以长久。翻译教材应是翻译科研与翻译教学的最佳结合点，因此在翻译教材的编写中，我们要使翻译科研与翻译教学真正融合。2）在教学程序上，基于翻转课堂模式，提出翻转教材理念，即先进行翻译理论、翻译知识的讲解，然后进行语篇翻译实践，最后才讲解翻译策略与翻译技巧。也就是说，应先让学生了解翻译的整体面貌，知道翻译的大体样子、正确的翻译理念、翻译的标准、翻译的学习方式等，然后再进行翻译实践。我们认为这种自上而下（top-down）的翻译学习方式更符合翻译学习的基本规律，也更有效，会防止学生走盲人摸象、以偏概全的弯路。同时，这种翻转教材理念也符合当今全球高等教育发展的最新趋势。

本教程分上、下两编，上编主要包括：第一章 汉英翻译的基本知识、第二章 汉英翻译的过程、第三章 汉英翻译语篇实践；下编主要包括：第四章 汉英翻译的主要策略、第五章 汉英翻译常见错误例析、第六章 汉英翻译名家经验谈。

当然，也有老师和学生偏爱传统的汉译英教学模式。通过调整顺序，也可使用本教程，即先讲第四、五、六章，然后再讲第一、二、三章。

本书中的部分照片来自百度等，“第六章 汉英翻译名家经验谈”引用了程镇球、王弄笙、刘士聪等翻译名家的文章，在此一并致谢。

编 者

2018 年 5 月

目 录
CONTENTS

上编

下编

上 编

第一章 汉英翻译的基本知识

第一节 "翻译"的由来

根据《翻译文化史论》(王克非，1997：1)，"翻译"二字由来的简单历史如下：翻译之事，由来已久，古籍中早有记载。《礼记·王制》篇中说，中国"五方之民，言语不通，嗜欲不同，达其志，通其欲……北方曰译"。之后，佛教译者在"译"字前加上"翻"字，遂有"翻译"一词，沿用至今。

香港学者孔慧怡(2005)在《重写翻译史》中对"译""翻""翻译"三个词的由来进行了更为详尽的考察。在我国历史上，"译""翻""翻译"这三个词并不是同时出现的，而是有先后顺序，其顺序为："译"→"翻"→"翻译"。以下是孔慧怡(2005：19-23)对"译""翻""翻译"这三个词溯源的部分摘录。

"译"

有关中国古代翻译活动的记载，现有的翻译史书和资料都溯源至周代政府的对外事务，而最常引用的文献是《周礼》和《礼记》。其中"译"字作为政府外事工作的一部分，《礼记》列为职官编制的一种："五方之民，言语不通，嗜欲不同，达其志，通其欲，东方曰寄，南方曰象，西方曰狄鞮，北方曰译。"

在古籍之中，"译"字用来代表各种翻译活动和方法，既可以指笔译，也可以指口译；既可以指译音，也可以指译义。我们到底如何理解活动的详情，只能看上下文来判断。以"译"字覆盖不同翻译活动和不同翻译方式，不但不足以应付比较深入的讨论或技术性的叙事要求，而且如果翻译活动兴盛，"译"字作为名词、动词、职衔或工作人员不断在文中出现，就会破坏行文的流畅(此乃主流文化的大忌)。在主流文化并不关注外来事物的情况下，大而化之的"译"字不会让一般人感到有不足之处，但一旦翻译活动在某种层面或某种圈子里产生量和质的变化，引起较深入和带有技术性讨论的需要时，一个多功能的"译"字就不足以应付了。中文出现另一个代表语际转换的字——“翻”——也正是这个原因。

“翻”

“翻”字用作翻译的意思，起源于中国第一次大型文化翻译运动——佛经汉译。它和“译”字有两点重要的分别：1. 不作名词使用；2. 只代表译义，不代表译音。这两点都显示，“翻”字着眼于语际转换过程，特别是语意的传达。玄奘所说的“五不翻”，最能显示“翻”与“译”的分别：“不翻”，就是不译义，只译音或写音。由此“翻”字专指译义，显而易见。

“翻”字进入主流，是隋代的事，虽然仍然只用于佛经翻译活动，但随着政府致力监管佛教事务，佛教词汇也因此纳入官方语言，最好的例子莫如隋代政府所设的“翻经院”；此名唐代也沿用。还有隋代“翻经学士”，唐代“翻经大德”等头衔。这都说明，就佛教领域而言，“翻”字作为语际转换的动词已确立了。通过政府与佛教的种种关系，到了唐代，“翻”字的使用量明显提高，不但和“译”字达到相辅相成的程度，而且在佛学圈中有时比“译”字用得更多。

“翻译”

“翻译”一词在主要佛教典籍中出现，似乎以《出三藏记集》为先，但全书只见此词一次。比《出三藏记集》成书稍晚的《高僧传》(成书约在530年),不但以“翻”字代表翻译的次数较《出三藏记集》多，而且也较多用上“翻译”这个双音节词，总数共8次。例如：“舍利弗阿毗云，以伪秦弘始九年出书梵书文，至十六年翻译方竟。”

至于，“翻译”这个双音节词如何逐渐脱离佛学范围，进入汉语主流，我们可以用二十五史为探讨的基础。下面列出“翻译”在各朝断代史出现的条目数字：《隋书》: 2；《旧唐书》: 8；《宋史》: 1；《元史》: 3；《明史》: 1；《清史稿》: 83。

二十五史在《隋唐》以前未见“翻译”一词，此词进入汉语主流在隋、唐之世。由此可见,《隋书》及《唐书》中所有用“翻译”一词的地方，都和佛经翻译有关，而政府翻译事务则只用“译”字。但到了《元史》,“翻译”就不再限于佛学了。例如元代翰林学士阿鄰帖本儿“善国书”(即蒙古文),“翻译诸经”(指儒家经典)；资善大夫“鲁直班则为翻译”(指在元代儒家经筵为皇帝充当传译)，可见“翻译”一词已推展到佛学以外的范围，而且用以代表笔译和口译两种工作。

到了清代，“翻译”一词已完全确立，既用作动词，亦用作名词，政府官员和外国驻华使馆译者都以“翻译”为职衔，是其站稳主流地位的最佳佐证；而“翻译”一词在《清史稿》的出现频率激增，更是此词在20世纪占领主流位置的好证明。

由此可见，“翻译”二字在我国历史上有着上千年的漫长演化史。“翻译”二字最早出现于佛教翻译中，到了清代才完全确立为今天我们所称的翻译的统称。了解“翻译”二字在我国的历史发展，将有利于我们正确理解我国语境下的翻译内涵。特别是“翻”字着眼于语际转换，尤其强调语意的传达，更应引起我们的重视。

此外，我国著名学者钱钟书先生（1985：2）在《林纾的翻译》一文中也讨论了“译”的来源，现摘录如下：

> 汉代文字学者许慎有一节关于翻译的训诂，义蕴颇为丰富。《说文解字》卷六《口》部第二十六字：“囮，译也。从‘口’，‘化’声。率鸟者系生鸟以来之，名曰‘囮’，读若‘譌’。”南唐以来，“小学”家都申说“译”就是“传四夷及鸟兽之语”，好比“鸟媒”对“禽鸟”所施的引“诱”，“譌”、“讹”、“化”和“囮”是同一个字。“译”“诱”“媒”“讹”“化”这些一脉通连、彼此呼应的意义，组成了研究诗歌语言的人所谓“虚涵数意”(manifold meaning)，把翻译能起的作用（“诱”）、难于避免的毛病（“讹”）、所向往的最高境界（“化”），仿佛一一透示出来了。

在此，钱钟书先生不仅探索了《说文解字》中“译”的意义，而且更重要的是，还由此阐发了翻译能起的作用（“诱”）、难于避免的毛病（“讹”）和所向往的最高境界（“化”）。当然，钱钟书先生在此所讲的主要是文学翻译。

综上所述，我们可以看出，“翻译”二字有着丰富的文化内涵，并不仅仅限于我们通常所说的直译和意译，还应包括各种形式的摘译、编译等。因此，翻译也不仅仅是语言文字的转换，更重要的是其作为文化沟通和交流的桥梁。

练习题：

1. 查阅英语中 translation 的词汇来源及具体含义。
2. 思考并总结你所理解的“翻译”二字的含义，特别是“汉译英”的含义。

第二节 汉英翻译简史

1275 年，意大利旅行家马可·波罗来到中国，遍游中国各地。回国后，由他人整理出版了《马可·波罗游记》一书。根据谭载喜（2000：196）的考察，这是西方第一部以第一手材料介绍中国的著作；可以说，西方在较大范围内对中国文化的研究，是从这个时候开始的。到了 16 世纪末，中国作品开始被人译入西方。据马祖毅在《中国翻译简史》中的考察，现存最早的中国书西译本是罗明坚（Michael Ruggieri, 1543–1607）译成西班牙语的《明心宝鉴》（马祖毅，1998：298）。早期的汉籍外译的译者主要是耶稣会士。虽然他们最初都是欧洲各殖民帝国的先遣队，但在当时中国与欧洲正处于相互隔绝的状态下，耶稣会士竟成了中西两大文明交流的中间人（马祖毅，1998：302）。

下面，我们将从中国哲学、社会科学著作的英译、中国文学著作的英译及中国自然科学著作的英译三个方面简述我国的汉英翻译简史及我国汉籍外译的影响。

在中国哲学、社会科学著作的英译方面，最重要的当推中国儒家经典的英译，即“四书”（包括《大学》《中庸》《论语》《孟子》）和“五经”（包括《诗》《书》《礼》《易》《春秋》）的英译。在“四书”“五经”中，《论语》最具代表性，不仅在中国影响深远，而且在世界范围内产生了广泛的影响。目前，《论语》已被译入六十多种语言，其中英译本的数量最多。据李钢（2012）的考察，《论语》最早的英译本出现在17世纪末，是从拉丁文转译而来。目前尚存的早期《论语》英译本有1809年在印度传教的英国人马歇曼（Joshuma Marshman, 1768—1837）翻译的 *The Works of Confucius* 第一卷。此后，上百位西方传教士、西方汉学家和海内外华人都翻译过《论语》。在经书中，《诗经》和《易经》的英译本较多。

“四书”“五经”的英译首先主要是由明清来华传教的耶稣会士完成的。在19世纪至20世纪早期，西方出现了许多优秀的汉学家和翻译家。在儒家经典的英译方面，我们不得不提的是赫赫有名的英国第一代汉学家和翻译家理雅各。理雅各 (James Legge，1815—1897) 是一位杰出的来华传教士和汉学家，他出生于英国苏格兰的一个非国教家庭，于1835年获得阿伯丁国王学院文学硕士学位，在加入基督教公理会后，曾一度进入伦敦的海伯里神学院学习神学。此时理雅各便萌生了到国外做传教士的想法，21岁时，理雅各便向伦敦会提出申请，于1838年加入伦敦会，在伦敦会的安排下，理雅各师从伦敦大学的汉学教授基德（Samuel Kidd）开始学习汉语，不久理雅各便在伦敦会的派遣下赴马六甲出任英华书院院长。在此过程中，理雅各不但未中断汉语学习，还将一些基督教资料翻译成中文，并且立志要将中国的“十三经”翻译成英文。1842年《南京条约》使得英国对香港实行殖民统治，次年，理雅各便将英华书院迁至香港，此后的30年里，理雅各曾因身体原因三次回国，除此之外都是在香港度过。在港期间，除了传教，理雅各还改革香港教育、出版报刊，但最引人瞩目的成绩莫过于对《中国经典》的翻译。理雅各于1858年制订了具体的翻译计划，经过20年不辞劳苦的工作，他的鸿篇巨制《中国经典》于香港发行第一版，于1861至1872年间陆续问世。《中国经典》分五卷共八本，分别为：卷一《论语》《大学》《中庸》（1861年）、卷二《孟子》（1861年）、卷三《书经》（两本，1865年）、卷四《诗经》（两本，1871年）、卷五《春秋左氏传》（两本，1872年）。《中国经典》译文的出版奠定了理雅各在汉学研究中的地位，使其成为首届儒莲中国文学国际奖的获得者，并为他赢得了牛津大学首任汉学教授的席位。之后理雅各离港赴职，无暇监督印刷事宜，因此卷六《易经》和卷七《礼记》未能收进《中国经典》，而是分别在1882年和1885年被收进缪勒（Max Muller）主编的《东方圣典》丛书。理雅各的英译以精确著称，至今仍被西方奉为“标准译本”。例如，1871理雅各《诗经》英译本正文之前的绪论长达182页之多，内容包括五章。第一章介绍孔子对《诗经》的贡献，理雅各对“孔子删诗”

说表示怀疑，并举出例证，说明在孔子之前《诗经》就已经编纂成集，而非司马迁所说的孔子以礼义为标准将《诗经》从3 000篇删定成了305篇，在他看来，孔子对《诗经》最大的贡献在于"让弟子了解学《诗》的重要性,并将其保存下来"（James Legge,1871: 7）。另外，理雅各还对"鲁诗"、"齐诗"、"韩诗"和"毛诗"四家诗进行了讨论，附录部分为理雅各从沈德潜《古诗源》中选取的43首古诗的译文；第二章介绍了《诗经》研究的历史，包括《诗经》的搜集以及传播、《诗经》的作者、诗序等问题，附录部分是理雅各翻译的大序（即《毛诗》在首篇《关雎》的"小序"之后，概论全经的大段文字）和小序（即列在各诗之前，解释各篇主题的文字）以及部分的《韩诗外传》，除此之外，还按著成时间顺序将《诗经》中的诗歌排列成表；第三章介绍了《诗经》的语言特色，对《诗经》的韵律、古汉语的发音和韵律种类进行了详细介绍，并对《诗经》的诗学价值和写作特点等问题进行探讨，附录中选译了各种格律的中国诗作为对照；第四章介绍了《诗经》时代的中国社会，包括周朝的疆域、政治、宗教以及社会现状，附录是法国汉学家毕奥（M. Edouard Biot）研究《诗经》中所描述的中国社会风俗的文章；第五章列举了参考书目，中文部分共55个条目，包括郑玄《毛诗故训传》、孔颖达《毛诗正义》、朱熹《诗集传》、康熙帝命王鸿绪等撰写的《钦定诗经传说汇纂》以及王韬手稿《毛诗集释》等等，此外还列举了《诗经》的其他语言译本以及相关研究资料。因此，可以说，理雅各翻译的《中国经典》是儒经英译至今仍无法逾越的一座高峰。

在中国文学著作的英译方面，我们将其分为两个阶段：一是我国古典文学的译介，二是我国现当代文学的译介。根据马祖毅、任荣珍（2003：223–225）的考察，在18世纪英国翻译的第一部中国古典小说是《好逑传》。同时，《好逑传》也是第一部传入欧洲的中国古典小说。实际上，英国《好逑传》的英译本并不是从中文原文直接翻译为英文的，而是由法文版转译过来的。《好逑传》是我国明末清初的白话长篇小说，共十八回。内容是写男女主人公铁中玉和水冰心不畏强暴、敢于抗争的侠义行为和婚姻故事。这本小说在我国当时并不属于名著，却被偶然地译介到了英国。由此可见，直到18世纪，中国文学在英语世界中的译介是非常落后和不严谨的。直到19世纪后半叶起，中国文学才从真正意义上被译介到英语世界。在这一时期，较早进行中国文学翻译的是剑桥大学的第二任汉学教授翟理斯（Herbert Allen Giles, 1845–1935）。1873年，翟理斯出版了第一部汉译英作品——《两首中国诗》（*Two Chinese Poems*），其中收录了韵体《三字经》和《千字文》的英译文。1878年，翟理斯完成了蒲松龄《聊斋志异》的选译工作。翟理斯翻译了其中164则故事，迄今为止，仍然是最全的一个英译本。1883年，翟理斯自费印刷了一本《古文选珍》（*Gems of Chinese Literature*）。在这本书中，翟理斯翻译了不同时期中国著名散文作家的散文片段。1898年10月，翟理斯又出版了一本《古今诗选》（*Chinese Poetry in English Verse*），其中选译了大量中国古诗。由于其杰出的翻译成就，翟理斯于1897年和1911年两度荣获法兰西学院儒莲奖。继理雅各和翟理斯之后，英国又培养出了第二代和第三代的汉学家和翻译大师，如阿瑟·韦利（Arthur Waley, 1888—1966)、霍克思（David

Hawkes, 1923—2009）等。阿瑟·韦利一生都未来过中国，但他翻译的《诗经》《西游记》《论语》《一百七十首中国诗》等在英语世界广泛流传。马祖毅、任荣珍（2003：229）总结了西方翻译界对这位多产的翻译家的评论，主要有三方面：一是他对所译作品的语言有很深的造诣；二是他对所译作品有透彻的研究；三是他对翻译工作热情极高。霍克思是阿瑟·韦利的学生，于20世纪50年代毕业于中国北京大学，能用中文写旧体诗词。霍克思最伟大的翻译成就是将我国的四大文学名著之一《红楼梦》第一次完整地译入了英语世界，改变了以往《红楼梦》的英译本只有节译的情况，让西方读者得以见其全貌。1973年至1980年，英国企鹅出版社出版了《红楼梦》全译五卷本，霍克思翻译了前三卷的八十回，后两卷的四十回由其女婿在其指导下翻译完成。在该英译本中，霍克思将书名改为了《石头记》(*The Story of the Stone*)。该英译本出版后立即受到普遍欢迎，并陆续再版，现已成为英语翻译文学的经典之一。《泰晤士报教育增刊》认为霍克思的译本是当代最佳英文译作之一（马祖毅、任荣珍，2003：267）。2009年10月9日，时任中国驻英国大使傅莹在《人民日报》发表《忆霍克思先生》一文，指出"他将中国人民最钟爱的古典小说以通俗易懂的方式引荐给西方读者，为中英两国人民架起一座文化沟通的桥梁，他的贡献将永为世人铭记"。在19世纪末至20世纪，美国翻译中国古典文学作品的主要成就在诗歌方面。美国翻译中国古典诗词的第一部诗集是庞德(Ezra Pound, 1885–1972)翻译的《华夏集》(*Cathay*)。在当时，庞德并不懂中文，其翻译的许多诗歌都经过了改写和加工，并保留了中国的异国情调。《华夏集》这本仅有18首诗的薄薄小册子，被人称为庞德本人对文学的"最持久的贡献"，在美国现代文学中总忘不了要提及这本书（马祖毅、任荣珍，2003：350）。1965年，美国"垮掉的一代"的著名诗人加里·斯奈德(Gary Snyder)出版了《砌石与寒山诗》(*Riprap and Cold Mountain Poems*)，向美国介绍了唐代僧人寒山的诗作。1981年，美国汉学家斯蒂芬·欧文（Stephen Owen）出版了《盛唐诗》(*The Great Age of Chinese Poetry: the High Tang*)。1986年，被誉为美国"翻译中国古典文学的泰山北斗"的波顿·沃森（Burton Watson）出版了其所编译的《中国诗选》(*The Columbia Book of Chinese Poetry: From Early Times to the Thirteenth Century*)。在此时期，中国的古典名著小说在美国也都有译介，但成就不如诗歌方面突出。美籍华裔翻译家王良志、王际真分别于1927年和1929年出版了《红楼梦》的节译本。1933年，美国女作家赛珍珠（Pearl Buck）出版了其翻译的《水浒传》，将书名改为了《四海之内皆兄弟》(*All Men Are Brothers*)。1937年，杰克逊（J. N. Jackson）也出版了其翻译的《水浒传》，书名为*The Water Margin*。1983年，美籍华裔学者余国藩出版的四卷英文版《西游记》，成为英语世界上第一个英文《西游记》全译本。在中国现当代文学的译介方面，美国译者的成就更为突出，特别是在小说翻译方面。在美国，我国作家鲁迅、老舍、萧红、钱钟书、茅盾、莫言、王蒙、余华、贾平凹、张洁等的作品都有译介。英国翻译的中国现当代作家有鲁迅、老舍、丁玲等。在中国现当代文学的译介方面，我们不能不提的一位译者就是美国汉学家葛浩文（Howard Goldblatt）。葛浩文是我国2012年诺贝尔文学奖得主莫言作品的英文译者，其翻译过萧红、陈若曦、白先勇、张洁、冯骥才、贾平凹、李锐、刘恒、苏童、老鬼、王朔、莫言、刘震云、虹影、阿来、朱天文、朱天心、姜戎等 20 多位名家的 50 多部作品。葛浩文被美国著名的中国小说评论家夏志清教授称为“公认的中国现代、当代文学之首席翻译家”。

相对于文学和社科作品的英译，我国自然科学著作的英译作品数量较少。明代宋应星所著《天工开物》可谓是中国 17 世纪的工艺百科全书，特别是在 17 世纪后半叶传入日本后影响较大。但直到 1966 年，美国宾州州立大学出版社才出版了该大学历史系任以都和她丈夫孙宋全译出的英文版《天工开物》，题目为：*Sung Ying-hsing's Tien-kung Kai-Wu, Chinese Technology in the Seventeenth Century*。20 世纪初，美国米尔斯（Ralph Mills）和伊博恩（Bernard Emms Read）教授翻译了我国的药物巨典《本草纲目》的一部分。此外，我国造纸技术、地理学、农学等方面的自然科学著作也有部分英译作品，但数量不多。

当然，中国国内也对汉籍英译作出了重要贡献。例如，在哲学和文学方面，辜鸿铭翻译了《论语》、林语堂翻译了《墨子》《老残游记》等、杨宪益与其夫人戴乃迭合译了《红楼梦》，许渊冲英译了唐宋诗词、张培基英译了当代散文，等等。在政治作品方面，我国翻译出版了《毛泽东选集》《周恩来选集》《邓小平文选》等。在自然科学著作方面，我国也英译了大量作品。在机构方面，新中国成立后，我国政府高度重视汉籍外译的出版。1978 年以前，国内从事外文书刊编译和发行的出版社仅有外文出版社和新世界出版社两家。1979 年后，我国先后成立了中国文学出版社、今日中国出版社等几十家出版社从事中文作品的英译工作。

根据马祖毅、任荣珍（2003），我国汉籍外译的影响主要有两方面。一是汉籍翻译对西方思潮的影响。我国大量典籍的外译对西方的启蒙思想家都产生了广泛的影响，如德国的莱布尼茨、法国的孟德斯鸠、伏尔泰等都认识到中国文化和中国思想的价值，并从中吸取养料。19 世纪的英国生物学家达尔文还在其《物种起源》等著作中引用了多条有关中国的资料，来证实其生物进化论。二是汉籍外译在世界文学领域内产生的影响。德国诗人歌德和席勒是最早发现和推崇中国文学的西方文学家。歌德在读了《好逑传》后便为中国古老的文明所倾倒。在英语世界，庞德所译的《华夏集》对美国意象派诗歌的创作产生了决定性影响。20 世纪中叶，唐代僧人寒山的诗歌的译介在美国也曾掀起了一股“寒山热”，引来美国“垮掉的一代”的诗人纷纷效仿。

理雅各

理雅各（James Legge，1815—1897）是近代英国著名汉学家，曾任香港英华书院校长，伦敦布道会传教士。他是第一个系统研究、翻译中国古代经典的人，从 1861 年到 1886

年的25年间，将“四书”“五经”等中国主要典籍全部译出，共计28卷。当他离开中国时，已是著作等身。理雅格的多卷本《中国经典》、《法显行传》、《中国的宗教：儒教、道教与基督教的对比》和《中国编年史》等著作在西方汉学界占有重要地位。他与法国学者顾赛芬、德国学者卫礼贤并称汉籍欧译三大师，他本人也是第一个儒莲翻译奖的获得者。

艾兹拉·庞德（Ezra Pound，1885年10月30日—1972年11月1日）是美国著名诗人、文学家，意象主义诗歌的主要代表人物。庞德还是一个热衷于介绍中国古典诗歌和哲学的翻译家，他自称为儒者。他改编并翻译了《华夏集》《诗经》《论语》等儒家经典。

庞德

葛浩文

葛浩文及其译作

Howard Goldblatt的中文名是葛浩文，美国著名的汉学家，是2012年诺贝尔文学奖得主莫言作品的英文译者。葛浩文出生于1939年，20世纪60年代服役期间在台湾学习汉语，后获得印第安纳大学中国文学博士学位，目前是英语世界地位最高的中国文学翻译家。他的翻译严谨而讲究，“让中国文学披上了当代英美文学的色彩”。葛浩文翻译了萧红、陈若曦、白先勇、李昂、张洁、杨绛、冯骥才、古华、贾平凹、李锐、刘恒、苏童、老鬼、王朔、莫言、刘震云、虹影、阿来、朱天文、朱天心、姜戎等20多位名家的50多部作品。

霍克思及其译作《红楼梦》

霍克思为著名的汉学家，年轻时即翻译《楚辞》(*The Songs of the South*)，其著作 *A Little Primer of Tu Fu* 更是极具权威且广为人知的唐诗翻译作品。而他的《红楼梦》译本 *The Story of the Stone* 更是身为翻译家的非凡成就。

杨宪益、戴乃迭及其译作《红楼梦》

杨宪益，1953年调任北京外文出版社翻译专家，曾与夫人戴乃迭（英籍中国文化学者）合作翻译中国古典小说《魏晋南北朝小说选》、《唐代传奇选》、《宋明平话小说选》、《聊斋选》、全本《儒林外史》以及全本《红楼梦》等，均先后由北京外文出版社出版。20世纪60年代初，杨宪益和戴乃迭夫妇开始翻译《红楼梦》，其间曾一度中断，最后于1974年完成，于1978—1980年由外文出版社分三卷出版，译文书名为 *A Dream of Red Mansions*。

韦利

阿瑟·韦利（Arthur Waley）是一位多产的翻译家，被称为没有到过中国的中国通。他对中国古典诗词的翻译尤其值得称道，他的翻译流畅优美，具体可见 *A Hundred and Seventy Chinese Poems, More Translations from the Chinese* 和 *The Book of Songs*。

辜鸿铭

辜鸿铭（1857 年 7 月 18 日—1928 年 4 月 30 日），字汤生，号立诚。祖籍福建省同安县，生于南洋英属马来西亚槟榔屿。学博中西，号称“清末怪杰”，精通英、法、德、拉丁、希腊、马来等 9 种语言，获 13 个博士学位，是清朝精通西洋科学、语言兼及东方华学的中国第一人。他翻译了中国“四书”中的三部——《论语》、《中庸》和《大学》，创获甚巨；并著有《中国的牛津运动》（原名《清流传》）和《中国人的精神》（原名《春秋大义》）等英文书，向西方人宣传东方的文化和精神，并产生了重大的影响。西方人曾流传一句话：到中国可以不看三大殿，不可不看辜鸿铭。

练习题：

1. 查阅理雅各英译的《论语》，并与汉语原文进行比较分析。
2. 查阅《红楼梦》霍克思和杨宪益两个英译本，选择书中的一回进行详细比较，并与汉语原文对比。

第三节 我国学生汉译英学习的基本性质：译入二语

在西方文化中，翻译的惯例是译入母语。译入外语（translating into a non-mother tongue），或称为逆向翻译（inverse translation）往往是一项值得怀疑的翻译活动，且人们认为其注定会失败。特别是对文学文本的翻译，西方的文化传统更是很难容忍译入外语的做法。这就是国际翻译界约定俗成的“母语原则”。

马士奎（2012）指出国际翻译界这一不成文的母语原则体现在两方面。一是一些行业组织和机构明确不承认非母语翻译的可行性。联合国教科文组织于 1976 年发布的关于依法保护译者和译作权利以及提高译者地位的建议（《内罗毕宣言》）主张“译者应尽可能将作品译入其母语或其有同等程度掌握的语言”。国际翻译家联盟在其网站上特别强调“职业译者应该从事译入母语的工作”。许多国家的翻译协会在其职业行为规范中明确要求成员译入自己的母语，除非译者真正拥有双语背景。在西方口译界，按照惯例，译员原则上只译入母语。英国著名的 Ask Translation 翻译公司对自己公司的介绍如下：

High quality professional translation services from one of the UK's leading translation services companies.

As one of the UK's leading translation companies we translate many millions of words every year between all major languages, and translate a broad spectrum of subjects.

Established in 1988, and with a quarter of a century's expertise and experience behind us our translation services are provided to the ISO9001 and EN15038 international standards.

We only use highly qualified mother tongue professional translators who translate into their native language. They are of the very highest standard, with a proven track record in their specialist translation field.

All of our translation services are handled by an experienced project management team, who will advise you and keep you informed of your project's status at all times. Quality, customer service and strict client confidentiality are our founding principles; which combined with the expertise of our staff and depth of our resources means that we can handle the most complex of translation projects in any language to almost any turnaround.

As you would expect from a company that started trading in 1988, we have a large in-house library of resources ensuring that our translation services always meet our customers' requirements.

Not only do **we only use mother tongue translators**, but unlike many of our competitors we aim to **perform translations in the countries where your work will be read**. Using translators who reside in the countries where the translation will be used helps to produce a higher calibre of translation, as residents inevitably have a better knowledge of the current nuances in language and culture in their country. For example, the vast majority of our French translation is performed by French translators who grew up speaking French as their first language, have English language or translation degrees, and are now resident in France.

To ensure consistency in future projects, we always aim to use the same translation team. Glossaries are routinely compiled and any necessary research is included as part of our translation service. Trados, Transit, SDLX and other CAT tools can also be used where applicable.

Translations requiring proofreading are carefully checked by a proofreader or second independent mother tongue translator prior to dispatch, not just for accuracy, spelling and grammar, but also for consistency in terminology.

Our interpreters have a wealth of experience and are highly qualified professionals, being affiliated to recognised professional bodies including the Institute of Translation and Interpreting and the Institute of Linguists.

We are confident that ASK's commitment to translation quality, service and long-term partnerships will make us an invaluable asset to your team, whatever type of translation service you require.

(http://www.translate.co.uk/translation.htm, accessed september 5, 2014)

从以上该翻译公司的介绍中，我们可以清楚地看到，该翻译公司明确指出仅聘用母语译者，且要求译员应生活在将使用译作的国家。

二是许多业内人士，包括欧美翻译、语言学和文学界一些学者否认非母语翻译行为的合理性，或者对此类译作的质量持怀疑态度。当中国现当代文学最杰出的翻译家葛浩文在被问及从母语译入外语与从外语译入母语这两种翻译形态哪一种更理想时，葛浩文的回答是："毫无疑问，译者理想的目标语言是自己的母语。总体而言，由中国译者把中国文学翻译成外语并不是最好的选择，而且也很难真正成功。"（孟祥春，2013：47）

那接下来的问题就是：既然国际翻译界的惯例是母语原则，那我国学生是否还可以学习汉译英，是否还可以做汉译英。

马士奎（2012：21）指出，"母语原则"在理论上无可厚非，但在翻译实践中却难以完全贯彻。因为这一原则明显忽视了非通用语言使用国的文化诉求，也与翻译实践的历史及现状不符。由于双方都有众多熟谙双方语言的人士，因此像德语、法语和英语间的互译一般不需要非母语翻译。但对于非主要语言来说，非母语翻译就成为了一种现实需要，因为现实中无法找到足够熟谙双方语言的人士。澳大利亚坎贝尔（Stuart Campbell，1998: 27）指出，在俄罗斯、挪威等国家找到足够的熟悉俄语、挪威语的英语本族人士是不切实际的。日本翻译协会的主席 William Lise 指出，几乎大部分的日译英作品都是由以英语作为外语的日本人完成的（Lise, 1997: 27）。在澳大利亚，根据其国家译员认证委员会（NATTI）的规章，许多译员可以进行译入母语和译入非母语的双向翻译。在北欧，各国绝大多数译者的工作以译出母语为主，如在丹麦，这一比例超过 90%。由此可见，非母语翻译并非个别现象，而是一种普遍的国际性现象。在我国，由于熟谙我国语言文化的英语母语人士远远不足，因此我国人士从事汉译英有着现实的必要性。孔慧怡（2000）对全国暑期英汉翻译高级讲习班学员的调查发现，90% 的学员在平时承接的翻译任务中需要同时应付中译外和外译中的双向翻译。马士奎（2012：24）指出，非母语翻译是弥补因语言和文化差异等因素导致的翻译不平衡现象的积极手段，其意义毋庸置疑，因此我们应该理性看待国内外部分学者针对我国对外翻译事业的质疑和批评。

但我们要谨记的是：译入二语与译入母语有着本质的差异，而不仅仅是翻译方向上的差异。在译入母语时，最大的困难是理解原文，因为母语的表达相对容易。但在译入二语时，对母语文本的理解相对容易，最大的困难则是避免出语法错误，并写出地道的目的语文本。在汉译英方面，也就是如何避免汉化英语（Chinglish）的问题。

联合国总部

1971 年 11 月 15 日，中华人民共和国代表团出席联大会议

1983 年，口译员陶见章和董叙林为大会做同声传译

1971年11月15日，以乔冠华为团长的中华人民共和国代表团正式出席联大会议，标志着中国在联合国合法地位的恢复，同时这也给联合国中文工作带来了新的机遇。

联合国为了储备人才，于1979年在北京外国语学院成立“联合国译员训练班”，由联合国提供经费、设备和教材，集中培训中文的笔译和口译人员。训练班学员在结训时参加联合国举行的严格考试。考试及格者列入名册，等候联合国征聘。这个训练班一直维持到20世纪90年代中期，造就了几百名年轻的高翻人员。今天在联合国各地中文单位任职的翻译人员大半出身这个训练班。

欧洲联盟，简称欧盟（EU），总部设在比利时首都布鲁塞尔（Brussels），是由欧洲共同体（European Community，又称欧洲共同市场，简称欧共体）发展而来的，初始成员国有6个，分别为法国、德国、意大利、荷兰、比利时和卢森堡。如今该联盟现拥有28个会员国，正式官方语言有24种。

练习题：

1. 思考并总结中国学生进行汉译英时常犯的错误有哪些方面。
2. 思考并总结中国学生进行汉译英实践时的主要困难有哪几方面。

第四节 汉译英的标准

翻译标准是译者在翻译活动中应该遵守的准绳，是衡量译文的尺度。因此，了解并掌握翻译标准，对提高翻译质量、充分发挥翻译的作用有重要意义。在翻译标准方面，中外翻译学者都进行了不懈的探索，下面我们对翻译标准有代表性的论述进行简介。

在西方，1790 年，英国出版了泰特勒（Alexander Fraser Tytler）的专著《论翻译的原则》（*Essay on the Principles of Translation*）。在该书中，泰特勒提出了著名的翻译的三大原则：

1. 译作应完全复写出原作的思想（The translation should give a complete transcript of the ideas of the original work.）；
2. 译作的风格和手法应和原作属于同一性质（The style and manner of the writing should be of the same character with that of the original.）；
3. 译作应具备原作所具有的通顺（The translation should have all the ease of the original composition.）。

在这三项原则中，泰特勒不仅论述了翻译要忠实和通顺，还论及了翻译的风格，论述较为全面，在西方有着重要的影响。在西方的现代翻译理论中，1969 年美国翻译家奈达（Eugene Nida）和泰伯（Charles Taber）在其专著 *The Theory and Practice of Translation* 中提出了著名的"动态对等"（dynamic equivalence）翻译原则。动态对等指的是"quality of a translation in which the message of the original text has been so transported into the receptor language that the response of the receptor is essentially like that of the original receptors."也就是说，一部译作的成功与否，主要取决于译文读者对译作作出反应是否基本等同于原文读者对原作的反应。因此，在一定程度上来说，奈达的动态对等理论也是读者反应论。奈达的翻译理论是我国引进较早的翻译理论，自 20 世纪 80 年代引进我国以来，对我国翻译界影响极大，有一段时间甚至到了言必称奈达的程度。但奈达的翻译理论主要是基于其《圣经》的翻译实践，因此未必适合普通文本的翻译实践。

在我国，1898 年，清末启蒙思想家严复在其译作《天演论》的"译例言"中提出了"信、达、雅"的三字翻译标准。原文如下：

译事三难：信、达、雅。求其信已大难矣，顾信矣不达，虽译犹不译也，则达尚焉。

此后，这三个字似乎成为我国翻译界颠扑不破的三字真经，后人无法逾越。“信”就是指忠实于原文，“达”就是指表达要流畅。一般来说，这两点争议较小，但“雅”字争议就较大。在当时中国的社会环境下，严复的求“雅”是一种刻意的翻译方法，主要是指译文要用汉代以前的字法、句法，目的是吸引并影响当时厚古薄今的士大夫阶层（有的说“宋以后之书不读”，有的说“唐以后之书不读”）。现在，我们对“雅”的理解主要是指要有文采。事实上，中文历来就有“雅”的传统，我国古代先贤孔子就说过“言之无文，行而不远”。就是说，文章没有文采，就不能流传很远。换言之，“雅”是中文作为目的语文本的内在要求。因此，我们可以说，“信、达、雅”的三字翻译标准是适合外译汉的实际的，这也符合严复的翻译实践。严复的译作主要是英译汉方面，商务印书馆辑为《严译名著丛刊》，共有八部：《天演论》《群已权界论》《原富》《群学肄言》《法意》《社会通诠》《名学浅说》《穆勒名学》。由此可见，严复的“信、达、雅”的翻译标准是适合英译汉的，但未必适合汉译英。

严复（1854 年 1 月 8 日—1921 年 10 月 27 日），字又陵，后名复，中国近代启蒙思想家、翻译家。严复系统地将西方的社会学、政治学、政治经济学、哲学和自然科学介绍到中国，他翻译了《天演论》《原富》《群学肄言》《群已权界论》《社会通诠》《法意》《名学浅说》《穆勒名学》等著作。他的译著在当时影响巨大，是中国 20 世纪最重要启蒙译著。严复的翻译考究、严谨，每个译称都经深思熟虑，他提出的“信、达、雅”的翻译标准对后世的翻译工作产生了深远影响。

严复

在我国现阶段，许多学者也对翻译标准进行了探讨。吕瑞昌等（1983）在《汉英翻译教程》中提出了汉英翻译的两条标准：信和顺。“信”是指忠实于原文的内容，包括思想、感情、风格等，即把原文完整而准确地表达于译文中，对原文内容尽可能不增不减。“顺”是指用词正确得体，行文流畅通顺，符合英语习惯；避免逐字死译、生搬硬套，使不懂汉语的英语读者也能看懂。此外，吕瑞昌等（1983）还指出，不同题材的翻译可能标准有所不同。例如文学翻译必须尽可能地保持原作的艺术特色；政治翻译必须特别注意在措辞和语气方面的立场和观点；科技翻译必须说理清楚，公式、数据、术语正确无误。联合国语文部门是世界上最重要的专业翻译机构之一，其中文翻译部门对翻译质量有何要求，可能对我们的翻译学习有所帮助。我国外交部前翻译室主任、前中国常驻联合国代表团资深翻译（1971 年—1981 年）过家鼎（2004）提出，翻译的基本要求是“忠实准确，通顺易懂”。

联合国驻日内瓦办事处中文科资深译员赵兴民（2011）在其所著《联合国文件翻译》一书中总结了联合国语文部门翻译方面的六点守则：完整、准确、通顺、术语、一致、风格。“完整”指译文完整，不随意减译或增译。“准确”指意思准确，忠实于原文。不但要忠实于原文的基本意思，还要忠实于原文的感情色彩、细微差别，如不能随便使用修饰语或限定语。“通顺”指语句通顺，符合现代汉语习惯，因为中国人在联合国从事的翻译主要是英译汉。“术语”指尽可能沿用国际组织固定的术语译法，避免制造一些新的译法。“一致”指术语、专有名词及其他固定用语在译文里须前后一致。“风格”指译文风格应与原文风格相符。由以上可以看出，大家基本一致同意的汉译英的一般标准应是：忠实与通顺。

当然“忠实与通顺”这两个翻译标准，说起来容易，做起来难。我国著名的《毛泽东选集》英译大家程镇球先生（2002：214）讨论了《毛选》英译过程中这两个翻译标准间的矛盾：

> 《毛选》翻译要求在文字和精神上均完全忠实于原文。信与达是统一的，要信就要求达，不达也就难以做到信。这样讲，在理论上说无疑是正确的。但在具体翻译实践中，更为重要的是：信与达往往又是矛盾的。翻译中的难处就在于，译文既要信又要达，很不容易，尤其是汉英两种文字，它们之间存在着文化和社会方面的巨大差异。解决信与达的矛盾也就是在两者之间找到最佳的平衡点。尽善尽美的译文只是我们追求的理想。有一位英国学者曾经指出：“All translation is compromise.”（“翻译就是妥协。”）当然，这不是说翻译因此可以马马虎虎，草率从事。恰恰相反，翻译应该精益求精，这方面是永无止境的。

下面，我们看下汉译英的翻译教学标准。目前，对汉译英提出教学标准的主要是英语专业及翻译专业的汉译英教学。根据《高校英语专业八级考试大纲》（2004 年新版），汉译英的测试要求是：能运用汉译英的理论和技巧，翻译我国报刊杂志上的文章和一般文学作品。速度为每小时 250 至 300 个汉字。译文必须忠实原意，语言通顺、流畅。根据《高等学校翻译专业本科教学要求》（试行），翻译本科专业翻译能力的要求是：能翻译一般难度、普通文体的外、汉段落，掌握常用的笔译技巧；外译汉速度约为 200 汉字 / 小时，汉译外速度约为 150 汉字 / 小时；要求译文忠实于原文，表达流畅；无重大语言理解和表述错误。根据《翻译硕士专业学位（MTI）入学考试全国联考指南》，对翻译硕士专业学位的汉译英要求是：汉译英要求考生运用有关理论和技巧，翻译我国报纸杂志上的论述文、国际会议文件、应用文、国情介绍以及一般文学作品的节录。速度为 250 汉字 / 小时，译文必须忠实于原文，语言通顺，比较地道。从这三个汉译英的翻译教学要求来看，汉译英的基本标准也是忠实与通顺。

下面是英国埃克斯特大学（University of Exeter）的翻译教学评分标准（摘自 (http://intranet.exeter.ac.uk/humanities/studying/subjecthandbooks/ml/translations/)。

Marking Criteria for Translations

1. Marking criteria for translation into English（译入英语的翻译评分标准）

The criteria below give an indication of how module tutors and examiners grade translation work from the language of study into English. The criteria are cumulative (a higher grade implies the possession of the skills described at lower grades, as well as the absence of deficiencies described at lower grades). At the same time, the grade profiles are necessarily general and typical: a candidate need not fit all aspects of a profile to fall into that grade band and there may be elements that do not apply to every translation exercise. In specialist translation exercises (e.g. literary translation, applied translation), additional criteria may apply.

Please note the following in applying these criteria:

In coursework (as opposed to examination) a higher degree of accuracy is expected in each of the grade bands and marks are deducted for poor dictionary skills.

Repeated or consequential errors are not penalized.

Gaps are penalized.

Marking is not purely "negative": marks are deducted for mistakes but marks are also awarded for good translation ability as defined below.

High 1st 90+%

No errors in comprehension of the passage. Rendition of the passage into English conveys, as far as is possible for a translated text, all aspects of the sense of the original, including nuances of style, register, metaphor and cultural reference.

Good 1st 80-89%

Virtually no problems of comprehension of the passage. The English version shows flair in use of English, which accurately renders the original in an appropriate register. The student correctly identifies all points of difficulty in the translation and shows imagination in dealing with them. Only one or two imperfections. Work which would be judged as excellent or very good at the next highest level of study.

Low 1st 70-79%

Very good comprehension of the passage; any problems are handled resourcefully, resulting in an English version that reads clearly and convincingly with no mistranslations or awkwardness of style.

2:1 60-69%

Good comprehension of the majority of structures and no significant difficulties with vocabulary. Demonstrates sensitivity to the mismatch between structures existing/in common use in the language of study and those existing/in common use in English. There may be a few mistranslations and one or two examples of awkwardness of style.

2:2 50-59%

Good comprehension of the majority of structures and vocabulary, but attempts to overcome translation problems posed by the passage are not always successful. The English version reads well but shows some areas of unsuitable register, mistranslations and awkwardness of style. The student sometimes assumes wrongly that a grammatical or idiomatic structure that exists in the language of study also exists, or is in common use, in English.

3rd 40-49%

General comprehension of a reasonable range of structures and vocabulary, but with evidence of inability to handle some or the more difficult areas. Evidence of a reasonable attempt to handle areas of difficulty should be awarded a mark at the top of the range. The English version shows awkwardness and tendency to literal translation. Where some of the English lacks sense and there is a lack of ability to handle some basic grammar in the language of study, the work should be awarded a mark at the bottom of the range.

Fail 26-39%

Satisfactory understanding of the original but shows inability to handle relatively common structures and vocabulary. There may be serious misunderstanding of part of the passage. The translation is literal, showing several instances of failure to produce a comprehensible English text.

Lowest fail 0-25%

Understanding of a minority of the passage demonstrates inability to comprehend basic grammatical structures and vocabulary in context. The English version is not able to convey the gist of the passage, lacks sense and is disjointed.

2. Marking criteria for translation into the language of study（译入所学语言的翻译评分标准）

The criteria below are generic to exercises in translation from English into any of the languages taught by DML. Your language discipline may also supply you with language-specific criteria. The criteria are cumulative (a higher grade implies the possession of the skills described at lower grades, as well as the absence of deficiencies described at lower grades). At the same time, the grade profiles are necessarily general and typical: a candidate need not fit all aspects of a profile to fall into that grade band and there may be elements that do not apply to every kind of translation exercise. In specialist translation exercises (e.g. literary translation, applied translation), additional criteria may apply.

Please note the following in applying these criteria:

In coursework (as opposed to examination) a higher degree of accuracy is expected in each of the grade bands and marks are deducted for poor dictionary skills.

Repeated or consequential errors are not penalized.

Gaps are penalized.

Marking is not purely "negative": marks are deducted for mistakes but marks are also awarded for good translation ability as defined below.

High 1st 90+%

The sense of the passage is conveyed fully and accurately, and register is appropriate throughout. Language is virtually error-free and demonstrates ability to handle complex syntax. Shows ability to reflect the style of the original passage to a considerable degree and to reproduce certain stylistic effects. Demonstrates an impressive range of vocabulary and an awareness as to how and when it should be deployed.

Good 1st 80-89%

The sense of the passage is conveyed fully and accurately, and register is appropriate throughout. Language is generally error-free, although there may be slips. Demonstrates ability to handle complex syntax. Shows an awareness of stylistic features of the original passage and makes some successful attempts to reproduce them. Demonstrates a good range of vocabulary. Work which would be judged as excellent or very good at the next highest level of study.

Low 1st 70-79%

The sense of the passage is conveyed fully, and register is generally appropriate. Language is generally error-free, although there may be slips, and more complex constructions may generate more significant errors. Shows an awareness of stylistic features of the original passage and makes some attempt to reproduce them. Range of vocabulary is adequate to convey the sense.

2:1 60-69%

The sense of the passage is broadly conveyed with clarity, and register is generally appropriate. Few major mistakes of syntax and morphology are made, and generally the incidence of errors is low, although some of the more complex sections generate significant errors. Will generally be able to use appropriate vocabulary, though there may be gaps in knowledge or in understanding of usage. Displays an understanding that not all grammatical or idiomatic structures that exist in English have a direct counterpart in the language of study, and that the exercise of translation involves finding equivalent structures where necessary.

At the higher end of the range, work will contain few errors and the student will handle register well, with an attempt to reproduce stylistic features of the original. At the lower end of the range there will be less proficient mastery of appropriate vocabulary and syntax, and little attempt will be made to reproduce the style of the original.

2:2 50-59%

Whilst the sense of the passage will be clear for the most part, there are moments where translation breaks down. Register is generally appropriate, but some errors appear. A general command of syntactical and morphological features of the language of study will be evident, but there may be a number of errors, and complex syntactical elements cause problems. Little awareness of stylistic issues is evident. The student sometimes wrongly assumes that a grammatical or idiomatic structure that exists in the English source text also exists in the language of study. At the higher end of the range the student will generally convey the sense successfully, and will demonstrate an adequate range of vocabulary. A lower mark will be awarded to scripts where the incidence of errors is high and complex syntax regularly causes problems.

3rd 40-49%

Errors of register, syntax and morphology are frequent, but some ability to handle basic syntactical and morphological features of the language is demonstrated. The literal sense of the original passage is conveyed to some degree. Little or no evidence of an awareness of the structural differences between the two languages or of stylistic issues. At the higher end of the range the student will be successful more often in conveying the sense of the original, and will be able to construct some sentences with few errors. At the lower end of the range the work will contain frequent errors.

Fail 26-39%

Demonstrates the ability to handle basic syntactical and morphological features of the language, but struggles to convey the sense of the passage. To a large degree, lacks the vocabulary required by the passage for translation, but some relevant vocabulary is present.

Lowest fail 0-25%

Script is incomprehensible or significantly incomplete. Demonstrates inability to reconstruct any of the sense of the passage to be translated. Clear inability to handle syntax and morphology.

埃塞克斯大学（University of Essex）于 1965 年建立，是英国一所综合性大学，拥有来自超过 100 个国家的学生就读。埃塞克斯大学在最近一次的 2008 年英国官方大学科研实力 RAE 排名居全英第 9 位，在 2014《泰晤士报》（*TIMES*）英国大学排名上位居全英第 39 位，在 2013/2014QS 世界大学排名上位居世界第 338 位，在 2013—2014 泰晤士高等教育世界大学排名上位居世界第 251—275 位。

练习题：

1. 汉译英是否存在一种客观的标准？阐述你的观点并作出合理的解释。
2. 文学翻译和非文学翻译是否可用同一个翻译标准？阐述你的观点并作出合理的解释。

第五节　汉译英翻译能力

新世纪以来，随着教育的重点逐渐转移到素质和能力上，在翻译学习中，翻译能力的概念也越来越受到重视。在翻译学习中，学习的不应只是翻译知识，更重要的是翻译能力的习得。因此，我们要了解翻译能力的构成成分，特别是汉译英翻译能力的构成成分。

国际著名的西班牙巴塞罗那自治大学翻译能力习得过程和评估研究小组（PACTE）给翻译能力下的定义是“胜任翻译所需要的潜在的知识和技能体系”（PACTE, 2000：100）。对于翻译能力的研究，Pym（2003）认为可归纳为 4 大类：1）不存在翻译能力；2）翻译能力是语言能力的总和；3）翻译能力由多种子能力构成；4）翻译能力就是一种能力。目前，多数研究认为翻译能力是由多种成分构成的，也就是说，翻译能力可以分解为若干子能力。但翻译能力究竟由何成分构成，由几种成分构成，目前学界意见不一。Campbell（1998）认为翻译能力由 3 部分构成：一是译入语语篇能力；二是译者个性；三是监控能力。Bell（2001: 38-42）认为译者能力包括：1）双语能力；2）专家技能系统；3）交际能力。Neubert（2000: 6）认为翻译能力包括语言能力、语篇能力、语域能力、文化能力和转换能力。Pym（2003）提出了翻译能力的最简方案，认为翻译能力由两方面组成：一是能够针对一个源语文本生成多个译语文本的能力；二是能够从多个译语文本中挑选出一个最佳译语文本的能力。Hatim & Mason（1997）认为翻译能力应包括 3 部分：源语文本处理技能、目的语文本处理技能以及转换技能。我国学者文军（2004）认为，翻译能力由 3 部分构成：语言 / 文本能力、策略能力和自我评估能力。经过两次修订，PACTE（2003，2005）的翻译能力模型共由 5 种子能力构成：1）双语子能力。该项能力主要是指翻译学习者的源语和目的语的语法、词汇、语篇、社会语言学及语用学的知识水平。2）语言外子能力。该项能力主要是陈述性知识，主要是关于世界和专门领域的显性知识和隐性知识，主要包括关于两种文化的知识、百科知识和主题知识。3）翻译知识子能力。该项能力主要是陈述性知识，主要是关于翻译是什么以及翻译职业的显性知识和隐性知识，主要包括翻译如何运作的知识和翻译职业实践的知识。4）工具子能力。该项能力主要是程序性知识，主要是关于如何使用参考资料、信息和交际技术等的能力，如如何使用词典、百科全书、平行文本、电子语料以及文本格式等。5）策略子能力。该项能力主要是程序性知识，主要是保证翻译过程的效率以及确保翻译过程中遇到的问题得到有效解决。该项能力是翻译能力的核心成分，因为该项能力能够影响其他子能力，并使其发生相互作用。该项能力的主要功能包括：一是规划翻译过程并实施翻译项目；二是评估翻译过程及结果；三是激活各项子能力，并使其相互弥补；四是找出翻译问题并实施解决方案。6）心理生理成分。该项能力主要指的是翻译学习者的各种认知、态度和心理运动机制。主要包括：1）认知成分，如感知、记忆、情绪及注意等；2）各种态度，如严谨性、自信心、动机、好奇心等；3）创造性、逻辑推理、分析和整合等能力。具体图示如下：

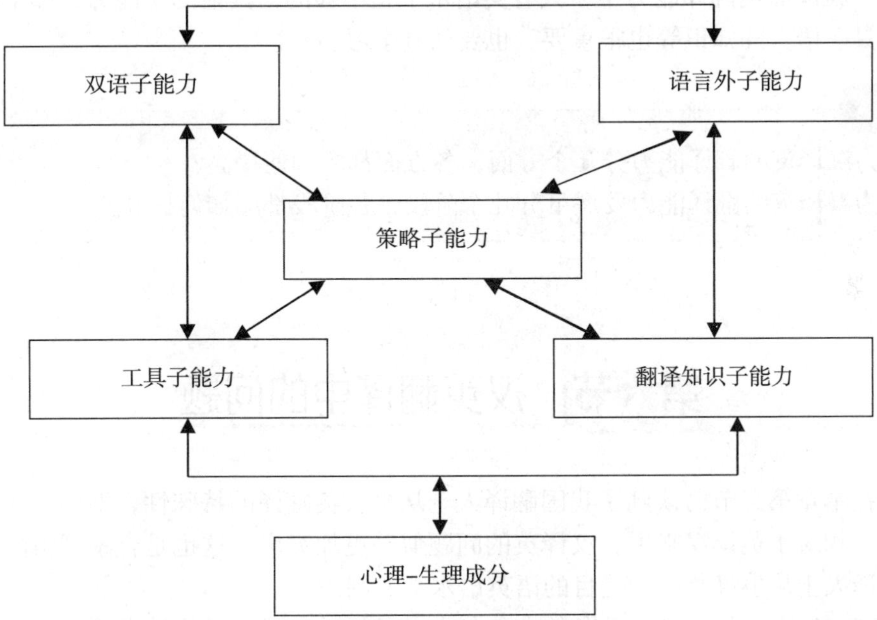

PACTE 翻译能力模型

在汉译英翻译能力方面，根据北京外国语大学马会娟（2013）的考察，对于中国学习者来说，汉译英的难点和主要问题在于译入语的表达能力。因此，在汉译英翻译能力的构成成分中，语言交际能力应占有绝对核心的地位。一个译者如果不具备基本的语言能力，学汉英翻译只能是本末倒置、缘木求鱼，达不到学习的根本目的。在西方的翻译培训或教育中，学员的双语语言能力已达到了较为熟练的程度，达到了翻译培训的基本要求。但我国的翻译学习者在翻译培训前目的语水平普遍不高，因此其目的语水平的提升是翻译的必要条件。马会娟（2013：74）通过对北京外国语大学翻译系本科三年级学生进行的问卷调查发现，几乎100%的同学都认为汉译英的难点在于英语的表达。马会娟（2013：74）还总结了我国从事翻译教学的一线教师和学者对汉译英学习中英语水平重要性的阐述。单其昌指出："无论英译汉或汉译英，都必须有较高的英语水平，汉英翻译尤其如此——也许可以这么说：如果一个人的英文水平低，别的条件都具备，他只不过具备了全部翻译条件的百分之三十，还是不能进行翻译的；反之，如果一个人的英文水平较高，那么他就具备了翻译条件的百分之七十，也就是说，英文水平的高低是搞好汉英翻译的关键。"杨晓荣进一步阐述道："有了这'百分之七十'，其余'百分之三十'才能发挥作用，翻译训练也才有效果。如果满篇都是语言错误，翻译水平的提高从何谈起？"孙海晨也指出："如果没有足够的中英文水平，尤其是英文水平作为基础，无论对汉译英的原则理解得多么透彻，学了多少翻译技巧，都不过是纸上谈兵。原则可以很快地理解，技巧可以通过机械的训练得以速成，语言表达能力则靠多年的学习积累，无捷径可循。"

当然，在汉译英翻译能力中，只有英语水平是不够的，其他的子能力，如策略、翻译知识、工具、语言外知识等也很重要，也要认真学习。

练习题：

1. 你认为汉译英的翻译能力分几个方面，各方面都应如何提高？
2. 你认为汉译英的翻译能力发展可分几个阶段，各阶段都应如何提高？

第六节 汉英翻译中的问题

我们在本章第三节已谈到了我国翻译人士从事汉英翻译的特殊性，即译入非母语，因此在我国，相对于英译汉来说，汉译英的问题似乎更加突出。这也是合乎逻辑的结果，因为我国翻译人士从事汉英翻译受目的语英语水平的制约。

1990年12月，中国翻译工作者协会在北京召开了全国中译英学术研讨会，与会代表就汉译英问题以及汉译英教学和人才培养等问题进行了认真的讨论和交流。在这次大会上，段连城先生宣读了其发表在《中国翻译》1990年第5期上题为《呼吁：请译界同仁都来关心对外宣传》的文章，引起了大家对汉译英问题的重视和广泛讨论。在该文中，段连城先生将汉译英的"常见病"分为了两类：甲型病状和乙型病状。甲型病状明显易见，主要表现为"白字"连篇，语法错误和用词不当；乙型病状指拼写无误，语法不错，但外国读者会感到难懂甚至不懂，更谈不上喜闻乐见的译文。如果说甲型病是汉译英的"外伤"的话，那么乙型病则是汉译英的"内伤"。相对于外伤而言，内伤更难发现，也更难治愈。

参加过《毛泽东选集》《周恩来选集》《邓小平文选》英译的我国汉译英资深翻译家程镇球先生也就汉英翻译问题进行了深刻的阐述。程镇球先生（1992）认为，汉译英问题，总的来讲，可以概括为两个问题：1）应译未译，或译得有限，主要涉及当代和古代的文、史、哲名著；2）已译质量不高，有的很差，特别是在对外宣传方面。程镇球先生（1992：40）还进一步阐述到，汉英翻译质量的一个关键问题是避免所谓的“中文式英文”（Chinglish），翻译最大的课题之一就是摆脱原文字面的束缚。程镇球先生（1992：40）还引用了美国专家 Sol Adler 的话：“The main problem is that the language from which you are translating imposes itself on the language into which you are translating. This applies to all translation.”

曾在我国外文出版社和中央编译局工作过八年、专门为中国翻译工作者翻译的英译文作修改和润色的美国专家 Joan Pinkham 也认为汉译英的一个重大问题就是中式英语的问题，并著有《中式英语之鉴》（*The Translator's Guide to Chinglish*）一书。在该书中，作者将其八年中积累的大量典型的中式英语实例进行了分门别类的划分，并指出了其具体体现，对改进中式英语非常具有借鉴意义，该书已成为众多院校翻译方向本科生和研究生的必读书目。

虽然这些汉英翻译问题都是在 20 世纪 90 年代提出的问题，但我们感觉这些问题都还没有得到很好的解决，至今仍然存在。

程镇球，教授。1956 年以来，曾多次参加中共党代会、人代会文件及其他重要文献的英译定稿工作。1965 年调外交部，从事英文定稿工作。曾任翻译室副主任、顾问，外交部外语专家，外交学院兼职教授，外交学会理事，中国翻译工作者协会常务理事等职。自 1960 年起，程镇球曾分别参加《毛泽东选集》第 1—5 卷英文版的定稿及修订定稿工作。1980 年后，程镇球主持了《周恩来选集》上卷、《刘少奇选集》上卷的英译定稿工作，并参加《邓小平文选》英文版最后阶段的定稿通读，积累了丰富的翻译经验。撰有《翻译问题探索》《论汉译英的几个问题》等著作，参与翻译了《毛主席书信手迹选》（合译）。2001 年 1 月被中国译协表彰为资深翻译家。

程镇球

练习题：

1. 实地调研你所在地区两个景点的中文简介的英译，并找出其存在的主要问题。
2. 分析两部中国电影的字幕英译，并找出其存在的主要问题。

第二章 汉英翻译的过程

在翻译方面，我们必须更正的一个观点是：翻译不是一蹴而就的，而是一个过程。因此，我们将对汉英翻译过程作为单独的一章进行讲解，以突出其在翻译学习中的重要性。如果说前面第一章是翻译学习的陈述性知识的话，本章就是翻译学习的程序性知识。我们认为，翻译过程应分为狭义和广义两方面。

第一节 狭义的翻译过程

狭义的翻译过程指的是翻译活动本身。在狭义翻译过程方面，美国著名翻译理论家奈达（1969）提出的翻译过程如下：

However, a careful analysis of exactly what goes on in the process of translating, especially in the case of source and receptor languages having quite different grammatical and semantic structures, has shown that, instead of going directly from one set of surface structures to another, the competent translator actually goes through a seemingly roundabout process of analysis, transfer, and restructuring. That is to say, **the translator first analyzes the message of the SOURCE language into its simplest and structurally clearest forms, transfers it at this level, and then restructures it to the level in the RECEPTOR language which is most appropriate for the audience which he intends to reach.** Such a set of related procedures may be represented diagrammatically as in Figure 1. This roundabout procedure may be compared to the experience of the hiker who finds that a stream he must cross is so deep and the current so swift that he cannot risk crossing over directly from one point to another. Therefore, he goes downstream to a ford, at which point the transfer from one side to another can be made with the least possible danger to himself and his equipment. He can then go back upstream to the point which best suits him. The processes of analysis are, however, relatively complex, for they involve at least three different sets of features: (1) the grammatical relationships between constituent parts, (2) the referential meanings of the semantic units, and (3) the connotative values of the grammatical structures and the semantic units. (Nida, 1969: 484)

具体模型如下：

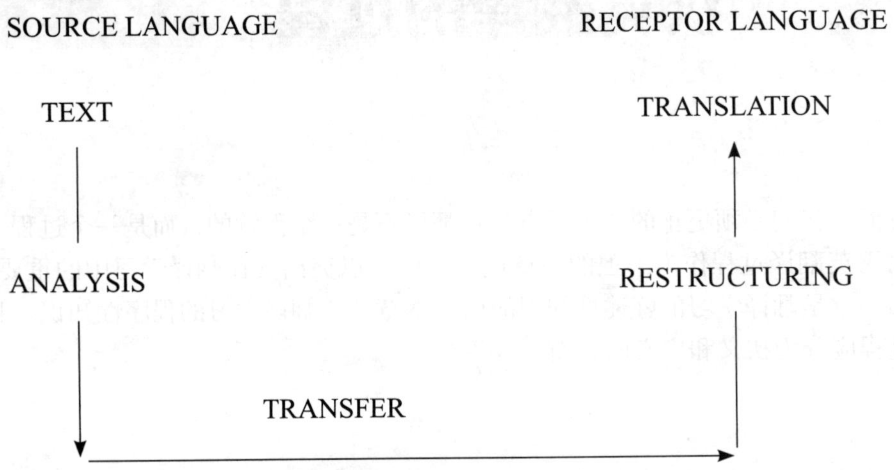

与直觉认识不同，根据奈达的此翻译过程模型，翻译过程并不是从源语的表层结构（surface structure）直接转换为译语的表层结构。实际的翻译过程是：译者首先将源语的信息分析（analyze）为其最简单和结构最清晰的形式，然后在此最基本的层面上进行语言转换（transfer），最后将此最基本的层面进行提升并重构（restructure）其为最适合译文读者的译文。（The translator first analyzes the message of the SOURCE language into its simplest and structurally clearest forms, transfers it at this level, and then restructures it to the level in the RECEPTOR language which is most appropriate for the audience which he intends to reach.）

我们认为，奈达的这一观点抓住了翻译过程的实质与要义。特别是在汉译英过程中，很多时候出现翻译卡壳的现象，就是因为对翻译过程的认识不正确，认为翻译就是源语和目的语间的表层转换，直接去找对应词。但由于英语和汉语差异巨大，英语和汉语中许多词语并没有直接的对应词。例如，有一次本人在四年级的一个汉译英课程的课堂上，问学生如何英译下面这句话："他是一个城府很深的人。"班里的同学都被汉语中的"城府"这个词卡住了，不知如何英译。究其原因，问题还是出在学生对翻译过程的错误认识上。根据奈达的翻译过程模型，首先我们不应直接去找"城府"的英语对应词，而是将"城府"分析为最简单的意义"掩盖自己的想法或感情等"。在这个最基本的层面上，向英语转换的瓶颈就突破了，因为大家基本都会将汉语的"掩盖自己的想法或感情等"转换为英语的 hide his opinions and feelings。因此，在最基本的层面上，汉语中的"他是一个城府很深的人。"就可转换为英语中的"He is a man who always hides his opinions and feelings."当然，在真实的语境中，这样的英语表达会显得较为啰唆，不够生动。因此，在一定语境下，我们可以进一步将此句英文提升为“He is a deep man.”。因此，我们可以看到“城府”并不难翻译，其对应的并不是一个很有难度的英语单词，而只是一个人人皆知的 deep。由此可见，许多同学感觉汉英翻译难的一个重要原因是对翻译过程的认识不正确，导致出现卡壳现象。

相对来说，我国学者对翻译过程的认识较为直接。大部分学者认为，翻译过程包括两个阶段：理解和表达。吕瑞昌等（1983）还对理解和表达两个阶段提出了明确的要求：理解原文词句不应脱离上下文；表达中最重要的一点是译者避免机械照搬的死译和望文生义的乱译。下面，我们以庄绎传（1980：2-3）列举的《毛选》英译中“世界”一词的英译来说明这两个问题。例句如下：

1. 世界上就是这样一个辩证法：又动又不动。
2. 我们总要相信，全世界也好，我们中国也好，多数人是好人。
3. 讲基本完成，是谨慎的讲法，世界上的事情总是谨慎一点好。
4. 实际上，世界上只有具体的自由，具体的民主，没有抽象的自由，抽象的民主。
5. 你要母鸡多生蛋，又不给它米吃，又要马儿跑得好，又要马儿不吃草。世界上那有这样的道理。

以上 5 个例句中都有“世界”这样一个普普通通的词。下面我们看看这五句话中的“世界”各是如何英译的。

1. All things are at once in motion and not in motion—such is the dialectics *of our world*.
2. We must believe that in China, *as everywhere else in the world*, the majority of the people are good.
3. To say it is basically accomplished is a prudent way of speaking; it is always better to be prudent in *everything we do*.
4. As a matter of fact, freedom and democracy exist not in the abstract, but only in the concrete.
5. You want the hen to lay more eggs and yet you don’t feed it, you want the horse to run fast and yet you don’t let it graze. What kind of logic is that！

从表面来看，作为一个地理概念，似乎汉语中的“世界”对应英语中的 world。但实际上，上述五句中的“世界”有时指一个地理概念，有时概括地指世界上的人和事，如果都机械地英译为 world，不仅不通顺，有时甚至是错误的。第一句中通过在 world 前增添 our，译文就使人脱离平面的地理概念，使人联想到我们所处的这个现实世界。第二句“全世界”为何不译作 the whole world 呢？中国是世界的一部分，说了中国再说 the whole world，在逻辑上就说不通了。第三句虽然说的是“世界上的事情”，但实际上指的是我们自己，everything we do 恰好表达了这个意思。在第四句和第五句中，“世界”没有体现在译文中，因为第四句是个一般性论断，泛指任何地方；而第五句也不是真的要在世界上找一找有没有这样的道理。在这两句汉语中，“世界”都是一种加强语气的说法。在英语翻译中，没有“世界”，语气才更强。

由此可见，即使像“世界”这样一个最普通的汉语词汇都有多种理解，在英语中都有多种译法，因此我们一定要注意汉译英中理解的准确性和翻译的灵活性。

奈达

尤金·奈达（Eugene A. Nida）于 1914 年出生于美国俄克拉何马州，当代著名语言学家和翻译理论家。尤金是当代翻译理论的主要奠基人，其理论核心是功能对等。尤金于 1943 年获语言学博士学位，后长期担任美国圣经协会翻译部的执行秘书，主持翻译部工作，并曾任美国语言学会会长。

练习题：

将下面这段话翻译为英语，并回溯你大脑中的翻译过程。

特区是个窗口，是技术的窗口，管理的窗口，知识的窗口，也是对外开放政策的窗口。从特区可以引进技术，获得知识，学到管理，管理也是知识。特区成为开放的基地，不仅在经济方面、培养人才方面使我们得到好处，而且会扩大我国的对外影响。听说深圳治安比过去好了，跑到香港去的人开始回来，原因之一是就业多，收入增加了，物质条件也好多了，可见精神文明说到底是从物质文明来的嘛！

第二节 广义的翻译过程

广义的翻译过程则不仅包括翻译活动本身，还包括译前和译后的各项工作。

1. 译前准备

我们认为一个完整的翻译过程应包括四个步骤：1）译前准备；2）原文理解；3）译文表达；4）译后校对。要保证并提高翻译质量，就要进行译前准备，目前国内翻译教材提及译前准备的还很少。

译前准备包括的内容有背景知识准备、专业知识准备、平行文本参阅、原文文本分析等。在译前，背景知识准备和专业知识准备是非常重要的。例如，法律文本的翻译就非常特殊。刘晓丹（2007）总结了法律语言的三方面特点：1）语篇结构特点。从语篇结构层面上看，法律语篇最突出的特点是它的高度程式化。语篇指超过一句话或超过一个句子的口语或书面语言的连续体，是话段或句子构成的语言整体。法律书面语篇包括立法文本（如法律法规）、司法文书（如庭审记录）、语言材料、可疑文本等。经过对比研究，我们可以发现英、汉立法语篇的结构大致相当，两类语篇都是由描写性成分过渡到规定性成分、由颁布命令和/或前言过渡到具体条文；其结构层次分明，都是采用从宏观到微观、从总论/总则到条文、从重要条文到次要条文的语篇结构。2）句法选择特点。在具体的语言操作层面上，法律英语语篇多用结构紧密、说理完整的长句，常常使用并列结构和复杂的同位语成分，为了保证表述的严谨准确性，有时会放弃简洁明了性和可读性。据专家统计，在英美普通法法系的法律文件中，句子的平均长度约为 271 个单词。相比之下，中文法律结构简练，其大量句子成分的省略，给人以简洁的感觉。此外，中文法律的条款还会用某个词或词组来充当多个动词的主语，形成在一个主语下的一系列动词短语结构，这样既体现了中文法律的简洁，又符合汉语意合的语言特点。3）词汇使用特点。在法律词语运用层面上，英文法律词汇的来源大致可以分为三大类：一类是现代通用的正式语言，它构成了英语法律的主体；第二类是其他文本中少用或是不用的中古英语，例如 aforesaid、hereby、notwithstanding、henceforth 等。另外一类就是大量借用的外来词，其中主要包括拉丁词语和法语词，例如：拉丁词语 amicus curiae（法庭之友，法庭的临时顾问）、decree nisi（非最终判决）、quasi（类似的，准的）、perse（自身）；法语词 estoppel（禁止反言）、plaintiff（原告）、defendant（被告）、mortgage（抵押）、lash（鞭笞刑）。法律英语频繁使用中古词汇及外来词汇，都是为了表达法律的正式、庄重。与之相比较，中文法律几乎没有外来词，至少没有直接借用的外来词，这是因为中文与那些法制健全的欧美国家语言属于不同语系，无法直接借用。所以中文法律仅凭少量的文言文，例如：兹、系、谨此、之、其等，以及大量的现代汉语中的正式语言来表达法律的正式、庄重。故此，中文法律用语来源要比法律英语少而简单。由此可见，法律翻译前如果没有英汉法律语言的背景知识准备和专业知识准备，法律文本的翻译几乎是不可能的。

译前查看目的语中的平行文本对翻译也会起到很大的作用。平行文本指的是不同语言中具有相似交际功能的语篇。虽然属于同一体裁，但由于语言文化的差异，同一体裁的不同语言的文本往往具有不同的语篇模式和文体风格。特别是在实用文本方面，英语中的平行文本对汉语文本的英译在语篇模式和文体风格上有非常大的借鉴意义。

卢小军（2012）比较了中国十家大型企业（包括中国石油化工集团公司、中国海洋石油总公司、中国石油天然气集团公司、中国第一汽车集团公司、上海汽车工业集团总公司、中国电信集团公司、中国移动通信集团、中国银行股份有限公司、中国建设银行股份有限公司、鸿海科技集团）网站的中英文企业概况和美国十家大型企业（包括 ExxonMobil、Chevron、ConocoPhillips、GM、GE、Verizon、AT&T、Wells Fargo & Company、Bank of America、HP）网站的企业概况的平行文本的不同，对我国中文企业概况的英译提供了很好的借鉴。

下面，先看下美国通用汽车公司的英文介绍：

GM

General Motors Company (NYSE: GM, TSX: GMM), one of the world's largest automakers, traces its roots back to 1908. With its global headquarters in Detroit, GM employs 209,000 people in every major region of the world and does business in more than 120 countries. GM and its strategic partners produce cars and trucks in 31 countries, and sell and service these vehicles through the following brands: Buick, Cadillac, Chevrolet, GMC, Daewoo, Holden, Isuzu, Jiefang, Opel, Vauxhall and Wuling. GM's largest national market is China, followed by the United States, Brazil, the United Kingdom, Germany, Canada and Russia. GM's OnStar subsidiary is the industry leader in vehicle safety, security and information services.

由以上可以看出，GM 公司概况非常简要地介绍了该公司的性质、规模、成立时间、业务范围、产品类型、海外市场等情况。叙述平实客观，不渲染不夸饰，不着政治色彩。

下面看看中国海洋石油总公司（CNOOC）英译文本中的一段：

During the "Eleventh Five-year Plan" period, while focusing on the "Eleventh Five-year Plan" objectives and highlighting the construction of an "offshore Daqing oilfield," the Company has firmly grasped the important strategic opportunities arising from China's economic and social development and responded effectively to the material adverse impact of the global financial crisis with the spirit of deepening reform and promoting development through innovation, and made outstanding achievements in capacity building in energy supply, construction of industry value chain, internationalization construction, modern enterprise system building and formation of soft power, thus the Company has entered into a new phase of development goals.

该段译文套话较多，且含有像"十一五规划""大庆油田"之类具有中国特色的信息，不太符合英文目标语受众的阅读期待和交际需求，应主要保留目标语受众关心的实质信息。

下面这段讲述中国石化主要业务活动的英文翻译，信息密密匝匝，可读性不强，不仅起不到应有的宣传效果，反而可能影响企业形象的国际传播。

Sinopec Group's key business activities include: industrial investment and investment management; the exploration, production, storage and transportation (including pipeline transportation), marketing and comprehensive utilization of oil and natural gas; oil refining; the wholesale of gasoline, kerosene and diesel; the production, marketing, storage, transportation of petrochemicals and other chemical products; the design, construction and installation of petroleum and petrochemical engineering projects; the overhaul and maintenance of petroleum and petrochemical equipment; the manufacturing of electrical and mechanical equipment; the research, development, application and consulting services of technology, information and alternative energy products, the import and export of commodities and technologies both for the Group and as a proxy (with the exception of those commodities and technologies that are either banned by the State or to be carried out by the State-designated companies).

实际上，英语中有类似的平行文本可以借鉴。美国能源巨头公司美国康菲国际石油有限公司 ConocoPhillips 讲述其公司活动的段落如下：

The company has four core activities:

* Petroleum exploration and production.

* Natural gas gathering, processing and marketing, including a 50 percent interest in DCP Midstream, LLC.

* Petroleum refining, marketing, supply and transportation.

* Chemicals and plastics production and distribution through a 50 percent interest in Chevron Phillips Chemical Co. LLC.

这段公司业务活动的讲述信息主次分明，尤其是列举项目符号的使用，一目了然。因此，以此平行文本为参照，对于业务活动的具体信息，筛选主要的，略去重复的和次要的，并以列举项目符号的文本样式呈现。卢小军（2012）将中国石化原有的英译文修改如下：

Sinopec Group has 6 core activities:

* Petroleum exploration and production.

* Natural gas gathering, processing and marketing.

* Petroleum refining, marketing, supply and transportation.

* Petrochemicals and other chemical products production and distribution.

* Industrial investment and investment management.

* Petroleum and petrochemical equipment overhaul and maintenance.

对原文文本的译前分析也很重要。美国著名的蒙特雷国际研究学院（Monterey Institute of International Studies）高级翻译学院施晓菁（Lynette Shi）教授认为动笔翻译前对原文的分析对翻译有较大的影响。原文本的分析一般有两种方法：一是文本类型分析，例如原文是记叙文、描写文、社论、议论文还是学术性文章；二是 5 个 W：who、why、when、where、what。许多学生的选词不当或译文文体不当等都是由于对原文的分析不够。施晓菁教授（2012：11-12）的原文如下：

Analysis of the source text (ST) has a huge influence on how the translation is carried out.

This analysis starts with text function. Generally texts can be divided into three functional categories: informative, expressive and vocative. Within these functions are a number of text types:

Narrative

Descriptive

Editorial

Persuasive

Academic

Of course, there is often overlap between the types within a text, which means the translator has to be alert to the varying requirements of different types.

Another way of expressing text analysis is with the 5Ws: who, why, when, where, what:

Who is the author? Who is commissioning the translation? Who is the readership?

Why was it written? Why is it being translated?

When was it written? When is it being translated?

Where is it going to be used or published?

What is it about? What are its special features? What are the circumstances under which it was written?

Some of the student translators have not analyzed the text enough before translating, resulting in inappropriate word choice and style, as well as lack of cohesion and coherence and obscured meaning.

2. 译后校对

施晓菁教授（2012：10-11）认为翻译绝不是一稿定终身，而是往往需要数稿。因为在第一稿的翻译中，由于忙于一个个具体的微观翻译问题，许多大的宏观问题就可能被忽视，如逻辑问题、搭配问题、风格问题、含义问题等。只有到了第二稿、第三稿，甚至更多稿时，这些被忽视的问题才会再浮现出来。因此，译后校对在翻译过程中不仅非常重要，而且必不可少。

下面，我们以施晓菁教授（2012）对一篇中国商务部网站上的前商务部副部长马秀红在中美贸易投资合作研讨会上的讲话的英译稿的修改为例说明译后校对的过程。

中文原稿：

马秀红在中美贸易投资合作研讨会上的讲话

2006 年 12 月 31 日

尊敬的各位中美企业家，

尊敬的各位来宾，

女士们、先生们，

非常高兴出席今天在克里夫兰举办的中美贸易投资合作研讨会。我谨代表张穹副主任，代表中华人民共和国商务部和中国政府法律交流代表团对研讨会的成功召开表示热烈祝贺，对美国商务部、俄亥俄州政府、克里夫兰市政府和克里夫兰市世贸中心为筹备此次研讨会所做出的努力表示衷心感谢。同时，我也要特别感谢中国机电产品进出口商会、美国中国总商会、中国驻美使馆经商处和中国驻纽约总领馆经商室，他们为此次研讨会成功举办做了大量工作。

促进中美企业间的合作是中国代表团访问俄亥俄州和克里夫兰市的主要目的之一。此次随访的中国企业家代表团由 36 家企业 51 人组成。这些企业都是中国知名企业，其中部分企业已在美国投资，但大多数企业希望通过此行在美国寻求投资机会或采购美国产品。此次中国政府和企业家代表团访问俄州，俄州人民对中国人民的友好情谊，俄州州政府和克里夫兰市政府促进对华经贸合作所做的不懈努力，给我们留下了深刻的印象。我相信，今天的研讨会，将进一步增进中国企业对俄州和克里夫兰市投资环境和产品的了解，并对扩大中国与俄州的贸易及相互投资，深化中国企业与俄州企业的经贸合作起到重要作用。

俄亥俄州是美国内陆水运和州际公路系统的交叉枢纽，具有得天独厚的地理优势，拥有较强的制造业、服务业、农业等产业基础，以及良好的营商环境、完善的基础设施、优越的办公条件和高素质的人力资源。俄亥俄州是美国三大工业基地之一，也是美国唯一自1998年来出口持续增长的州。目前俄州是全美第二大汽车产品和橡胶制品出口地、第三大钢铁制品出口地、第四大塑料产品出口地、第五大机械出口地。近10年来，俄州投资环境不断改善，经济迅速发展，为企业家提供了巨大的商机，成为外国企业在美制造业投资的重要地区之一。

中国是俄州的重要贸易伙伴。中国政府十分重视发展与俄州的经贸关系，采取积极措施，促进中国企业与俄州企业的交流与合作。近年来，俄州对华出口迅速增长，2005年俄州对华出口额达到9.34亿美元，比2001年增长了108%，目前中国已成为俄州第七大出口市场。双边投资合作也取得一定进展，目前，俄州有190多家企业在华投资，经营状况良好，在取得丰厚利润回报的同时，占有的中国市场份额不断扩大。中国企业在俄州投资也开始起步，尽管目前投资规模还不大，但越来越多的中国企业对俄州投资环境表现出浓厚的兴趣，积极寻求在俄州发展的机遇。俄州政府和克里夫兰市政府积极拓展与中国的合作，继在中国香港设立贸易办公室之后，最近又在中国上海设立了贸易办公室。这些举措必将对进一步促进中美企业的沟通、交流，加强企业间的合作，扩大双边贸易和投资起到重要作用。

英文译文初稿：

Address at China-US Trade and Investment Conference

Ma Xiuhong, Vice Minister of MOFCOM
(Cleveland, Dec.5, 2006)

Distinguished American and Chinese entrepreneurs,
Distinguished guests,
Ladies and Gentlemen,

I am very pleased to attend the China-US Trade and Investment Conference here in Cleveland. On behalf of Vice Minister Zhang Qiong, the Ministry of Commerce of China and the legal exchange delegation of the Chinese government, I would like to congratulate on the successful convening of the conference. I would like to thank the US Department of Commerce, the Ohio State Government, the Cleveland Municipal Government and the Cleveland World Trade Center for your preparation for the conference. At the same time, my thanks also go to CCCME, China General Chamber of Commerce in the US, the Economic and Commercial Counselor's Office of the Chinese Embassy in the US and the Economic and Commercial Counselor's Office of the Chinese Consulate General in New York for your tremendous efforts, which have made the success of the conference possible.

To promote cooperation between Chinese and American businesses is one of the major objectives of the Chinese delegation's visit to Ohio and Cleveland. The Chinese business delegation, which accompanies the government delegation, comprises of 51 entrepreneurs from 36 companies. The companies are mainly Chinese big names. Some have already invested in the US, while the majority wants to take this opportunity to seek investment opportunities in the US or buy products from the US. In visiting the State of Ohio, the Chinese government and business delegations are deeply impressed by the friendship of the Ohioan people and the unremitting efforts of the State Government and the Cleveland Municipal Government to promote US-China trade and economic cooperation. I believe today's conference will play an important role in enabling Chinese companies to learn more about the investment climate and product portfolio of Ohio and Cleveland, and boosting trade and mutual investment between China and Ohio, as well as deepening trade and economic cooperation between Ohioan and Chinese companies.

The State of Ohio is a hub of the US inland water transportation and the inter-state highway network, which gives it a unique geographical edge. The state possesses a comparatively strong industrial foundation in areas such as manufacturing, services and agriculture, a favorable business climate, well-established infrastructure, superb office facilities and high-quality human resources. Ohio is one the three industrial bases in the US and the only state seeing a sustained export increase. Currently, Ohio is the second largest exporting state of automobile products and rubber products to China, the third largest of iron and steel products, the fourth of plastic products and the fifth of machinery. In the past decade, the investment climate in Ohio has been improving and the economy growing quickly, which has created huge business opportunities for entrepreneurs, making the state one of the major areas for foreign investment in manufacturing.

China is an important trading partner for Ohio. The Chinese government attaches great importance to the trade and economic relationship with Ohio, and has taken positive steps to strengthen communication and cooperation between Ohio and Chinese businesses. In recent years, Ohio's export to China has been increasing quickly. In 2005, Ohio's export to China stood at $934 million with a year-on-year increase of 108%. At present, China is the seventh largest export market for Ohio. Two-way investment has also scored certain achievements. So far, more than 190 Ohio companies have made presence in China, performing quite well. While gaining big returns, their market share is enlarging. Chinese companies also began to invest in Ohio, though the scale is not big yet. But more and more Chinese companies are showing interest in Ohio's investment environment and seeking for development opportunities. The state government of Ohio and Cleveland municipal government have been actively exploring cooperation with China. After the Trade Office in Hong Kong, another trade office was set up in Shanghai. The moves will play a pivotal role in strengthening communication and exchanges and promoting cooperation between American and Chinese businesses, as well as increasing bilateral trade and investment.

施晓菁教授修改后的英文译稿如下：

Address at China-U.S. Trade and Investment Conference[1]

Ma Xiuhong, Vice Minister of MOFCOM

Distinguished American and Chinese entrepreneurs,

Distinguished guests,

Ladies and gentlemen,

I am delighted to attend the China-U.S. Trade and Investment Conference here in Cleveland. On behalf of Vice Minister Zhang Qiong, the Ministry of Commerce of China, and the Governmental Legal Exchange Delegation, I would like to congratulate you on the successful convening of this conference. I would also like to thank the U.S. Department of Commerce, the state government of Ohio, the Cleveland municipal government, and the Cleveland World Trade Center for all their hard work preparing this event.[2] At the same time, my thanks also go to[3] CCCME, China General Chamber of Commerce in the U.S., the Economic and Commercial Counselor's Office of the Chinese Embassy in the U.S., and the Economic and Commercial Counselor's Office of the Chinese Consulate General in New York for their tremendous efforts, which have all made this meeting possible.[4]

One of the major objectives of the Chinese delegation's visit to Ohio and Cleveland is to promote cooperation between Chinese and American businesses.[5] The Chinese business delegation, which is accompanying the government one, is made up of fifty-one entrepreneurs from thirty-six companies.[6] These are all big-name enterprises in China. Some have already invested in the U.S., but most wish to use this visit to seek out investment opportunities here or to buy American products.[7] We have been deeply impressed by the friendship of the people of Ohio and the unremitting efforts of the State and Cleveland municipal governments to promote U.S.-China trade and economic cooperation.[8] I believe today's conference will play an important role in enabling Chinese companies to learn more about the investment climate and product portfolio of Ohio and Cleveland, in boosting trade and mutual investment, and in increasing trade and economic cooperation between our respective companies.[9]

The State of Ohio is a hub of U.S. inland water transportation and of the interstate highway network, giving it a unique geographical edge. The state is relatively strong in sectors such as manufacturing, services, and agriculture; it has a favorable business climate, well-established infrastructure, excellent office facilities, and highly skilled human resources.[10] Ohio is one of the three industrial bases of the U.S., [11] and the only state that has experienced sustained export increases since 1998. [12] Currently, Ohio is the second largest exporter of automobile and rubber products, the third largest for iron and steel products, the fourth for plastic products, and the fifth for machinery. In the past decade, the investment climate in Ohio has improved and the economy has grown rapidly, creating huge business opportunities and making the state one of the most attractive for foreign manufacturing investment.[13]

China is an important trading partner for Ohio. The Chinese government attaches great importance to our trade and economic relationship with you and has taken active measures to strengthen communication and cooperation between our businesses.[14] In recent years, Ohio's exports to China have increased rapidly. In 2005, these were worth USD 934 million, an increase of 108 percent compared to 2001. At present, China is the seventh largest export market for Ohio. Two-way investment has also been fruitful. So far, more than 190 Ohio companies have investments in China, and they are performing quite well. [15] Returns have been good, and market share is growing. [16] Chinese companies have also begun to invest in Ohio, though not on a very large scale yet. However, more and more are showing interest in Ohio's investment environment and are seeking development opportunities. The state government and the Cleveland municipal government have been actively exploring cooperation with China. Following the opening of the Trade Office in Hong Kong, [17] another one has been set up in Shanghai. [18] These [19] will be pivotal in strengthening communication and exchanges and in promoting cooperation between American and Chinese businesses to increase bilateral trade and investment. [20]

(Adapted by Shi Xiaojing)

对于修改的具体原因，施晓菁教授（2011）的解释如下（原文为英文，现译为中文）：

1. 文本分析及翻译策略：本文为商务部的官方讲话，文体较为正式，译文应是中立、客观的文体风格。
2. 修改稿中在此增添了 also，原因是 I would like... 在本句前后有两次重复，I would like... 第二次出现时加上 also 后英文行文更流畅。“筹备……所做出的努力”在英文原稿中为 for your preparation for the conference，但在修改稿中改为了 for all their hard work preparing this event，增添了 hard work 和 event，目的是避免 conference 的重复。
3. 译者在此受到了源语的影响，频繁地重复 I would like。在修改稿中改为 my thanks go to，避免了重复。
4. 修改稿将英文原稿中的物主代词 your 改为了 their。这是一个常见的汉译英时的代词使用错误。原稿中的 success of the conference 在修改稿中改为了 successful convening。英文原稿中的 success of the conference 是不合逻辑的，因会议刚开始，还不知是否成功。修改稿中的 successful convening 指“成功召集”，这是中文原文的本意。

5. 在英文原稿中，本段开头作主语的是 to promote，这是典型的汉化英语。在英语中，一句话的开头，特别是一段的开头，一般需要一个明确的主语。因此，修改稿中改为了 One of the major objectives。这是汉译英中的一个常见的陷阱，译者要特别留意。
6. 英文原稿中 delegation 在很短的篇幅内重复了两次。汉语不介意重复，但英语忌讳重复。因此，修改稿中改为了代词形式 government one。修改稿将 accompany 改为了 is accompanying，因为动作正在进行。
7. 在修改稿中，第二个 companies 改为了代词 these。
8. 这是一个长句。英文原稿的问题是衔接不好，紧跟中文原文的结构，用 Chinese government and business delegations 作主语，好像指的不是代表团的人。实际上，讲话者是代表团的一员，因此在修改稿中增添了 we，以与前一句话衔接。
9. 这是一个长句，主要动词是：增进、扩大、深化，在英文原稿中译为了：role in enabling、and boosting、as well as deepening，逻辑显得较为松散。修改稿改为了：in enabling、in boosting、and in increasing。
10. 英文原稿中的"the state possesses a comparative strong industrial foundation"明显地沿用了中文原文"拥有……基础"，在英文中难于理解。因此，修改稿中将其拆解为了"the state is relatively strong in sectors such as"。
11. 修改稿中将 industrial bases in the U. S. 中的介词改为了 of，原因是中文原文明确地指出了所有，而不仅仅指地理概念。
12. 在英文原稿中，Seeing...increase 是别扭的搭配，同时时态也是错误的。
13. 注意时态的使用，英文原稿中的 has been improving 在修改稿中改为了 has improved，因为是已完成的动作。
14. 注意视角和人称的变化。英文原稿将讲话者及听众都作为第三方，而修改稿将讲话者作为第一人称，Ohio 作为第二人称。
15. 英文原稿将"在华投资"译为了 have made presence in China，是不正确的翻译，修改稿改为了 have investments in China。
16. 在英文原稿中"While gaining big returns, their market share is enlarging."是个语法错误（悬垂分词），gaining 的真正主语不是 market share。修改稿避开了这一陷阱，将其译为了一个复合句"Returns have been good, and market share is growing."。
17. 英文原稿中的 After the Trade Office in Hong Kong 改为了修改稿中的 Following the opening of the Trade Office in Hong Kong。
18. 修改稿使用了代词 another one。
19. 英文原稿紧跟中文原文将"举措"译为 moves。moves 在英语中指临时性的措施，很明显这不是中文原文的本意。修改稿改为了指代 trade offices 的 these。

20. 在英文原稿中，对“起重要作用”的翻译是硬译 (rigid translation) “play a pivotal role”。实际上，“作用”不一定总是译为 role。修改稿将此改为了 these will be pivotal in。

施晓菁（Lynette Shi），美国蒙特雷国际研究学院（MIIS）高级翻译学院副教授（也有译为“助理教授”的）(associate professor)、国际会议口译员协会（AIIC）会员及亚太区主管、联合国资深同传译员、AIIC 会员、中国外文局教育培训中心顾问。主要译著有《骆驼祥子》及多部翻译辞书。

练习题：

根据本节讲述的广义翻译过程， 将下面这个段落翻译为英语。

在人际关系问题上我们不要太浪漫主义。人是很有趣的，往往在接触一个人时首先看到的都是他或她的优点。这一点颇像是在餐馆里用餐的经验。开始吃头盘或冷碟的时候，印象很好。吃头两个主菜时，也是赞不绝口。愈吃愈趋于冷静，吃完了这顿筵席，缺点就都找出来了。于是转喜为怒，转赞美为责备挑剔，转首肯为摇头。这是因为，第一，开始吃的时候你正处于饥饿状态，而饿了吃糠甜如蜜，饱了吃蜜也不甜。第二，你初到一个餐馆，开始举筷时有新鲜感，新盖的茅房三天香，这也可以叫作“陌生化效应”。

第三章
汉英翻译语篇实践

根据奈达的说法，文学翻译在全部翻译中所占比例不超过 5%；根据 Scarpa, 文学翻译仅占世界翻译总量的 1%（转引自李长栓，2004：20）。换言之，在现实世界中，翻译材料绝大多数为非文学材料。因此，在本章中，在题材上我们强调非文学翻译，但这并不是因为非文学翻译比文学翻译容易。关于非文学翻译，北京外国语大学李长栓教授有如下评价：

有人认为非文学翻译比文学翻译容易，这是一种误解。任何翻译都需要艰苦、细致的工作，克服各种各样的语言障碍和文化障碍，非文学翻译也不例外。文学翻译有其特点和难处，非文学翻译也一样。（李长栓，2004：68）

非文学翻译涉及的文体主要有：应用文翻译、商务翻译、政治翻译、法律翻译、新闻翻译。同时，在非文学翻译方面，我们强调交际翻译的理念。也就是说，非文学翻译的译文要是有效的目的语文本，要让目的语读者看得懂，能够实现其在目的语环境中的交际功能，而不是仅仅忠实地一字不漏地把原文转换为译文。

在实际翻译中，文学翻译所占比例虽然不高，但其在翻译中的地位举足轻重，不可忽视。文学翻译不同于一般类型的翻译，最根本的区别是文学作品使用的不是一般的语言，而是一种艺术的、具有美学感染力的语言（姜倩、何刚强，2008：98）。

这就要求文学翻译不仅要忠实于原文，还要具有一定的创造性。正如茅盾（1984：10）所说：

这样的翻译，自然不是单纯技术性的语言外形的变易，而是要求译者通过原作的语言外形，深刻地体会原作者的艺术创作的过程，把握原作的精神，在自己的思想、感情、生活体验中找到最适合的印证，然后运用适合于原作的文学语言，把原作的内容与形式正确无疑地再现出来。这样的翻译的过程，是把翻译者和原作者合二为一，好像原作者用另外一国文字写自己的作品。这样的翻译既需要译者发挥工作上的创造性，而又要完全忠实于原作的意图，——这是一种困难的工作。但是文学翻译的主要任务，既然在于把原作的精神、面貌忠实地复制出来，那么，这种艺术创造性的翻译就完全是必要的。

第一节 应用文翻译

应用文种类繁多，但共同点是用语规范，行文以书面语为主，措辞严谨，句式整齐，概念明确，内容和观点力求客观，避免个人感情的渗入，在形式上往往有特定的文本样式和表达程式（姜倩、何刚强，2008：99）。根据应用文的这些特点，姜倩、何刚强（2008：99）进一步指出应用文翻译时应注意的两方面问题：一是译者需要注意形式问题，在文章格式、体例等方面译文和原文原则上要保持一致；二是在语言表达上，不求华美优雅，但求明确清晰，注意语言规范。

1. 澳门大学简介英译

中文原文：

澳门大学（澳大）是一所国际化综合大学，前身为1981年创立的私立东亚大学，1988年由政府收购后改为公立大学，1991年改名为澳门大学，成为澳门唯一的一所公立大学。设有工商管理学院、教育学院、社会科学及人文学院、法学院、科技学院、中华医药研究院和荣誉学院。澳大开办学士、硕士、博士等约100个学位课程，主要的教学语言为英语。设两个教学中心，包括持续进修中心和英语中心。目前在校学生6 900多名，其中本科生约5 100人。澳大拥有一支400多人的国际化教师队伍，大部分教师拥有博士学位，其中许多教师是在世界著名的大学取得博士学位，拥有丰富的国际教学经验和卓越的学术背景。

澳大位于珠海横琴岛的新校区将于3年后落成，并将由澳门特区法律实施管辖。新校区对于推进澳门高等教育事业的发展，具有重要的意义和长远的影响，并为澳大带来新的课程、新的设施、新的校园文化和新的管理模式。这千载难逢的历史契机将有助于澳大实践精品本科教育、优秀师资团队、卓越科研和高效环保的办学理念，创建成为一所具有区域特色、高水准的世界一流大学。

参考译文：

The University of Macau (UM) is a comprehensive university of international standing. Formerly a private institution established in 1981 with the name of University of East Asia (UEA), the university was purchased by the local government in 1988 and was renamed the University of Macau in 1991, becoming the only public university in Macao. Presently, major academic units of UM include: Faculty of Business Administration, Faculty of Education, Faculty of Social Sciences and Humanities, Faculty of Law, Faculty of Science and Technology, Institute of Chinese Medical Sciences, and Honours College. UM offers approximately 100 bachelor's, master's and Ph.D degree programmes with English being the main medium of instruction. It also has two teaching centers, namely Center for Continuing Education and English Language Center.

Presently UM has more than 6,900 students, approximately 5,100 of whom are undergraduate students. UM boasts a strong faculty team comprised of more than 400 academics from around the world, most of whom have Ph.D degrees granted by renowned universities as well as rich teaching experience and impressive academic backgrounds.

Construction of the new UM campus on Hengqin Island will be completed within three years. Upon completion, it will come under the jurisdiction of Macao SAR. The new campus project will have a far-reaching impact on the future development of Macao's higher education. It will bring new academic programmes, new facilities, a new culture and new management models for the university. The unprecedented opportunity presented by the new campus project will help UM to develop into a world-class university with distinctive regional features and realize elite undergraduate education, outstanding faculty, research excellence and environmental efficiency.

2. 上海世博会团队票 "注意事项" 英译

中文原文：

注意事项

· 园区开放时间 9：00—24：00，21：00 起停止入园。上海世博局有权调整园区、展馆开放时间和活动安排，或采取临时限制入园措施。

· 本票为团队纪念票，不作入园使用。本票请妥善保管，请勿弯折、浸水或置于强磁场环境。

· 不准携带动物及上海世博局规定的其他禁带物品入园。

· 入园后请保留本票以备查验及他用。

· 请遵守上海世博局的有关规定，遵从工作人员的现场引导。

上海世博会事务协调局

网址：www.expo2010.cn 服务热线：+86-21-962010

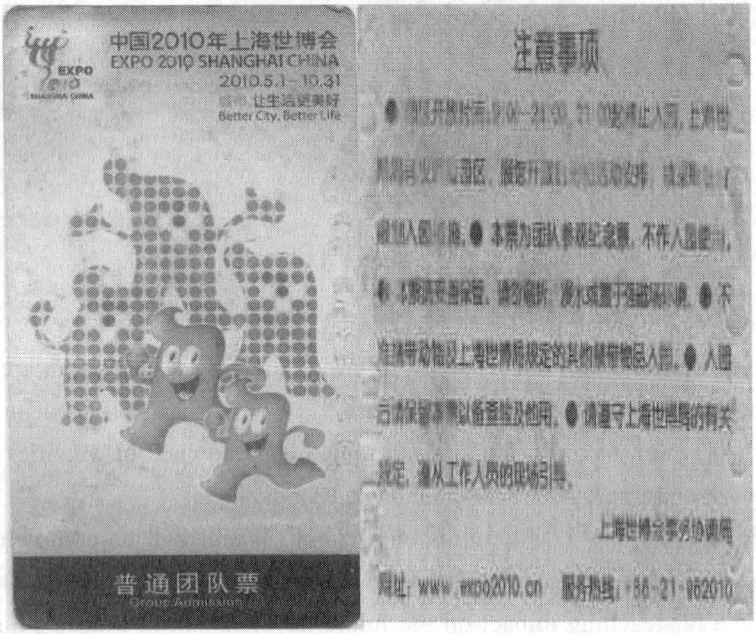

参考译文：

NOTICE

· Park operating hours: 9:00–24:00, last entry: 21:00. The Expo Bureau reserves the right to reschedule the operating hours of the Park and pavilions and to limit admission on a temporary base.

· This ticket is only used as a souvenir ticket for group visitors, not for entry into the Park.

· Please maintain the ticket properly. Any improper acts, such as bending, moistening or exposing to strong magnetic forces, should be avoided.

· No animals or any other item prohibited by the Expo Bureau are allowed in the Park.

· Please keep the ticket for further check or other uses.

· Please observe the regulations by the Expo Bureau and follow the instructions of staff on-site.

Bureau of Shanghai World Expo Coordination

Website: www.expo2010.cn　Hotline:+86-21-962010

3. 中文演讲的英译：国家主席胡锦涛在美国耶鲁大学演讲的部分内容英译

2006年4月21日，国家主席胡锦涛在美国耶鲁大学发表重要演讲。

在美国耶鲁大学的演讲

（2006年4月21日，纽黑文）

中华人民共和国国家主席胡锦涛

尊敬的理查德·莱文校长，同学们，老师们，女士们，先生们：

首先，我感谢莱文校长的邀请，使我有机会来到世界著名学府耶鲁大学，同青年朋友和老师们相聚在一起。

进入耶鲁大学的校园，看到莘莘学子青春洋溢的脸庞，呼吸着书香浓郁的空气，我不由回想起40年前在清华大学度过的美好时光。学生时代，对人的一生都会产生重要影响。当年老师们对我的教诲，同学们给我的启发，我至今仍受用不尽。

耶鲁大学以悠久的发展历史、独特的办学风格、卓著的学术成就闻名于世。如果时光能够倒流几十年，我真希望成为你们中的一员。

耶鲁大学校训强调追求光明和真理，这符合人类进步的法则，也符合每个有志青年的心愿。300多年来，耶鲁大学培养出一大批杰出人才，其中包括20位诺贝尔奖获得者、5位美国总统。美国民族英雄内森·黑尔是耶鲁校友，他的名言——"我唯一的憾事，就是没有第二次生命献给我的祖国"，深深感染了我和许多中国人。我衷心祝愿贵校培养出更多英才，为美国经济社会发展、为人类进步事业作出更大贡献！

女士们、先生们、朋友们！

长期以来，中美两国人民一直相互抱有浓厚的兴趣和友好的感情。中国人民欣赏美国人民的开拓进取精神，钦佩美国人民在建设国家中取得的骄人业绩。随着中国的快速发展和中美合作的不断拓展，越来越多的美国人也把目光投向中国，更加关注中国的发展进步。

了解是信任的基础。今天，我愿从中华文明历史流变和现实发展的角度，谈谈当代中国的发展战略和前进方向，希望有助于美国人民更全面、更深入地了解中国。

在5 000多年的历史长河中，中华民族为人类文明进步做出了巨大贡献，同时也走过了曲折艰辛的道路。特别是从1840年鸦片战争以来的160多年间，中国人民为摆脱积贫积弱的境遇，实现民族复兴，前仆后继，顽强斗争，使中华民族的命运发生了深刻变化。95年前，中国人民通过辛亥革命推翻了统治中国几千年的君主专制制度，为中国的进步打开了闸门。57年前，中国人民经过长期浴血奋斗实现了民族独立和人民解放，建立了人民当家做主的新中国。28年前，中国人民开始了改革开放和现代化建设的伟大历史进程，经过艰苦创业取得了举世瞩目的巨大成就，从1978年到2005年，中国国内生产总值从1 473亿美元增长到22 257亿美元，进出口总额从206亿美元增长到14 221亿美元，国家外汇储备从1.67亿美元增加到8 189亿美元，农村贫困人口由2.5亿人减少到2 300多万人。回顾这160多年来中国发生的沧桑巨变，可以说，中国人民经过艰苦探索和顽强奋斗，既改变了自己的命运，也推动了人类进步事业。

参考译文：

Speech by Chinese President Hu Jintao at Yale University

New Haven, April 21，2006

Dear Mr. Richard Levin, President of Yale University,
Dear Students and Faculty Members, Ladies and Gentlemen,

Let me begin by thanking you, Mr. Levin, for your kind invitation and the opportunity to come to Yale to meet young friends and teachers of this world-renowned university.

Coming to the Yale campus with its distinctive academic flavor and looking at the eager young faces in the audience, I cannot but recall my great experience studying at Qinghua University in Beijing 40 years ago. Indeed, what happens during one's school years will influence his whole life. I still benefit greatly from the instruction of my teachers and my interaction with other students.

Yale is renowned for its long history, unique way of teaching and excellence in academic pursuit. If time could go back several decades, I would really like to be a student of Yale just like you.

Yale's motto, "Light and Truth," which is a calling for human progress, represents the aspiration of every motivated young man and woman. Over the past three centuries, Yale has produced a galaxy of outstanding figures, including 20 Nobel laureates and five American presidents. The words of Nathan Hale, an American hero and Yale alumnus, "I only regret that I have but one life to lose for my country" have also inspired me and many other Chinese. I sincerely hope that Yale will produce more talents and contribute further to the social and economic development of the United States and the cause of human progress.

Ladies and Gentlemen, Dear friends,

The Chinese and Americans have always had an intense interest in and cared deeply about each other. The Chinese admire the pioneering and enterprising spirit of the Americans and their proud achievements in national development. As China develops rapidly and steady headway is made in China-U.S. cooperation, more and more Americans are following with great interest China's progress and development.

Understanding leads to trust. Today, I would like to speak to you about China's development strategy and its future against the backdrop of the evolution of the Chinese civilization and China's current development endeavor. I hope this will help you gain a better understanding of China.

In a history that spans more than five millennia, the Chinese nation has contributed significantly to the progress of human civilization. But its course of national development has been an arduous one. In particular, in the 160 years and more since the Opium War in 1840, the Chinese people have fought courageously and unyieldingly to rid themselves of poverty and backwardness and to realize national rejuvenation, thus profoundly changing the destiny of the Chinese nation. Ninety-five years ago, the Chinese people launched the Revolution of 1911 that overthrew the feudal autocracy which had ruled China for several thousand years and opened the door to China's progress. Fifty-seven years ago, the Chinese people succeeded in winning liberation after protracted and hard struggle and founded New China in which people became their own masters. Twenty-eight years ago, the Chinese people embarked upon the historic drive of reform, opening-up and modernization and have made phenomenal progress through unremitting efforts. Between 1978 and 2005, China's GDP grew from US$147.3 billion to US$2.2257 trillion. Its import and export volume went up from US$20.6 billion to US$1.4221 trillion, and its foreign exchange reserve soared from US$167 million to US$818.9 billion. During this period, the number of its poor rural population dropped from 250 million to 23 million. The above review of the profound changes in these 160 years shows one thing, namely, by carrying out persistent and hard struggle, the Chinese people have both changed their own destiny and advanced the cause of human progress.

（译文摘自外交部网站 http://www.mfa.gov.cn/eng/zxxx/t259224.htm）

练习题：

一、将以下应用文翻译为英语。

1. 澳门简介

澳门以前是个小渔村，它的本名为濠镜或濠镜澳，因为当时泊口可称为“澳”。澳门及其附近盛产蠔（即牡蛎），蠔壳内壁光亮如镜，澳门因此被称为蠔镜。后人把这个名称改为较文雅的“濠镜”。从这个名称中，又引申出濠江、海镜、镜海等一连串澳门的别名。

澳门的名字源于渔民非常敬仰的一位中国女神——天后，她又名娘妈。后人在其登岸的地方建了一座庙宇供奉这位娘妈。

16 世纪中叶，第一批葡萄牙人抵澳时，询问居民当地的名称，居民误以为指庙宇，答称“妈阁”。葡萄牙人以其音而译成“MACAU”，成为澳门葡文名称的由来。在后来的 400 多年的时间里，东西文化一直在此地相互交融，留下了许多历史文化遗产，使澳门成为一个独特的城市。

自 1999 年 12 月 20 日起，澳门成为中华人民共和国的一个特别行政区。在“一国两制”政策的指引下，澳门实行高度自治，享有行政管理权、立法权、独立的司法权和终审权，而澳门在社会和经济方面的特色会予以保留并得以延续。

澳门的面积很小，是世界上人口最稠密的地方之一，也是亚洲人均收入较高的地区。

地理位置

澳门特别行政区是中国领土的一部分，位于中国广东省东南沿海的珠江三角洲，毗邻广东省，与香港相距 60 公里，距离广州 145 公里。

面积

澳门的总面积因为沿岸填海造地而一直扩大，已由 19 世纪的 10.28 平方公里逐步扩展至今日的 28.6 平方公里，面积约是香港的 1/40、新加坡的 1/23。澳门包括澳门半岛、氹仔和路环两个离岛。半岛北面与中国大陆相连，南面分别由嘉乐庇大桥、友谊大桥和西湾大桥与氹仔岛连接；至于氹仔岛与路环岛，则由全长 2.2 公里、6 线行车的路连贯公路相接。

中西文化、民情风俗

澳门是 19 世纪前中国主要的对外港口，也是亚洲地区重要的国际港口。贸易活动的兴盛吸引了世界各地的人前来，一个融合欧、亚、非、美四洲人民的“华洋杂居”的国际城市于是就诞生了。

在这种机遇下，澳门得风气之先，成为中国境内接触近代西方器物与文化最早、最多、最重要的地方，是当时中国接触西方文化的桥头堡。与此同时，居住在澳门的外国人，也以各种方式，向世界各国介绍在澳门见到的一切中国文化思想与生活习俗。澳门，也是一道外国认识中国的门户。

澳门开创了许多“中国第一”的事业，如中国第一所西式大学（圣保禄学院）、中国第一所西式医院（白马行医院）、中国第一所西式印刷厂（圣保禄学院附属印刷所）、中国第一份外文报纸（《蜜蜂华报》）（*A Abelha da China*）等等。

在 400 多年的历史里，中国人与葡萄牙人在澳门历史城区内，合力营造了不同的生活社区。这些生活社区，除了展示澳门的中、西式建筑艺术特色外，更展现了中葡两国人民不同宗教、文化以至生活习惯的交融与尊重。这种中葡人民共同酝酿出来的温情、淳朴、包容的社区气息，是澳门最具特色、最有价值的地方。

世界遗产

2005 年 7 月 15 日，在南非德班市举行的第 29 届世界遗产委员会议上，“澳门历史城区”正式获得通过，成为中国第 31 处世界遗产项目。《中国国家地理》杂志评选中国最美的五个古城区时，澳门名列第三。历史城区拥有 25 个历史建筑物，正是澳门居民聚居和生活的地方，这亦是吸引游客之处。

澳门历史城区是中国现存最古老的西式建筑遗产，是东西方建筑艺术的综合体现。澳门历史城区见证了西方宗教文化在中国以至远东地区的发展，也见证了向西方传播中国民间宗教的历史渊源。

澳门历史城区是中西文化多元共存的独特反映，是中国历史城市中极具特色的组合。澳门历史城区是中西生活社区有序的组合，从历史到今天，都与居民的生活习俗、文化传统密不可分。

澳门历史城区保存了澳门 400 多年中西文化交流的历史精髓。它是中国境内现存年代最远、规模最大、保存最完整和最集中，以西式建筑为主、中西式建筑互相辉映的历史城区；是西方宗教文化在中国和远东地区传播历史重要的见证；更是 400 多年来中西文化交流互补、多元共存的结晶。

欲查询更多有关澳门历史城区的资料，请登录以下网址：

http://www.macauheritage.net/mherit/indexC.asp

2. 粤剧简介

粤剧发源和流行于广东和广西地区，已经有近 300 年的历史。它是集文学、历史、音乐、舞蹈、美术和武术于一身的综合表演艺术。在粤剧演出中，舞台美术是一个重要组成部分，包括戏服、盔头、化妆、道具、布景和灯光等，用于突出剧中人物的角色形象和营造舞台情景气氛。

本次展览透过展出的戏服、盔头、靴鞋、头饰和道具等，让游客对粤剧舞台美术有扼要的认识。

3. 香港机场世贸中心简介

香港机场世贸中心是世界一流、服务专业、设备齐全的商务中心、会议中心及会员会所。

香港国际机场世贸中心位于全球有名的国际枢纽，地点优越，交通方便，为商务旅客提供一站式完善及高弹性的工作环境，除了设有一应俱全的办公室、会议设施、贸易资料库等，中心内的会员会所（机场世贸中心会所）更提供高级餐饮服务。你只需安坐在这配套完善的办公室，便可即时投入工作。办公室可作私人办公或商务会议用途，收费甚至可以按时计算。在繁重的商务会议结束后，你还可前往会员会所享用佳肴美膳。会所餐厅供应的中式菜肴屡获殊荣，是款待客户及业务伙伴的最佳选择。香港国际机场世贸中心是世贸中心协会的正式会员。 该协会会员数目与日俱增，目前已于超过 90 个国家设立逾 300 个世贸中心，为超过 75 万个国际业务机场提供服务。

网址：www.wtchkia.com　　电邮地址：info@wtchkia.com

4. 香港浸会大学年报摘译

培植知识种子

于 2012 年 9 月，浸大迎来“3+3+4”新学制下的变班年。为迎接这历史性的一年，浸大在过去数年一直悉心筹划，以确保教学设施能应付激增的学生人数，以及行政系统能顺利应付三年制和四年制的本科课程同时并行。尽管过程繁复、挑战重重，但因规划得宜，新学制得以顺利推行。

为进一步推行浸大“全人教育”理念，大学设计了全新的四年制课程，以加强知识面的广度和深度，提供学习果效良好的通识课程，让学生可从更多的选修科和跨学科课程中选择。大学更采纳“果效为本”的教学方式，确保所有课程内容均有助培育浸大的毕业生七大特质。此外，大部分学院改为执行“联合收生”制，让学生在大学首年可全面认识心仪的学科，帮助他们于第二年选科时，能做出明智而合适的选择。

浸大的多元化通识课程为学生日后的整全大学教育奠定了良好基础。于 2012—2013 学年，浸大共有 142 个通识课程提供同学选修，其中六个为跨学科课程；并于 2013—2014 学年推行“GE Off Campus”计划，鼓励学生参加具启发性的活动，如话剧欣赏、艺术表演、体验学习等，从而把通识教育所学到的应用到个人和专业发展上。 在浸大尚志会（HKBU Century Club）赞助下，将推出“通识教育杰出学生奖励计划”，以奖励在通识教育课程上有优秀学术表现、积极参与通识教育活动及热心投入社区服务的学生。

培植知識種子

於2012年9月，浸大迎來3+3+4新學制下的雙班年。為迎接這歷史性的一年，浸大在過去數年一直悉心籌劃，以確保教學設施能應付激增的學生人數，以及行政系統能順利應付三年制和四年制的本科課程同時並行。儘管過程繁複，挑戰重重，但因規劃得宜，新學制得以順利推行。

為進一步推行浸大的「全人教育」理念，大學設計了全新的四年制課程，以加強知識面的廣度和深度，提供學習果效良好的通識課程，讓學生可從更多的選修科和跨學科課程中選擇。大學更採納「果效為本」的教學方式，確保所有課程內容均有助培育浸大的畢業生七大特質。此外，大部分學院改為執行「聯合收生」制，讓學生在大學首年可全面認識心儀的學科，幫助他們於第二年選科時，能作出明智而合適的選擇。

浸大的多元化通識課程為學生日後的整全大學教育奠定良好基礎。於2012-13學年，浸大共有142個通識課程供同學選修，其中六個為跨學科課程；並於2013-14學年推行「GE Off Campus」計劃，鼓勵學生參加具啟發性的活動，如話劇欣賞、藝術表演、體驗學習等，從而把通識教育所學到的應用到個人和專業發展上。在浸大尚志會贊助下，將推出「通識教育傑出學生獎勵計劃」，以獎勵在通識教育課程上有優秀學術表現、積極參與通識教育活動及熱心投入社區服務的學生。

二、分析并总结中文应用文的文体特点及其英译对策。

第二节 中文商务、经济类文章的英译

商务翻译属于专门用途翻译的一种，包括外经贸函电、招商引资对外宣传、市场营销、对外劳务契约与合同、国际金融、涉外保险、国际旅游、国际运输、国际金融与会计核算、涉外法律条文、WTO 文献等。 商务翻译在所有翻译活动中占据着相当的比例，具有举足轻重的地位。商务翻译有如下特点：1）准确性。准确性是商务翻译的最基本要求。如果翻译出错，轻则影响商务沟通，重则会带来巨大的经济损失。因此在商务翻译中，译文必

须准确地传递原文的信息。2）得体性。商务文本措辞严谨，语气委婉，注重礼节，行文正式。因此，在翻译商务、经济类文章时要注意这些特点。

1.《澳门贸易投资快讯》2010 年 6 月 249 期

中文原文：

首季 GDP 增长 30.1%

今年第 1 季本地生产总值取得 30.1% 的实质增长，高于去年第 4 季的 27.4%。其中，今年第 1 季博彩旅游业表现理想，其中博彩毛收入（不计赏钱）较去年同季名义升幅达 57.1%，旅客消费总额（不包括博彩消费）的增幅由去年第 4 季的 0.8% 上升至 14.3%；货物出口的跌幅由去年第 4 季的 41.8% 收窄至 12.8%；但固定资本形成总额持续收缩，减幅达 38.9%。

参考译文：

GDP for the first quarter of 2010 grew by 30.1% in real terms, up from the 27.4% growth of the fourth quarter of 2009. The gaming and tourism sector saw vibrant growth in the first quarter, with gross gaming revenues (excluding gratuities) soaring by 57.1% year-on-year in nominal terms and total visitor spending (excluding gaming expenses) rising further from a 0.8% increase in the fourth quarter of 2009 to 14.3%. Exports decrease tapered off from 41.8% in the previous quarter to 12.8%; however, gross fixed capital shrank steadily to post a decrease of 38.9%.

2. 港澳与内地的经贸关系（昆士兰大学提供）

中文原文：

内地改革开放三十年来，港澳的经济发展和内地的经贸合作令人鼓舞，内地与港澳已经形成唇齿相依、密不可分的经贸关系。特别是 2003 年以来，《关于建立更紧密经贸关系的安排》及其四个补充协议的签署与实施，更标志着内地与港澳的经贸合作进入了一个新阶段。

安排和协议的实施减少了内地与港澳在经贸交流中的体制性障碍，加快了相互间资本、货物、人员的流动，对港澳经济的复苏和与内地的经贸交流起到了积极的促进作用，具体表现在以下两个方面：

一是增强了港澳市民投资、消费信心，推动了港澳经济的增长，稳定了房地产市场并拉动股票市场上扬。困扰香港多年的通货紧缩问题也已随着经济的强劲复苏而消失。

二是促进了港澳制造业的专业升级，推动了澳门经济适度多元发展。同时，也使香港日益成为跨国公司拓展内地与亚洲业务的首选之地，不少内地企业和海外企业相继以香港作为地区总部。

近年来，港澳开放对内地游客的自由行更是加强了与内地的人员和经济交流。

参考译文：

Hong Kong and Macao's Economic and Trade Relations with the Chinese mainland

For the past 30 years, as the Chinese mainland has reformed and opened up, the economic development of Hong Kong and Macao and their economic and trade cooperation with the Chinese mainland have been encouraging. The Chinese mainland has formed interdependent and close-knit economic and trade links with Hong Kong and Macao. In particular, since 2003, the signing and implementation of the Mainland and Hong Kong Closer Economic Partnership Arrangement (CEPA) and its four supplementary agreements are a clearer indication still that the Chinese mainland's economic and trade cooperation with Hong Kong and Macao have entered a new phase.

The implementation of the CEPA and its agreements has reduced the systemic/institutional obstacles/barriers in the Chinese mainland's trade and economic exchanges with Hong Kong and Macao, [has] accelerated the mutual circulation of capital, goods, and personnel, and [has] been a positive/active impetus for [both] the recovery of the economies of Hong Kong and Macao as well as their economic and trade exchanges with the Chinese mainland. In particular this can be seen in the following two areas:

In the first place, it has strengthened/enhanced investment and consumer confidence among the local people of Hong Kong and Macao, promoted the economic growth of Hong Kong and Macao, brought the property market back to stability, and enhanced the stock market. The problem of deflation that had been troubling Hong Kong for many years has already disappeared with the powerful economic improvement and recovery.

In the second place, it has impelled the transforming and the upgrading of the manufacturing sector in Hong Kong and Macao, and promoted a moderate degree of diversified development in Macao's economy. At the same time, it is increasingly making Hong Kong the first choice for multinational companies who are developing their business with the Chinese mainland and Asia. One after the other, numerous mainland Chinese and foreign corporations have been establishing their regional headquarters in Hong Kong.

In recent years, Hong Kong and Macao have been accepting independent tourists from the Chinese mainland which has enhanced Hong Kong and Macao's personnel and economic exchange with the Chinese mainland.

3. 国际化大都市（昆士兰大学提供）

中文原文：

"国际化大都市"从何建起？

近年来，随着中国经济社会的发展、城市化进程的不断加快，国内一些城市纷纷提出建设"国际化大都市"的口号。日前，中国人事科学研究院院长王通讯指出，对照国际化大都市标准，中国真正可以称得上"国际化大都市"的城市可能一个也没有。中国城市国际化还有一段较长的路要走。

何谓"国际化大都市"？具体来讲，它应该具有超群的政治、经济、科技和文化实力，并且与全世界或绝大多数国家在经济、政治、科技和文化上有密切的联系，具有强大的全球影响力。更重要的是，国际化大都市是一种能量的聚合体，能在国际舞台上扮演举足轻重的角色。

由此可见，建设国际化大都市绝非一朝一夕之功，也不是短短几年就能一蹴而就的。

一个城市的发展是与其经济发展水平相适应的。尽管中国经济有了很大发展，但国际化大都市不应成为所有城市发展的目标。

城市化无疑是中国走向现代化的必然选择，但一窝蜂的"国际化"造城运动将给城市建设带来致命伤。

参考译文：

How Does One Begin to Build "Major International[ized] Cities"?

In recent years, following the constant acceleration of both the development of China's economy and society, and the progress/course of its urbanization, some cities in China have, one after the other, been coming out with slogans about constructing "major internationalized cities." A few days ago, Wang Tongxun, director of the Chinese Academy of Personnel Science, pointed out that there was perhaps no city in China that could truly be called/described as a "major internationalized city" in comparison with the standards for such a major internationalized city. The internationalization of Chinese cities still has rather a long way to go.

What is meant by a "major internationalized city"? To be specific, such a city should possess exceptional political, economic, scientific, technological and cultural power, and it should also have close economic, political, scientific, technological and cultural ties with the rest of the world or the majority of countries, as well as strong global influence. More importantly, a major internationalized city is an aggregate of energies, and is able to play a decisive role on the international stage.

From this it can be seen that the construction of a "major internationalized city" is by no means the work of a single day, nor is it even something that can be accomplished in one step in the space of a few short years.

A city's development corresponds to the level of its economic development. Even though the economy has developed greatly in China, a "major internationalized city" should not however become the developmental objective of every city.

Urbanization is, undoubtedly, a necessity in China's move towards modernization. However, swarming into a campaign to create "internationalized" cities will fatally damage the construction of Chinese cities.

4. 香港《南华早报》2010年9月出版的《会展商务》（*Mice Biz*）杂志

中文原文：

会展产业借世博提升

随着新酒店和基建的落成，2010 年世博成功推动上海的会展旅游产业。如 2008 年北京奥运会所展现，盛大活动可以将一个国家对商务旅游的吸引力提升至崭新的高度。如今，中国正借力为期半年的 2010 年上海世博会，使其地位更上层楼。

就此采取的策略之一是借此世博会发展旅游业，为上海树立一个新形象。

"这次盛事不仅催生了新的会展旅游场所及费尔蒙和平饭店等豪华酒店，也使本市交通基建设施取得改善，”上海市旅游局国际旅游促进处助理处长陈平说，“这有助于让全球关注我们的最新发展。”

上海的努力无疑得到了回报。“去年 5 月，我们成功争取到国际会议协会会议于 2013 年 11 月在上海举行，”陈先生表示，“随着基建设施大为改善，奖励旅游方面的潜力不断增长，目前已确认日本安利将于 2011 年底安排由 8 000 人组成的团队访沪。”

此次世博会就奖励旅游和商务会议所派生出来的业务，也让企业旅游管理公司 Hogg Robinson Group 印象深刻。“我们全球各地的企业客户大多在世博期间筹办更多活动，”公司亚太地区执行副总裁詹姆斯 · 史蒂文森表示，“譬如，许多公司利用上海举办其各项活动，其中甚至有部分公司将活动安排在世博会展馆举行。还有公司与上海世博会主办方携手合作，以推动设立特别通道和解决拥挤问题。”

上海市旅游局的统计资料显示，今年 6 月份上海游客数量增长 61.2%，酒店平均客房入住率高达 85.23%，增幅为 26.46。

“由于北京邻近上海，世博会外溢效应由此产生，因为赴沪游客通常也希望到中国首都游历一番，”史蒂文森表示，“这对于远道而来的英美游客更是如此，他们往往会在中国游览多个城市。”

Hogg Robinson 还注意到，目前游客人数已重返 2008 年经济衰退前的水平。“商务游客数量在 2010 年上半年迅速好转，我们预料 2010 年第 3 季还会有较为温和的上升，史蒂文森称。

鉴于 10 月份世博会将落下帷幕，有些人担忧随后会出现后继乏人的情况。“这到世博会快结束时，我们才能知道，”上海浦东丽斯卡尔顿酒店总经理 Rainer Burkle 说，“世博会期间，部分公司由于业务水平已较高而延后在上海举行的会议。”

香港四海旅行社大中华区商旅业务总经理高思伟坚信世博会后将有某种效应产生——问题只是以何种形式产生。“由于这里五星级酒店林立，因此有可能出现供过于求的局面。不过，我不认为情况会像北京在奥运会闭幕后那样严重，原因是上海的跨国企业正在不断扩展而且数目也在不断增加，所以将能够吸收部分供应。我认为，世博会闭幕后上海能提供可供选择的各种会议地点和价格也更灵活，从而有利于会展旅游入境业务。”

约有三项世博会设施之后将变成永久活动场地。如上海市旅游局陈先生所言：“世博中心将会建成一个可容纳 6 000 至 7 000 人的会议中心，用于承办各种论坛和会议。外形酷似 UFO 的演艺中心届时将变身为设有 18 000 个座位的活动场所，用于举办体育赛事等娱乐活动。”

高思伟等旅游业行政人员对此举表示欢迎。“除了新建成的五星级酒店外，新活动场地其实并没有那么多，”他说，“我认为，其原因在于上海和香港一样，市中心区域的场地已捉襟见肘，或是房地产价格节节攀升。这些新的活动地点必将有利于上海会展旅游业务的未来发展，因为它让活动策划者在考虑以上海为目的地时拥有更多的选择。”

参考译文：

Expo Raises Great Expectations

Event boosts Shanghai's reputation as a top Mice destination, thanks to new luxury hotels and an improved transport infrastructure. Big events can lift a country as a delegate destination to new heights—as the 2008 Beijing Olympics showed. Now, China is drawing on the six-month World Expo 2010 in Shanghai to raise that profile even higher.

One of the strategies being adopted is to treat the Expo as the voice of tourism and build a new image for Shanghai.

"The event has given birth to new Mice sites, as well as luxury hotels such as Peace Hotel by Fairmont, and the makeover of our transportation infrastructure," says Patrick Chen Ping, deputy director of Shanghai Municipal Tourism Administration's International Tourism Promotion Department. "This has helped capture global attention to our new development here."

The city's efforts have paid dividends. "Last May, we won an International Congress and Convention Association meeting to be held in November 2013," Chen says. "Incentive-wise, the potential keeps growing with improved infrastructure, and an 8,000-person group from Amway Japan is confirmed for the end of 2011."

The spinoffs from the Expo for incentive trips and business meetings have also impressed corporate level management company Hogg Robinson Group. "Most of our corporate clients around the world are organizing more activities during the period," says James Stevenson, executive vice-president for Asia-Pacific. "Corporates are utilizing Shanghai as the city to hold many of their activities, some of which are held in the pavilions of the Expo. Corporates also work with the organizers of the Shanghai World Expo to facilitate special entry and overcome crowd issues."

Statistics from the Shanghai Municipal Tourism Administration indicate a 61.2 percent increase in travelers to Shanghai in June this year, with average room occupancy at 85.23 percent—an increase of 26.46 percent.

"With the proximity of Beijing to Shanghai, there is a spillover from the World Expo as visitors to Shanghai are also interested in visiting the capital city of China," Stevenson says. "This is especially so for long-haul travelers from the United States and Britain who tend to visit multiple cities in China."

Hogg Robinson has seen travel volume returning to the pre-recession level of 2008. "Business travel volumes have experienced a steep improvement in the first half of 2010. We also predict a gentler improvement in the third quarter," Stevenson says.

With the Expo ending next month, there is concern about a draining post-Expo effect.

"We will not know until closer to the closing date," says Ritz-Carlton Shanghai Pudong general manager Rainer Burkle. "During the expo, some companies held back meetings and conventions in Shanghai due to the already high business levels.

Jonathan Kao See-Wai, general manager for Greater China business travel at Shanghai Four Seas Travel, has no doubts about a post-Expo effect. "As a lot of five-star hotels were built here, there will most likely be an oversupply. However, I do not believe it will be as serious as Beijing after the Olympics, as Shanghai's multinational enterprises are expanding and growing in number and will be able to absorb some of the supply. I think it will be good with the different choices of venue and flexibility in pricing."

Companies with access to bigger budgets seized the opportunity to stage their events at the Expo, while others looked elsewhere. "I believe most of the large-scale convention and exhibition [organizer] avoid the crowds and the high price tag," Kao says. "This diverted mainly meetings traffic to Beijing primarily and some second-tier cities."

Several Expo facilities will be turned into permanent event space. As Mr. Chen of Shanghai Tourism Bureau says: "The World Expo Center will be converted to a convention center for forums and meetings with a capacity for 6,000 to 7,000 people. The Performance Center in a UFO shape will then become an events venue for entertainment with 18,000 seats."

Travel industry executives, such as Kao, welcome the move. "Other than the new five-star hotels, there are not that many new venues. I believe the reason is that Shanghai, like Hong Kong, is running out of space in the city center area or that the price of real estate is going up. These new event spaces will definitely be good for the future of Mice in Shanghai as they give more alternatives to event planners when choosing Shanghai as a destination," he says.

5. 中国人民银行一次国际会议的材料
中文原文：

金融业发展需要有良好的宏观经济环境

经济决定金融，金融又促进经济发展。中央银行可以通过货币政策工具调节货币供应量，但货币流通归根到底是居民、工商企业、商业银行、政府的资金收支的综合反映。因此，为了使金融业稳定发展，必须要有良好的宏观经济环境，要依法确定城乡居民、工商企业、商业银行和政府的行为。

在建立良好的宏观经济环境方面，最重要的是国民经济的发展速度和结构要相对合理、对内对外债务总量和结构须比较合理、本币的兑换机制应实行循序渐进的原则。从1993年到1995年，中国采取控制货币供应、增加有效供给的政策，克服了严重的通货膨胀。从1996年5月1日起到1999年初，中国人民银行6次降低利率，1998年又适当增加货币供应并采取积极的财政政策，从而避免了出现较大的通货紧缩，促进了国民经济的平稳发展。中国鼓励外商对华直接投资，控制外债总量和结构，努力提高外汇储备。中国于 1996 年宣布人民币在经常项目下可兑换，对资本项目实行循序渐进原则。这些措施对我国金融业稳定发展和避免亚洲金融危机对我国的直接冲击，发挥了重要作用。相反，1992 年和 1993 年上半年的房地产过热，近一两年出售中小企业中的逃废债务增加以及国有企业资本过少、负债过多，已成为形成和扩大金融业风险的重要原因。

参考译文：

The Financial Industry Can Only Develop in a Healthy Macroeconomic Environment

The economy sets the tune, whereas financial developments interact with the economy. Although the central bank may adjust the money supply through monetary policy instruments, monetary aggregates eventually reflect the composite fund flows of the households, enterprises, commercial banks and the government agencies. Therefore, sound financial developments call for a healthy macroeconomic environment, in which the behavior of the households, enterprises, commercial banks and the government is legally defined.

In creating such an environment, it is most important to maintain a reasonable relationship between the growth and structure of the economy and a sustainable level and structure of the internal debt and external debt. The principle of gradualism should be applied to local currency convertibility. During 1993–1995, China managed to bring the serious inflation under control by tightening monetary policy and increasing effective supply. Since May 1, 1996, the People's Bank of China has cut interest rates on six occasions. Last year, the money supply was increased appropriately while more proactive fiscal policies were adopted, which helped fend off severe deflation and maintaining steady growth of the national economy. China encourages foreign direct investment, while striving to control the size and structure of its external debt and to increase its foreign exchange reserves. In 1996, China declared the current account convertibility of the Renminbi and adopted the principle of gradualism with regard to capital account convertibility. These measures played an important role in promoting the steady development of the financial sector in China and staving off the direct blast of the Asian Financial Crisis. On the other hand, the legacy of the overheated real estate markets in 1992 and the first half of 1993, the abusive asset stripping and repayment evasion in the recent couple of years, citing enterprise restructuring as an excuse, and the high leverage ratio for state-owned enterprises are major sources of financial risk.

练习题：

1. 把下面的短文译为英语。（中文原文摘自《中国经济改革发展之路》，厉以宁、凌原译，外研社，2010，pp.340-341）

在传统经济运行机制下，资源的有效利用受到严重的限制。市场不完善和企业缺乏活力，不可避免地造成资源的低效率利用，无效供给难以依靠经济内在的力量加以制止。这时，只有依赖政府采取非经济的手段来干预经济。但经济运行机制不转换，即使政府以非经济的手段来暂时缓和因资源利用效率低下而造成的矛盾，问题也只会越积越多。当问题积累到一定程度以后，资源供求之间的矛盾便充分暴露出来。经济的混乱迫使企业不得不为了自身的利益（甚至是为了本单位职工的利益），通过地下交易活动而谋求出路。对个别企业来说，资源利用效率也许有所提高，但对全社会而言，资源利用效率仍然是低下的，甚至还会因地下交易活动而变得更差。这是因为地下市场可能使一些企业为了进行有利于自己的交易而付出昂贵得多的代价，还可能使资源配置的方向进一步扭偏。

2. 把下面的短文译为英语。（中文原文为《中国海洋石油 2009 年可持续发展报告》“经济责任与业绩”中的一部分）

2009 年，中国海油克服了国内外严峻的宏观经济困难及台风等给生产经营带来的不利影响，取得了好于预期的业绩。公司的发展质量和财务健康状况继续保持良好水平。实现销售收入 2 096 亿元，利润总额 524 亿元，截至 2009 年底，公司总资产达 5 183 亿元，增长 20.4%。实现了储量、产量同步增长，上中下游协同发展，进一步完善了公司一体化的产业布局，上游的油气产量，中下游的化肥、甲醇、乙烯、天然气发电等产量都较上年有所增加。

截至 2009 年底，中国海油所属的中国海洋石油有限公司共有净探明储量 26.6 亿桶油当量。

2009 年，中国海油在中国海域自营勘探共获得 15 个新发现，并成功评价了 11 个油气构造；合作勘探取得 2 个新发现并成功评价了 1 个含油气构造。

2009 年，深水勘探获得新突破，流花 34-2 气田获得天然气新发现，并成功评价荔湾 3-1 气田。

此外，垦利 10-1 构造的评价成效显著；文昌油田群周围发现多个小油田，有望带动整体开发。

2009 年，中国海油有 20 多个海上油田项目在建，实现了大部分新建油气田按时投产，并有 3 个新项目提前投产；顺利完成了年度生产目标，油气净产量达 227.7 百万桶油当量，比上年同期增长 17.2%。

在海外，中国海油于印度尼西亚、澳大利亚、尼日利亚和其他国家的油气区块持有权益。

为进一步优化公司下游资源配置，推进上下游一体化战略，中国海油成立了炼化事业部，集中管理公司炼油、石化、重油利用和成品油及化工品销售业务。

2009 年，中国海油惠州炼厂一期 1 200 万吨 / 年炼油项目建成投产，结束了中国海油“有采无炼”的历史。重油利用业绩优异，中海油 36-1 沥青以优异的质量中标长安街改造工程，并且获得 50% 以上的沥青供销量；新开发的环烷基环保高芳橡胶油填补国内空白，生产销售了 1 459 吨，实现了产业化；原有差异化产品形成了规模化，其中 50 号沥青年度产销量达到 4.8 万吨，同比增长 79%，中国海油成为国内最大的 50 号沥青生产商和供应商；商业化的沥青品种由 6 个增加到 10 个。

2009 年中国海油实现销售和贸易实物量 1 924 万吨，销售收入 707 亿元，成功突破成品油销售市场壁垒。截至 2009 年底，中国海油在北京、上海、天津、广州、武汉等 23 个国内重要城市拥有分支机构，在香港拥有境外机构；在华东、华南、华北地区共计拥有 208 座加油站，库容 90 万立方米，油库 28 座。

2009 年 9 月 7 日，中国海油对山东海化集团有限公司实施重组，拥有海化集团 51% 的股份。海化集团组建于 20 世纪 90 年代中期，以发展海洋化工新兴产业为主导，是集煤化工、盐化工、石油化工为一体的大型国有企业。

3. 分析并总结中文商务、经济类文章的文体特点及其英译对策。

第三节 中文政治、外交类文章的英译

政治、外交类文章的翻译属于较难翻译的文章。这类文章的翻译要注意以下几点：1）要明确政治立场，要有政治敏感和政策头脑；2）忠实的标准更高，要紧扣原文，不能随意增词、减词，不能随便改变次序；3）要仔细衡量用词的褒贬含义及语气差别。

1.《邓小平文选》的英译

中文原文：

保持艰苦奋斗的传统

中国过去在很长的时间里处于封闭状态，经济发展受到限制，直到一九七八年底我们党的十一届三中全会，才把这个问题恰当地解决了。从那时到去年底的十年里，中国有了可喜的成就，经济发展和人民的生活水平都上了一个台阶。发展中也出现了新的失误，但主要的还是我们的成就，这是我们的根本观点。我们的国民生产总值翻了一番，这是不容易的，是由于我们坚持社会主义现代化建设的路线，坚持改革开放政策带来的。我们执行的路线、方针、政策是正确的。大错误没有犯，小错误没有断，因为我们没有经验，没有经验就要摔跟头，今后也难以避免。我们现在的问题是通货膨胀，物价上涨得太快，给国家和人民都带来了困难。我们已经注意到这个问题，准备用两年或更多的时间来解决问题。我们的一条经验是，发展顺利时要看到出现的新问题，发展要适度，经济过热就容易出毛病。总之，制定一切政策，要从实际出发。只要注意这一点，就不会犯大错误。如果发现错误，要赶快纠正，不要掩饰，不要回避。把错误纠正过来，就能为我们的经济发展创造更好的条件。我看我们中国还是有希望的，世界上许多国家的通货膨胀比我们厉害，只要全国人民思想统一，治理也不难。对到本世纪末达到国民生产总值翻两番的目标，我们是有信心的。

参考译文：

Maintain the Tradition of Hard Struggle

China was closed for a long time, which handicapped its economic development. Not until the Third Plenary Session of the Eleventh Central Committee, held at the end of 1978, did we solve this problem. During the ten years from that time to last December, our country scored gratifying achievements. Progress was made both in developing the economy and in raising living standards. Although we made new mistakes, our achievements were dominant. This is our basic assessment. We quadrupled the GNP. That was no small achievement. It can be attributed to our perseverance in socialist modernization, reform and the open policy. We have been following correct lines, principles and policies.

However, although we haven't made any major mistakes, we have made many minor ones, because we have no experience. Without experience, we couldn't help blundering and shall no doubt blunder again. The current problem is inflation. Prices have gone up very rapidly, making things difficult for the country and the people. We are aware of this problem and are prepared to spend two years or more solving it. One thing we have learned is that when development is going smoothly, we have to foresee new problems and keep to an appropriate pace; if the economy overheats, it may well cause trouble.

In short, in formulating a policy, we have to proceed from realities. If we take the realities into account, we shall not make major mistakes. Once we discover a mistake, we should not conceal or ignore it but correct it immediately, to create better conditions for economic development. I think the situation in China is promising, because inflation is more serious in many other countries. So long as the people of the whole country achieve unity of thinking, inflation will not be difficult to overcome. We are confident that we can quadruple the GNP by the end of this century.

2.《江泽民文选》的英译

再造一个山川秀美的西北地区

看了这个调查报告，感到很高兴。陕北地区治理水土流失，改善生态环境的措施和经验是好的。

我国是一个有几千年历史的文明古国。包括甘肃、陕西在内的黄河流域，是我们中华民族的主要发祥地。陕西曾经是周、秦、汉、唐等十三个王朝的建都之地，在古代历史上相当长的时间内，陕西、甘肃等西北地区，曾经是植被良好的繁荣富庶之地，所谓“山林川谷美，天材之利多”就是古来描绘陕西一带的自然风物的。司马光的《资治通鉴》中描述盛唐时期陕、甘的发展情景是“闾阎相望，桑麻翳野，天下称富庶者无如陇右”。后来由于历经战乱的破坏，加上自然灾害和滥砍滥伐造成的损失，导致了陕、甘等西北地区的严重沙化、荒漠化，经济文化的发展也因此受到极大制约。

历史遗留下来的这种恶劣的生态环境，要靠我们发挥社会主义制度的优越性，发扬艰苦创业的精神，齐心协力地大抓植树造林，绿化荒漠，建设生态农业去加以根本的改观。经过一代一代人长期地、持续地奋斗，再造一个山川秀美的西北地区，应该是可以实现的。

1997 年 8 月 5 日

参考译文：

Restore the Beautiful Landscape of Northwest China

Reading this investigative report made me very happy. The measures taken to control soil erosion and improve the ecosystem in northern Shaanxi Province and the experience gained therefrom have both been good.

China is an ancient civilization with a history that spans thousands of years. The Yellow River Valley, which includes Gansu and Shaanxi provinces, is the main birthplace of the Chinese nation. Thirteen dynasties, including the Zhou, Qin, Han and Tang, founded their capitals in Shaanxi.

Shaanxi, Gansu and other areas in northwest China were flourishing and prosperous, with lush vegetation, for quite a long time in ancient history. "It is endowed with beautiful mountains, forests, rivers and valleys and a great wealth of natural resources." This passage describes natural scenery in and around Shaanxi in ancient times. In his *Comprehensive Mirror for Aid in Government*, Sima Guang depicted the state of the development of Shaanxi and Gansu in the flourishing period of the Tang Dynasty as follows: "There are numerous households and dense mulberry trees and hemp plants. There is no other place under heaven more prosperous than the area around Shaanxi and Gansu." However, the ravages of war and damage from natural disasters and excessive logging later caused severe desertification in Shaanxi, Gansu and other parts of northwest China, thereby greatly hindering the region's economic and cultural development.

We need to make use of the superiority of socialism, foster a hard-working and enterprising spirit, and work hard together to reforest the region, green the desert wastes and develop eco-friendly agriculture to fundamentally transform the region's poor ecosystem bequeathed to us by history. It should be possible to restore northwest China's beautiful landscape through the prolonged and sustained efforts of generations of Chinese.

3. 国务委员戴秉国 2010 年 12 月发表的署名文章：坚持走和平发展道路

中文原文：

快速发展的中国如何处理与其他国家的关系？

中国有句俗话，在同一个锅里吃饭，哪有锅盖不碰碗勺的。我们生活在同一个地球村，国家之间难免有这样那样的矛盾和摩擦，没什么值得大惊小怪的。关键是问题出现了，本着什么原则处理，是睚眦必报，或是小题大做，还是采取完全不同的办法？我们处理国际关系的基本原则有这么几条，几十年来证明也行之有效：一是坚持按照和平共处五项原则发展同所有国家的关系。不搞干涉内政那一套，不搞使用或威胁使用武力那一套，不搞厚此薄彼、拉帮结派那一套。二是坚持奉行互利共赢的开放战略。不做以邻为壑、损人利己的事，注重共同利益、发展共同利益、维护共同利益，把共同利益的蛋糕做大做好。三是坚持以求同存异、对话协商的方式解决矛盾分歧。这些年我们在这方面做了大量工作，同美国、欧洲、日本以及一些新兴大国都建立了战略对话和磋商机制，就事关当今世界、事关双边关系的一些全局性和长期性重大问题深入交换意见，以增进相互理解、信任，寻求战略共识，扩大共同利益，减少麻烦和波折。对于暂时解决不了的问题，我们主张先放一放，等条件和时机成熟时再说，有些问题也可以让我们的子孙后代去解决。

参考译文：

How Will a Fast Developing China Handle Its Relations with Other Countries?

As a Chinese saying goes, "Scooping rice from the same pot, the ladles may inevitably knock against each other." As we live in a global village, frictions and clashes of various kinds are inevitable. It is nothing alarming. What matters is the principles that one follows in trying to tackle the problems: A tit-for-tat tactic or making a fuss of a minor problem, or rather, a totally different approach? We have our basic principles in our external relations, which have proven effective over the past decades. First, we follow the Five Principles of Peaceful Co-existence. To be specific, we reject interference in others' internal affairs and the use or threat of use of force and we do not enter into alliance with any country. Second, we follow the win-win strategy of opening-up and never adopt the beggar-thy-neighbor policy. We value, develop and protect common interests and strive to make the pie of common interests bigger and better. Third, we stand for settlement of disputes and conflicts through dialogue and negotiation and by seeking common ground while shelving differences. That is what we have been doing over the past years. We have set up strategic dialogue and consultation mechanisms with the United States, Europe, Japan and some emerging countries and have been engaged in in-depth exchange of views with them on important overarching and long-term issues concerning the world situation and bilateral relations. Those discussions have helped to enhance mutual understanding and trust, seek strategic consensus, expand common interests and reduce troubles and setbacks. For knotty problems, we have proposed that they be put aside until conditions are ripe for solution. Some issues can even be left to future generations.

练习题：

1. 将下面的短文译为英语。（摘自 2010 年温家宝总理的《政府工作报告》中关于港澳台的部分）

我们将坚定不移地贯彻"一国两制"、"港人治港"、"澳人治澳"、高度自治的方针，全力支持香港、澳门保持长期繁荣稳定。支持香港巩固并提升国际金融、贸易、航运中心地位，发展优势产业，培育新的经济增长点。支持澳门发展旅游休闲产业，促进经济适度多元化。要认真实施《珠江三角洲地区改革发展规划纲要》，积极推进港珠澳大桥等大型跨境基础设施建设和珠海横琴岛开发，深化粤港澳合作，密切内地与港澳的经济联系。伟大祖国永远是香港、澳门的坚强后盾。只要特别行政区政府与各界人士同心协力，包容共济，共同维护繁荣稳定发展的大局，香港、澳门的明天一定会更加美好。

过去的一年，两岸关系在新的历史起点上取得重要进展，呈现和平发展良好势头。两岸交流合作不断深入，全面直接双向“三通”得以实现。经济关系正常化迈出重要步伐，经济合作制度化建设逐步推进。两岸关系持续改善和发展，给两岸同胞带来了实实在在的利益。在新的一年里，我们要继续坚持发展两岸关系、促进祖国和平统一的大政方针，牢牢把握两岸关系和平发展的主题，不断开创两岸关系和平发展新局面。密切两岸经贸金融交往，深化产业合作，支持在大陆的台资企业发展，维护台胞合法权益。鼓励有条件的大陆企业赴台投资。支持海峡西岸经济区在两岸交流合作中发挥先行先试作用。通过商签两岸经济合作框架协议，促进互利共赢，建立具有两岸特色的经济合作机制。拓展文化教育交流，共同弘扬中华文化。加强两岸民众和社会各界交流，共同分享两岸关系和平发展成果，进一步凝聚推动两岸关系和平发展的共识。坚持大陆和台湾同属一个中国，巩固两岸关系和平发展的政治基础，增强两岸政治互信。我们坚信，全体中华儿女同心协力，祖国完全统一的宏伟大业一定能够实现！

2. 将下面的短文译为英语。（摘自《中美联合公报》）

双方回顾了中美两国之间长期存在的严重争端。中国方面重申自己的立场：台湾问题是阻碍中美两国关系正常化的关键问题；中华人民共和国政府是中国的唯一合法政府；台湾是中国的一个省，早已归还祖国；解放台湾是中国内政，别国无权干涉；全部美国武装力量和军事设施必须从台湾撤走。中国政府坚决反对任何旨在制造“一中一台”、“一个中国、两个政府”、“两个中国”、“台湾独立”和鼓吹“台湾地位未定”的活动。

美国方面声明：美国认识到，在台湾海峡两边的所有中国人都认为只有一个中国，台湾是中国的一部分。美国政府对这一立场不提出异议。它重申它对由中国人自己和平解决台湾问题的关心。考虑到这一前景，它确认从台湾撤出全部美国武装力量和军事设施的最终目标。在此期间，它将随着这个地区紧张局势的缓和逐步减少它在台湾的武装力量和军事设施。

3. 分析并总结中文政治、外交文章的文体特点及其英译对策。

第四节 中文法律类文章的英译

法律语言用词准确严谨，客观规范，句式较长，术语较多。此外，在中文法律文章英译时还应注意以下特点：1）书面语较多；2）英语旧体词和外来词频率较高；3）使用具有不同意义的常用词；4）大量使用命令词和情态动词；5）法律术语、行话、套话较多。

1.《中华人民共和国环境保护法》

中文原文：

第一章 总则

第一条 为保护和改善生活环境与生态环境，防治污染和其他公害，保障人体健康，促进社会主义现代化建设的发展，制定本法。

第二条 本法所称环境，是指影响人类生存和发展的各种天然的和经过人工改造的自然因素的总体，包括大气、水、海洋、土地、矿藏、森林、草原、野生生物、自然遗迹、人文遗迹、自然保护区、风景名胜区、城市和乡村等。

第三条 本法适用于中华人民共和国领域和中华人民共和国管辖的其他海域。

第四条 国家制定的环境保护规划必须纳入国民经济和社会发展计划，国家采取有利于环境保护的经济、技术政策和措施，使环境保护工作同经济建设和社会发展相协调。

第五条 国家鼓励环境保护科学教育事业的发展，加强环境保护科学技术的研究和开发，提高环境保护科学技术水平，普及环境保护的科学知识。

第六条 一切单位和个人都有保护环境的义务，并有权对污染和破坏环境的单位和个人进行检举和控告。

第七条 国务院环境保护行政主管部门，对全国环境保护工作实施统一监督管理。

县级以上地方人民政府环境保护行政主管部门，对本辖区的环境保护工作实施统一监督管理。

国家海洋行政主管部门、港务监督、渔政渔港监督、军队环境保护部门和各级公安、交通、铁道、民航管理部门，依照有关法律的规定对环境污染防治实施监督管理。

县级以上人民政府的土地、矿产、林业、农业、水利行政主管部门，依照有关法律的规定对资源的保护实施监督管理。

第八条 对保护和改善环境有显著成绩的单位和个人，由人民政府给予奖励。

参考译文：

Chapter I General Provisions

Article 1

This Law is formulated for the purpose of protecting and improving people's environment and the ecological environment, preventing and controlling pollution and other public hazards, safeguarding human health and facilitating the development of socialist modernization.

Article 2

"Environment" as used in this Law refers to the total body of all natural elements and artificially transformed natural elements affecting human existence and development, which includes the atmosphere, water, seas, land, minerals, forests, grasslands, wildlife, natural and human remains, nature reserves, historic sites and scenic spots, and urban and rural areas.

Article 3

This Law shall apply to the territory of the People's Republic of China and other sea areas under the jurisdiction of the People's Republic of China.

Article 4

The plans for environmental protection formulated by the state must be incorporated into the national economic and social development plans; the state shall adopt economic and technological policies and measures favourable for environmental protection so as to coordinate the work of environmental protection with economic construction and social development.

Article 5

The state shall encourage the development of education in the science of environmental protection, strengthen the study and development of the science and technology of environmental protection, raise the scientific and technological level of environmental protection and popularize scientific knowledge of environmental protection.

Article 6

All units and individuals shall have the obligation to protect the environment and shall have the right to report on or file charges against units or individuals that cause pollution or damage to the environment.

Article 7

The competent department of environmental protection administration under the State Council shall conduct unified supervision and management of the environmental protection work throughout the country.

The competent departments of environmental protection administration of the local people's governments at or above the county level shall conduct unified supervision and management of the environmental protection work within areas under their jurisdiction.

The state administrative department of marine affairs, the harbour superintendency administration, the fisheries administration and fishing harbour superintendency agencies, the environmental protection department of the armed forces and the administrative departments of public security, transportation, railways and civil aviation at various levels shall, in accordance with the provisions of relevant laws, conduct supervision and management of the prevention and control of environmental pollution.

The competent administrative departments of land, minerals, forestry, agriculture and water conservancy of the people's governments at or above the county level shall, in accordance with the provisions of relevant laws, conduct supervision and management of the protection of natural resources.

Article 8

The people's government shall give awards to units and individuals that have made outstanding achievements in protecting and improving the environment.

2. 香港基本法

中文原文：

中华人民共和国香港特别行政区基本法

（1990 年 4 月 4 日第七届全国人民代表大会第三次会议通过 1990 年 4 月 4 日中华人民共和国主席令第二十六号公布 自 1997 年 7 月 1 日起施行）

序言

香港自古以来就是中国的领土，一八四零年鸦片战争以后被英国占领。一九八四年十二月十九日，中英两国政府签署了关于香港问题的联合声明，确认中华人民共和国政府于一九九七年七月一日恢复对香港行使主权，从而实现了长期以来中国人民收回香港的共同愿望。

为了维护国家的统一和领土完整，保持香港的繁荣和稳定，并考虑到香港的历史和现实情况，国家决定，在对香港恢复行使主权时，根据中华人民共和国宪法第三十一条的规定，设立香港特别行政区，并按照“一个国家，两种制度”的方针，不在香港实行社会主义的制度和政策。国家对香港的基本方针政策，已由中国政府在中英联合声明中予以阐明。

根据中华人民共和国宪法，全国人民代表大会特制定中华人民共和国香港特别行政区基本法，规定香港特别行政区实行的制度，以保障国家对香港的基本方针政策的实施。

第一章　总则

第一条　香港特别行政区是中华人民共和国不可分离的部分。

第二条　全国人民代表大会授权香港特别行政区依照本法的规定实行高度自治，享有行政管理权、立法权、独立的司法权和终审权。

第三条　香港特别行政区的行政机关和立法机关由香港永久性居民依照本法有关规定组成。

第四条　香港特别行政区依法保障香港特别行政区居民和其他人的权利和自由。

第五条　香港特别行政区不实行社会主义制度和政策，保持原有的资本主义制度和生活方式，五十年不变。

第六条　香港特别行政区依法保护私有财产权。

第七条　香港特别行政区境内的土地和自然资源属于国家所有，由香港特别行政区政府负责管理、使用、开发、出租或批给个人、法人或团体使用或开发，其收入全归香港特别行政区政府支配。

第八条　香港原有法律，即普通法、衡平法、条例、附属立法和习惯法，除同本法相抵触或经香港特别行政区的立法机关作出修改者外，予以保留。

第九条　香港特别行政区的行政机关、立法机关和司法机关，除使用中文外，还可使用英文，英文也是正式语文。

第十条　香港特别行政区除悬挂中华人民共和国国旗和国徽外，还可使用香港特别行政区区旗和区徽。

香港特别行政区的区旗是五星花蕊的紫荆花红旗。

香港特别行政区的区徽，中间是五星花蕊的紫荆花，周围写有“中华人民共和国香港特别行政区”和英文“香港”。

第十一条　根据中华人民共和国宪法第三十一条，香港特别行政区的制度和政策，包括社会、经济制度，有关保障居民的基本权利和自由的制度，行政管理、立法和司法方面的制度，以及有关政策，均以本法的规定为依据。

香港特别行政区立法机关制定的任何法律，均不得同本法相抵触。

参考译文：

THE BASIC LAW OF THE HONG KONG SPECIAL ADMINISTRATIVE REGION OF THE PEOPLE'S REPUBLIC OF CHINA

(Adopted at the Third Session of the Seventh National People's Congress on April 4, 1990, promulgated by Order No. 26 of the President of the People's Republic of China on April 4, 1990, and effective as of July 1, 1997)

Preamble

Hong Kong has been part of the territory of China since ancient times; it was occupied by Britain after the Opium War in 1840. On 19 December 1984, the Chinese and British Governments signed the Joint Declaration on the Question of Hong Kong, affirming that the Government of the People's Republic of China will resume the exercise of sovereignty over Hong Kong with effect from 1 July 1997, thus fulfilling the long-cherished common aspiration of the Chinese people for the recovery of Hong Kong.

Upholding national unity and territorial integrity, maintaining the prosperity and stability of Hong Kong, and taking account of its history and realities, the People's Republic of China has decided that upon China's resumption of the exercise of sovereignty over Hong Kong, a Hong Kong Special Administrative Region will be established in accordance with the provisions of Article 31 of the Constitution of the People's Republic of China, and that under the principle of "one country, two systems," the socialist system and policies will not be practised in Hong Kong. The basic policies of the People's Republic of China regarding Hong Kong have been elaborated by the Chinese Government in the Sino-British Joint Declaration.

In accordance with the Constitution of the People's Republic of China, the National People's Congress hereby enacts the Basic Law of the Hong Kong Special Administrative Region of the People's Republic of China, prescribing the systems to be practised in the Hong Kong Special Administrative Region, in order to ensure the implementation of the basic policies of the People's Republic of China regarding Hong Kong.

Chapter I General Principles

Article 1

The Hong Kong Special Administrative Region is an inalienable part of the people's Republic of China.

Article 2

The National People's Congress authorizes the Hong Kong Special Administrative Region to exercise a high degree of autonomy and enjoy executive, legislative and independent judicial power, including that of final adjudication, in accordance with the provisions of this Law.

Article 3

The executive authorities and legislature of the Hong Kong Special Administrative Region shall be composed of permanent residents of Hong Kong in accordance with the relevant provisions of this Law.

Article 4

The Hong Kong Special Administrative Region shall safeguard the rights and freedoms of the residents of the Hong Kong Special Administrative Region and of other persons in the Region in accordance with law.

Article 5

The socialist system and policies shall not be practised in the Hong Kong Special Administrative Region, and the previous capitalist system and way of life shall remain unchanged for 50 years.

Article 6

The Hong Kong Special Administrative Region shall protect the right of private ownership of property in accordance with law.

Article 7

The land and natural resources within the Hong Kong Special Administrative Region shall be State property. The Government of the Hong Kong Special Administrative Region shall be responsible for their management, use and development and for their lease or grant to individuals, legal persons or organizations for use or development. The revenues derived therefrom shall be exclusively at the disposal of the government of the Region.

Article 8

The laws previously in force in Hong Kong, that is, the common law, rules of equity, ordinances, subordinate legislation and customary law shall be maintained, except for any that contravene this Law, and subject to any amendment by the legislature of the Hong Kong Special Administrative Region.

Article 9

In addition to the Chinese language, English may also be used as an official language by the executive authorities, legislature and judiciary of the Hong Kong Special Administrative Region.

Article 10

Apart from displaying the national flag and national emblem of the People's Republic of China, the Hong Kong Special Administrative Region may also use a regional flag and regional emblem. The regional flag of the Hong Kong Special Administrative Region is a red flag with a bauhinia highlighted by five star-tipped stamens. The regional emblem of the Hong Kong Special Administrative Region is a bauhinia in the centre highlighted by five star-tipped stamens and encircled by the words "Hong Kong Special Administrative Region of the People's Republic of China" in Chinese and "HONG KONG" in English.

Article 11

In accordance with Article 31 of the Constitution of the People's Republic of China, the systems and policies practised in the Hong Kong Special Administrative Region, including the social and economic systems, the system for safeguarding the fundamental rights and freedoms of its residents, the executive, legislative and judicial systems, and the relevant policies, shall be based on the provisions of this Law. No law enacted by the legislature of the Hong Kong Special Administrative Region shall contravene this Law.

练习题：

1. 请将以下章程译为英语。

世界旅游城市联合会专家委员会章程
（征求意见稿）

第一章　总则

第一条　为进一步推进世界旅游事业的科学发展，提升世界旅游城市联合会的学术研究水平，推动联合会决策的民主化、科学化进程，充分发挥业界广大专家学者咨询建议的作用，更有效地组织专家资源开展旅游科研、人员培训和学术交流等活动，经世界旅游城市联合会同意，特设立世界旅游城市专家委员会，英文全称为 Expert Committee for World Tourism Cities Federation（以下简称"专家委员会"及 EC）。

第二条　专家委员会是联合会的高级顾问咨询机构和智囊团体，其业务活动接受世界旅游城市联合会（以下简称"联合会"）的指导。

第三条　专家委员会坚持实事求是、客观公正、科学严谨、大胆创新的工作态度。

第二章　职责

第四条　专家委员会受联合会和研究中心委托开展工作，主要职责如下：

（一）围绕联合会发展的重大战略和政策决定，对联合会发展规划、相关政策文件等提供咨询评议；

（二）积极促进联合会和各国旅游政府、业界企业、咨询机构间的交流，开展广泛的国际合作研讨，沟通联合会与业内外的关系；

（三）接受联合会委托，对关系世界旅游业及旅游城市发展的重大热点、难点问题进行跟踪和超前性研究，提供综合调研、项目评估和战略咨询服务；

（四）举办交流论坛和学术沙龙活动，研讨业界基础理论、行业实践、管制政策和法律法规等重大问题，向会员城市的发展提供发展咨询；

（五）根据会员申请，接受联合会委托，为会员提供相应的学术研究、咨询等工作；

（六）接受联合会委托，对世界旅游城市发展指数评价体系部分计量指标进行专家意见评分，为逐步完善评价体系提出科学合理的意见及建议，并参与评价体系的修订及评审；

（七）为联合会出版的电子或纸质版刊物提供业界最新研究成果；

（八）承担联合会和研究中心委托的其他工作。

第三章　组织机构

第五条　专家委员会委员由主任委员、副主任委员、委员组成。设主任委员 1 人、副主任委员 2 人（1 名中方专家，1 名外方专家），委员若干人，学术秘书 1 人。中方副主任委员主持专家委员会的全面工作。

第六条　专家委员会设立委员会秘书处，负责专家委员会的日常工作、沟通联络和其他组织协调工作。

第四章　成员的产生

第七条　专家委员会由国内外学术水平高、旅游业界经验丰富、责任心强，并具有较高威望和重要影响的学者、专家、业界精英组成。专家委员会委员候选人来自相关院校、科研机构、联合会成员及旅游系统推荐，经委员会审核并研讨通过后，由联合会颁发聘书聘任，并在联合会官方网站上专栏发布相关个人简介。

第八条　委员会成员应当具备下列条件：

（一）有高度责任感和事业心，有良好的职业道德，作风正派；

（二）在旅游专业领域有一定造诣，在行业中具有较高影响力；

（三）有丰富的理论知识和实践经验，较强的综合分析判断能力；

（四）身体健康，能够完成所承担的工作任务；

（五）专家委员会规定的其他条件。

第九条　委员会首期成员由筹备发起单位与专家个人协商产生，由联合会直接聘任，任期五年。任期届满后换届，依据专家本人意愿和委员会发展需要，可以延聘或终止。

第十条　每届专家委员会任期五年，委员可续聘续任。

第十一条　专家委员会成员本人或所在单位认为该成员不再适宜继续任职，经本人提出书面申请，提请联合会秘书处决定是否留任。

第十二条　专家委员会委员违反法律法规和本章程，或一年内三次以上无故缺席专家委员会活动的，由联合会秘书处解除聘任，并书面通知本人。

第十三条　专家委员会可根据需要提请联合会秘书处调整委员组成。

第五章　权利和义务

第十四条　专家委员会成员享有下列权利：

（一）参与专家委员会举行的各项活动，优先获得联合会年度报告等公开性成果文件，或其他研究中心提供的信息、资料、数据等；

（二）根据需要免费获取联合会或研究中心研究出版简报、电子期刊、出版杂志等；

（三）以专家委员会委员的身份参加国内外学术会议、开展学术交流和发表论文；

（四）获取与任务有关的文件、资料、数据、背景材料，优先参加联合会或研究中心主办的相关专业学术会议；

（五）在参与咨询、评鉴过程中充分发表个人意见，并可保留个人意见和建议；

（六）向联合会或专家委员会提出工作意见和建议。

（七）联合会赋予的其他权利。

第十五条　专家委员会成员承担下列义务：

（一）遵守有关法律法规和专家委员会的章程或规定；

（二）积极参加会议咨询、评审、学术研讨等各项活动，按时完成应承担的工作任务；

（三）向专家委员会和联合会提供相关的信息和动态，提出相应的工作意见和建议；

（四）遵守相关工作规定，未经授权，不得透露联合会相关数据资料、研究动向、科研成果、年度报告等文件，严守工作秘密；

（五）未经联合会秘书处和研究中心的同意或授权，专家委员会委员不得以联合会和专家委员会的名义从事商业性活动；

第六章　运行管理

第十六条　联合会为专家委员会提供日常运行经费，由专家委员会秘书处负责筹办专家委员会工作，提供必要的工作环境和条件，为委员提供必要的补助；

第十七条　专家委员会原则上每年召开一次全体会议，研讨世界旅游发展战略、趋势等问题，评审世界旅游城市发展指数报告，审议专家委员会年度工作报告和工作计划，研究专家委员会内部重大事项等。

第十八条　专家委员会主任委员可根据情况，召开临时工作会议。

第十九条　专家委员会负责不定期召开专家组研讨会对联合会委托的相关课题进行调查研究、信息反馈、专家咨询等。

第二十条　专家委员会采用集体决策方式产生咨询、评鉴意见。

第二十一条　凡为旅游学术研究和联合会发展做出重大贡献的专家委员会委员，经主任委员提名，联合会秘书处和专家委员会评审通过后，将获邀出席联合会年度会议、颁发相应奖励并书面通知所在机构或单位。

第七章　附则

第二十二条　本章程经专家委员会全体大会表决通过，世界旅游城市联合会发布之日起正式生效。

第二十三条　本章程修改需由专家委员会三分之二以上委员同意。

第二十四条　本章程由世界旅游城市联合会负责解释。

2. 分析并总结中文法律文章的文体特点及其英译对策。

第五节　中文新闻类文章的英译

刘新粦在《国际新闻界》（1987 年第 3 期）总结了新闻翻译的如下特点：1）特别要求译文必须准确，因为新闻翻译政治性强，如有差错可能引起严重后果。在文学翻译中，如果把小说里一个人物的澳大利亚国籍误译为奥地利籍，这自然是一个错误，但恐怕还不至于产生严重后果。可是，如果在新闻翻译中把一个甲国特务误译为乙国间谍，这恐怕就会招来麻烦了。2）要求译得快。一条新闻、一篇文章要求在几个小时甚至几分钟之内译出来，以便及时广播或见报，没有时间给译者逐字逐句慢慢推敲、向人请教或找人商量讨论，也没有很多时间查词典、找资料。翻译界的老前辈严复说过："一名之立，旬月踟躇"，这种严谨、认真的精神自然是好的，但在新闻翻译的实践中却很难这样做，因为时间不允许。第二次世界大战即将结束的时候，美国总统罗斯福病逝，一位记者为了抢先发这条新闻，写了一条只有七个英文字母的消息：FDRDEAD。如果译者平时不知道 FDR 是 Franklin Delano Roosevelt（富兰克林 · 德兰诺 · 罗斯福）的首字母缩略词，那他就势必东查词典，西找资料，不能立即把这条新闻译出来。3）翻译的内容庞杂，一堆电讯稿几乎是一部包罗万象的百科全书。天文、地理、军事、政治、外交、经济、法律、科技、技术、教育、卫生、文学、艺术、历史、哲学、宗教、风俗习惯、风土人情，几乎人类的各种知识，各门学科都同新闻有关。4）世界上最新的事物、最新的词汇往往首先在新闻里出现、介绍，词典里无现成译法，需要译者自己创造性地进行翻译。

此外，与一般翻译不同，进行新闻翻译时，要进行内容分析、媒介分析和受众与效果分析。

中文原文（第23届韩素音翻译大赛原文）：

摩天大楼指数——如影随形的经济危机

作为一种以巨大的经济力量为支撑的建筑物，摩天大楼常被民众和政客视为展示经济繁荣、社会进步的标志。有些经济学家则持完全相反的看法，认为摩天大楼的出现，特别是摩天大楼的纪录被刷新，往往预示着经济即将衰退。

“高楼建成之日，即是市场衰退之时”，这是德意志银行的证券分析师安德鲁·劳伦斯于1999年发表的判言。2006年2月15日，雷曼兄弟公司在北京召开全球经济会议，其全球首席经济学家卢埃林向我国客户提及“摩天大楼指数”的预言：“如果全球有发生经济危机的可能性，那很可能会在2007年或2008年。”

雷曼的首席经济学家预见了2007年到2008年的经济危机，但却不曾想到，雷曼的百年基业正是在这场危机中化为泡影。对于经济而言，摩天大楼是荣耀还是诅咒？其与经济危机之间是否真的存在这样密切的联系呢？

1999年，安德鲁·劳伦斯经过研究验证了摩天大楼与经济危机的关联，并将这种关联称为“摩天大楼指数”。每一幢刷新世界纪录的摩天大楼的崛起，往往都伴随着经济的衰退。自20世纪初以来，全球共出现了四轮摩天大楼热，而每一次，都伴随着经济危机或金融动荡。

20世纪20年代，美国经济转好，证券市场再度空前繁荣，民用、商用房产建设高歌猛进。这期间，三座刷新纪录的摩天大楼先后兴建。纽约的华尔街40号、克莱斯勒大厦和帝国大厦相继于1929年至1931年的三年中落成，但随之而来的不是新的繁荣，而是空前的大萧条。在经历了被美国人称之为“黄金时代”的20世纪60年代强劲、持续的经济繁荣后，纽约的世贸中心和芝加哥的西尔斯大厦开始兴建。1972年和1974年，两座再次刷新世界纪录的摩天大楼相继落成，随后，全球经济发生了严重滞胀。

摩天大楼与经济危机的关联如此密切，很难用巧合来理解，那么究竟是什么原因让经济危机总是与摩天大楼如影随形呢？

首先，人性使然。人性当中有盲目自信的一面，具体体现在对客观事物认识不足，偏执于对事物的主观看法上。劳伦斯把他发现的经济危机与摩天大楼的联系称为“百年病态关联”，但此类现象，在人类社会中又何止只存在了百年。以史为鉴，我们不难发现，在我国历史的长河中，此类现象早有体现。商朝兴盛时，纣王兴建鹿台，引得民怨四起，他本人最终于鹿台自焚；清代鼎盛时，乾隆帝大举修建园林，导致国力衰落最终丧权辱国。

其次，利益推动。在商业行为中，逐利是前提条件。在经济繁荣之前，通常有一个低利率的过程，这也是经济向繁荣周期转化的一个先决条件。而在经济繁荣的过程中，利率相对于人们对于未来收益的预期来说，一直都是低的。

所以，就会产生一系列的利益传导途径，也就是前面所提到的利益链条。经济的繁荣和相对较低的利率，对土地价值和资本成本有着直接的影响。在土地价格、企业需求和资金支撑三个因素所构成的利益链的作用下，可以刷新世界纪录的摩天大楼计划，就应运而生了。

就像日有昼夜、季有冬夏一样，经济也是存在景气周期的。任何商品的价格，都会受到供需关系的影响。否极泰来，盛极而衰，低廉的利率、膨胀的需求、上涨的资本价格，以及大多数人盲目乐观的心态，所集合产生的“黄金状态”构成了摩天大楼的需求，但这种状态是不可持续的。

所以，通常是在经济已经步入衰退的时候，摩天大楼才刚刚竣工；在它真正投入使用的时候，经济很可能已经深陷困境。这就导致了经济危机总是与摩天大楼的兴建如影随形，也常使全球第一建筑成为繁荣逝去的纪念碑。

参考译文（第 23 届韩素音翻译大赛参考译文）：

The Skyscraper Index: Rising Towers Foreshadow Economic Downturns[1]

Skyscrapers, as buildings supported by enormous economic power, are often regarded by the public and by politicians as hallmarks of economic boom and social progress. Some economists, however, hold the opposite view that newly-built skyscrapers, especially those record-breaking ones, often foreshadow an imminent economic recession.

“The world’s tallest buildings have risen on the eve of market downturns.”[2] This is a “verdict” delivered in 1999 by Andrew Lawrence, securities analyst at Deutsche Bank. On February 15, 2006, when Lehman Brothers had its global economic conference in Beijing, John Llewellyn, the investment bank’s global chief economist, mentioned to the Chinese audience his prediction based on the “skyscraper index”: “If there is any possibility of a global economic crisis, it is most

1 This essay is extracted from Chapter 6, *Something You Should Know About Investment* (Li Yijian, Zhejiang University Press, 2007). In rendering the title, the translator drew upon the title of Lawrence’s paper, *The Skyscraper Index: Faulty Towers* (Property Report, March 3, 1999), and his conclusion that “Economic downturns seem as inevitable as rising girders” (*The Curse Bites: The Skyscraper Index Strikes*. Property Report, March 3, 1999).

2 These words, though in quotation marks, are the author’s summary of Lawrence’s findings, not Lawrence’s exact words. Among the related comments from Lawrence is: “[T]he erratic construction of the world’s next tallest building has largely coincided with financial crises.” (*The Skyscraper Index: Faulty Towers*. Property Report, January 15, 1999.)

likely to occur in 2007 or 2008."[1]

Lehman Brothers' chief economist rightly foresaw the economic crisis of 2007–2008, but never imagined that the bank, established on a firm foundation exceeding a hundred years, was to go up in smoke during that crisis. Now, are skyscrapers a blessing or a curse for the world economy? Is there indeed so close a correlation between skyscrapers and economic crises?

In 1999, Andrew Lawrence, after careful study, identified a correlation between skyscrapers and economic crises and named it "the skyscraper index." The theory suggests that the construction of each world record-breaking skyscraper has been followed by an economic recession. Since the beginning of the 20th century, there have occurred four global skyscraper booms, and each preceded an economic crisis or a financial turmoil.

In the 1920s when the American economy took a turn for the better and the stock market enjoyed unprecedented prosperity again, real estate development, whether for civilian use or commercial purposes, made giant strides. During that period, three record-breaking skyscrapers—40 Wall Street, the Chrysler Building and the Empire State Building—were launched one after another and were completed within the three years from 1929 to 1931. That, however, was followed by the Great Depression instead of another boom. Then, after a strong, sustained boom in the 1960s, called the "Golden Age" by Americans, the construction of the World Trade Center and the Sears Tower began. These two record-breaking skyscrapers were completed in 1972 and 1974, but in their wake came global stagflation.

It follows that the correlation between skyscrapers and economic crises is too close to be explained away as a mere coincidence. So, what is it that makes an economic crisis invariably follow the building of the world's next tallest building?

First, it is the blind self-confidence of human nature, which is manifested in a stubborn adherence to subjective opinions without an adequate comprehension of objective matters. Lawrence describes the relation he has identified between skyscrapers and economic crises as an "unhealthy 100-year correlation."[2] In fact, this phenomenon has existed in human society much longer than a mere hundred years. Looking into the mirror of the past, we can easily

---

1 In his kind reply to an email inquiry about the original words of the quote, John Llewellyn said, "We have now found what I said in 2006: I was speaking from a PowerPoint slide, a copy of which I attach. The relevant words are: 'For what it is worth, the skyscraper theory suggests that any crisis is more likely in 2007/8 than in 2006.' That was apparently quite a good prediction!" [From: john.llewellyn@llewellyn-consulting.com Date: 2011-04-14 16:29:43 RE: May I ask you a question?]

2 "An unhealthy 100-year correlation exists between building the world's next tallest building and an impending financial crisis. Be it New York in 1930, Chicago in 1974 or Kuala Lumpur in 1997, almost all the tallest buildings have heralded a major financial correction." (Lawrence, *The Skyscraper Index: Faulty Towers.* Property Report, January 15, 1999.)

find similar occurrences in the long course of China's history. For example, at the height of the Shang Dynasty (16th–11th Century B.C.), Emperor Zhou ordered to construct the magnificent Stag Tower, provoking widespread anger among the people, which led to the emperor's self-immolation on the tower. Similarly, at the zenith of the Qing Dynasty (1616–1911), Emperor Qianlong had grandiose gardens and palaces built, resulting in the dynasty's decline and, consequently, its humiliation by foreign powers and its loss of sovereignty.

Second, it is the profit motive. The pursuit of profit is the precondition for all business practices. Prior to an economic boom, there is usually a period of low interest rates, which constitutes a prerequisite for the periodic economic growth that culminates in boom-time conditions. In the economic boom that follows, interest rates remain low in comparison to the expectations of future earnings. Therefore, a series of transmission channels of profit, the profit-transmitting chains discussed earlier, are formed. The economic boom and the comparatively low interest rates have a direct influence on land values and capital costs. Thus, by virtue of the profit-transmitting chain formed by the three factors—land prices, business needs and financial support, plans are conceived to build record-breaking skyscrapers.

Just as day is followed by night and summer alternates with winter, the economy follows the cycle of boom and bust. The prices of commodities are, without exception, affected by supply and demand. As the Chinese saying goes[1], "Good fortune emerges out of the depths of misfortune, while prosperity begins to decline at its zenith." The low interest rates, the expanding demand and the rising cost of capital, together with the popular mindset of blind optimism, work together to create the "golden state" of euphoria that generates and fuels the demand for skyscrapers. This state, however, is far from sustainable.

Therefore, the world's tallest building of each boom period is usually barely completed when the economy has already begun to slip into recession. As it is put into use, the economy is, in all probability, already experiencing great difficulty. This explains why an economic crisis invariably follows the construction of the world's next tallest building, often making the rising tower a monument to the bygone boom-time.

练习题：

1. 将以下短文翻译为英语。（摘自第二十五届韩素音翻译大赛汉译英部分）

传统百货会否成为“消失的行业”

数据显示，2011年中国电子商务市场整体交易规模达到7万亿元，同比增长

1 This introductory expression is added to make the translation less abrupt and more coherent.

46.4%。电商营销取得的成绩，对传统百货行业的市场占有率是极大的挑战。越来越多的人去网购，在需求短期之内没有大幅变化的情况下也就意味着相应的百货商场客源流失。业内人士表示，近年来百货业销售下滑较大的品类也正是方便网络购买的品类，比如家电、IT产品和纺织品，甚至是奢侈品。

同时，一些传统百货商场还面临沦为电商“试衣间”的尴尬。不少人去实体店确定了衣服等物品的款式、尺寸之后到网上支付购买，由此诞生了“抄号族”“偷拍党”。随着网购市场的日益庞大，服装、化妆品和家居用品等都已经纳入涉猎范围，消费者线下选货线上购买。

除了电商侵占市场之外，行业之内的激烈竞争也不容小觑。传统百货商场之间同质化较严重，造成同业之间竞争激烈。近年来全国多个城市都在大力建设购物中心等大型商场，使本来就竞争激烈的百货商场经营更加困难。走在城市的商业街区，几乎所有的百货商场在销售内容、店面设计和产品布局等方面大同小异。一博士生说，从北京走到福州，看到各个城市的商场几乎是一样的。

在“内忧外患”之下，传统百货是否会成为下一个“消失的行业”？多位受访专家表示，传统百货行业面临较大的竞争压力，但并非没有机会。依靠线上线下一体、差异化竞争、商业模式创新等方式，百货行业或可成功“逆袭”。

据了解，目前“触电”的百货商场并不在少数。2012年以来，北京的大型百货都相继上线了自己的电子商务平台。天津百货大楼的电子商务正在筹划实施中。

同时，百货商场应该针对目标客户群体走错位经营、差异化营销的路子。一博士生导师强调，尽管最近几年百货商场面临的商业环境更加严峻，来自电商和大型商业综合体的竞争更加激烈，但对百货商场的客户群体只是分流了一部分。百货商场应该深耕目前所占有的客户群体，完善售后服务，探索针对客户的个性化服务。

另外，传统百货应该借助购物中心的发展势头趁机转型。据了解，零售业的业态构成与人均GDP水平存在一定的对应规律。人均GDP处于3 000美元至5 000美元，以大型综合超市为主，在5 000美元至1万美元则以购物中心、专卖店、专业店、便利店为主。而2011年我国人均GDP已经超过5 000美元，传统百货业可以乘机向购物中心等方向转变。

2. 分析并总结中文新闻文章的文体特点及其英译对策。

第六节 中文文学类作品的英译

文学翻译在翻译市场中占的份额不是太高，但地位很重要。相对于前面提到的几种专门的翻译，文学翻译的自由度略大，且有一定的创造性。文学翻译的内容包括诗歌、散文、戏剧和小说等，其具有形象、抒情、含蓄、讽刺、象征和韵律等特点。由于文学作品自身的艺术性特点，文学翻译也要求具有艺术性。文学翻译不但要传达原文的内容，还要传达原文风格及审美功能。仅仅语言层面的转换难以完成这一任务。因此，文学翻译要对原文的词、句、篇进行重组，要注意风格的转换和叙事模式的契合，要注重作品的文学性，要达到神似与化境，要再现原作的艺术性。因此，文学翻译有着较高的翻译要求。

1. 葛浩文英译莫言《红高粱》第一章节选

中文原文：

一九三九年古历八月初九，我父亲这个土匪种十四岁多一点。他跟着后来名满天下的传奇英雄余占鳌司令的队伍去胶平公路伏击日本人的汽车队。奶奶披着夹袄，送他们到村头。余司令说：“立住吧。”奶奶就立住了。奶奶对我父亲说：“豆官，听你干爹的话。”父亲没吱声，他看着奶奶高大的身躯，嗅着奶奶的夹袄里散出的热烘烘的香味，突然感到凉气逼人，他打了一个战，肚子咕噜噜响一阵。余司令拍了一下父亲的头，说："走，干儿。"

天地混沌，景物影影绰绰，队伍的杂沓脚步声已响出很远。父亲眼前挂着蓝白色的雾幔，挡住他的视线，只闻队伍脚步声，不见队伍形和影。父亲紧紧扯住余司令的衣角，双腿快速挪动。奶奶像岸愈离愈远，雾像海水愈近愈汹涌，父亲抓住余司令，就像抓住一条船舷。

父亲就这样奔向了耸立在故乡通红的高粱地里属于他的那块无字的青石墓碑。他的坟头上已经枯草瑟瑟，曾经有一个光屁股的男孩牵着一只雪白的山羊来到这里，山羊不紧不忙地啃着坟头上的草，男孩子站在墓碑上，怒气冲冲地撒了一泡尿，然后放声高唱：高粱红了——日本来了——同胞们准备好——开枪开炮——

有人说这个放羊的男孩就是我，我不知道是不是我。我曾经对高密东北乡极端热爱，曾经对高密东北乡极端仇恨，长大后努力学习马克思主义，我终于悟到：高密东北乡无疑是地球上最美丽最丑陋、最超脱最世俗、最圣洁最龌龊、最英雄好汉最王八蛋、最能喝酒最能爱的地方。生存在这块土地上的我的父老乡亲们，喜食高粱，每年都大量种植。八月深秋，无边无际的高粱红成汪洋的血海。高粱高密辉煌，高粱凄婉可人，高粱爱情激荡。秋风苍凉，阳光很旺，瓦蓝的天上游荡着一朵朵丰满的白云，高粱上滑动着一朵朵丰满白云的紫红色影子。一队队暗红色的人在高粱棵子里穿梭拉网，几十年如一日。他们杀人越货，精忠报国，他们演出过一幕幕英勇悲壮的舞剧，使我们这些活着的不肖子孙相形见绌，在进步的同时，我真切感到种的退化。

参考译文：

THE NINTH DAY of the eighth lunar month, 1939. My father, a bandit's offspring who had passed his fourteenth birthday, was joining the forces Commander Yu Zhan'ao, a man destined to become a legendary hero, to ambush a Japanese convoy on the Jiao-Ping highway. Grandma, a padded jacket over her shoulders, saw them to the edge of the village. "Stop here," Commander Yu ordered her. She stopped.

"Douguan, mind your foster-dad," she told my father. The sight of her large frame and the warm fragrance of her lined jacket chilled him. He shivered. His stomach growled.

Commander Yu patted him on the head and said, "Let's go, foster-son."

Heaven and earth were in turmoil, the view was blurred. By then the soldiers' muffled footsteps had moved far down the road. Father could still hear them, but a curtain of blue mist obscured the men themselves. Gripping tightly to Commander Yu's coat, he nearly flew down the path on churning legs. Grandma receded like a distant shore as the approaching sea of mist grew more tempestuous; holding on to Commander Yu was like clinging to the railing of a boat.

That was how Father rushed toward the uncarved granite marker that would rise above his grave in the bright-red sorghum fields of his hometown. A bare-assed little boy once led a white billy goat up to the weed-covered grave, and as it grazed in unhurried contentment, the boy pissed furiously on the grave and sang out: "The sorghum is red—-the Japanese are coming—compatriots, get ready—fire your rifles and cannons—".

Someone said that the little goatherd was me, but I don't know. I had learned to love Northeast Gaomi Township with all my heart, and to hate it with unbridled fury. I didn't realize until I'd grown up that Northeast Gaomi Township is easily the most beautiful and most repulsive, most unusual and most common, most sacred and most corrupt, most heroic and most bastardly, hardest-drinking and hardest-loving place in the world. The people of my father's generation who lived there ate sorghum out of preference, planting as much of it as they could. In late autumn, during the eighth lunar month, vast stretches of red sorghum shimmered like a sea of blood. Tall and dense, it reeked of glory; cold and graceful, it promised enchantment; passionate and loving, it was tumultuous.

The autumn winds are cold and bleak, the sun's rays intense. White clouds, full and round, float in the tile-blue sky, casting full found purple shadows onto the sorghum fields below. Over decades that seem but a moment in time, lines of scarlet figures shuttled among the sorghum stalks to weave a vast human tapestry. They killed, they looted, and they defended their country in a valiant, stirring ballet that makes us unfilial descendants who now occupy the land pale by comparison. Surrounded by progress, I feel a nagging sense of our species' regression.

2.《雷雨》对话的英译　第三幕

中文原文：

贵：（咳嗽起来）他妈的！（兴奋地问着）你们想，你们哪一个对得起我？（向四凤同大海）你们不要不愿意听，你们哪一个人不是我辛辛苦苦养到大？可是现在你们哪一件事做的对得起我？（对大海）你说？（对四凤）你说？（对着站在中间圆桌旁的鲁妈）你也说说，这都是你的好孩子啊？

静默。听外面胡琴，同唱声。

大：（向四凤）这是谁？快十点半还在唱？

四：（随意地）一个瞎子同他老婆，每天在这儿卖唱的。（挥着扇，微微叹一口气）

贵：我是一辈子犯小人，不走运。刚在周家混了两年，孩子都安置好了，就叫你（指鲁妈）连累下去了。你回家一次就出一次事。刚才是怎么回事？我叫完电灯匠回公馆，凤儿的事没有了，连我的老根子也拔了。妈的，你不来，（指鲁妈）我能倒这样的霉？

大：（放下手枪）你要骂我就骂我，别指东说西，欺负妈好说话。

贵：我骂你？你是少爷！我骂你？你连人家有钱的人都当面骂了，我敢骂你？

大：（不耐烦）你喝了不到两盅酒，就叨叨叨，叨叨叨，这半点钟你够不够？

贵：够？哼，我一肚子的冤屈，一肚子的火，我没个够！当初你爸爸也不是没叫人伺候过，吃喝玩乐，我哪一样没讲究过！自从娶了你的妈，我是家败人亡，一天不如一天，一天不如一天，……

参考译文（王佐良、巴恩斯译）：

LU: (*coughing*): God almighty! (*Heatedly.*) Just look at you. There's not one of you can look me in the face!(*Turning to Dahai and Sifeng.*) It's no good you pretending not to hear, either. I've worked my fingers to the bone to bring you two up, both of you, but what have either of you ever done to show your gratitude? (*To Dahai.*) Eh?(*To Sifeng.*) Answer me that! (*To Lu Ma, who is standing by the round table in the center.*) Or perhaps you can tell me, seeing that they're your precious children?

(*Silence. From outside comes the sound of someone singing to the accompaniment of a Chinese fiddle.*)

HAI (to Sifeng): Who's that still singing at this time of night? It's almost half past ten.

FENG (*listlessly*): Oh, some blind man and his wife. They're round here every day. Street-singers. (*She heaves a faint sigh as she fans herself.*)

LU: All my life I've just had one patch of bad luck after another, and every time it's been because some miserable nobody has put a spoke in my wheel. Just when I've been with the Zhous two years and got my children fixed up with good jobs, you (*pointing at his wife*) have to come along and undo all that I've done. Every time you come home there's trouble. Look at what happened today: I go out to fetch an electrician and when I get back what do I find? Sifeng's lost her job and I'm out on my neck into the bargain. If you hadn't come home, damn you (*pointing at her again*), all this would never have happened!

HAI (*putting down the revolver*): If you want to swear at me, just get on with it. There is no need to take it out on Mother indeed.

LU: Me swear at you? As if I'd swear at a young gentleman like you! You, who even swear at rich people to their faces!

HAI (*losing patience with him*): You get two or three drinks inside you and you're off. You've been gabbling on and on for half an hour now. Can't you give it a rest?

LU: Give it a rest? Not on you life! I've just about had a bellyful of her, and I'm going to have my say. Oh no, I haven't finished yet! It's not as if your old dad had always been a servant: there was a time when I had people waiting on me. I lived like a lord and had a good time—only the best was good enough. But from the day I married your mother, I started going to rack and ruin. Things have been going from bad to worse. Yes, from bad to worse—

3.《红楼梦》第一章　两种译文的对比

中文原文：

原来女娲氏炼石补天之时，于大荒山无稽崖练成高经十二丈，方经二十四丈顽石三万六千五百零一块。娲皇氏只用了三万六千五百块，只单单剩了一块未用，便弃在此山青埂峰下。谁知此石自经煅炼之后，灵性已通，因见众石俱得补天，独自己无材不堪入选，遂自怨自叹，日夜悲号惭愧。

一日，正当嗟悼之际，俄见一僧一道远远而来，生得骨骼不凡，丰神迥异，说说笑笑来至峰下，坐于石边高谈快论。先是说些云山雾海神仙玄幻之事，后便说到红尘中荣华富贵。此石听了，不觉打动凡心，也想要到人间去享一享这荣华富贵，但自恨粗蠢，不得已，便口吐人言，向那僧道说道："大师，弟子蠢物，不能见礼了。适闻二位谈那人世间荣耀繁华，心切慕之。弟子质虽粗蠢，性却稍通，况见二师仙形道体，定非凡品，必有补天济世之材，利物济人之德。如蒙发一点慈心，携带弟子得入红尘，在那富贵场中，温柔乡里受享几年，自当永佩洪恩，万劫不忘也。"二仙师听毕，齐憨笑道："善哉，善哉！那红尘中有却有些乐事，但不能永远依恃，况又有'美中不足，好事多魔'八个字紧相连属，瞬息间则又乐极悲生，人非物换，究竟是到头一梦，万境归空，倒不如不去的好。"这石凡心已炽，那里听得进这话去，乃复苦求再四。二仙知不可强制，乃叹道："此亦静极思动，无中生有之数也。既如此，我们便携你去受享受享，只是到不得意时，切莫后悔。"石道："自然，自然。"那僧又道："若说你性灵，却又如此质蠢，并更无奇贵之处。如此也只好踮脚而已。也罢，我如今大施佛法助你助，待劫终之日，复还本质，以了此案。你道好否？"石头听了，感谢不尽。那僧便念咒书符，大展幻术，将一块大石登时变成一块鲜明莹洁的美玉，且又缩成扇坠大小的可佩可拿。那僧托于掌上，笑道："形体倒也是个宝物了！还只没有，实在的好处，须得再镌上数字，使人一见便知是奇物方妙。然后携你到那昌明隆盛之邦，诗礼簪缨之族，花柳繁华地，温柔富贵乡去安身乐业。"石头听了，喜不能禁，乃问："不知赐了弟子那几件奇处，又不知携了弟子到何地方？望乞明示，使弟子不惑。"那僧笑道："你且莫问，日后自然明白的。"说着，便袖了这石，同那道人飘然而去，竟不知投奔何方何舍。

后来，又不知过了几世几劫，因有个空空道人访道求仙，忽从这大荒山无稽崖青埂峰下经过，忽见一大块石上字迹分明，编述历历。空空道人乃从头一看，原来就是无材补天，幻形入世，蒙茫茫大士，渺渺真人携入红尘，历尽离合悲欢炎凉世态的一段故事。后面又有一首偈云：

> 无材可去补苍天，枉入红尘若许年。
> 此系身前身后事，倩谁记去作奇传？

译文一：杨宪益

When the goddess Nü Wa melted down rocks to repair the sky, at Baseless Cliff in the Great Waster Mountain she made thirty-six thousand five hundred and one blocks of stone, each a hundred and twenty feet high and two hundred and forty feet square. She used only thirty-six thousand five hundred of these and threw the remaining block down at the foot of Blue Bridge Peak. Strange to relate, this block of stone after tempering had acquired spiritual understanding.

Because all its fellow blocks had been chosen to mend the sky and it alone rejected, it lamented day and night in distress and shame.

One day as the Stone was brooding over its fate, it saw approaching from the distance a Buddhist monk and Taoist priest, both of striking demeanor and distinguished appearance. They came up to the Stone and sat down to chat.

When they saw the pure translucent Stone which had shrunk to the size of a fan-pendant, the monk took it up on the palm of his hand and said to it with a smile:

"You look like a precious object, but you still lack real value. I must engrave some characters on you so that people can see at a glance that you're something special. Then we can take you to some civilized and prosperous realm, to a cultured family of official status, a place where flowers and willows flourish, the home of pleasure and luxury where you can settle down in comfort."

The Stone was overjoyed.

"May I trouble you to enlighten me," it said, "as to what wonderful merits you will bestow on me? And where do you mean to take me?"

"Don't ask." The monk smiled. "You'll find out all in good time."

With that he tucked the Stone into his sleeve and hurried off with the Taoist. But where they went no one knows.

After on one knows how many generations or aeons, a Taoist known as Reverend Void, searching for the Way and immortality, came to Great Waste Mountain, Baseless Cliff and the foot of Blue Bridge Peak. His eye fell on the inscription on a large stone which was still discernible and he read it through. It was an account of the Stone's rejection for repairing heaven, its transformation and conveyance to the world of men by the Buddhist of Infinite Space and the Taoist of Boundless Time, and the joys and sorrows, partings and encounters, warm and cold treatment from others it had experienced there. On its back was a Buddhist verse:

Unfit to mend the azure sky,
I passed some years on earth to no avail;
My life in both worlds is recorded here;
Whom can I ask to pass on this romantic tale?

译文二：霍克思

Long ago, when the goddess Nǚ-wa was repairing the sky, she melted down a great quantity of rock and, on the Incredible Crags of the Great Fable Mountains, moulded the amalgam into thirty-six thousand, five hundred and one large building blocks, each measuring seventy-two feet by a hundred and forty-four feet square. She used thirty-six thousand five hundred of these blocks in the course of her building operations, leaving a single odd block unused, which lay, all on its own, at the foot of Greensickness Peak in the aforementioned mountains.

Now this block of stone, having undergone the melting and moulding of a goddess, possessed magic powers. It could move about at will and could grow or shrink to any size it wanted. Observing that all the other blocks had been used for celestial repairs and that it was the only one to have been rejected as unworthy, it became filled with shame and resentment and passed its days in sorrow and lamentation.

One day, in the midst of its lamentings, it saw a monk and a Taoist approaching from a great distance, each of them remarkable for certain eccentricities of manner and appearance. When they arrived at the foot of Greensickness Peak, they sat down on the ground and began to talk. The monk, catching sight of a lustrous, translucent stone—it was in fact the rejected building block which had now shrunk itself to the size of a fan-pendant and looked very attractive in its new shape—took it up on the palm of his hand and addressed it with a smile:

"Ha, I see you have magical properties! But nothing to recommend you. I shall have to cut a few words on you so that anyone seeing you will know at once that you are something special. After that I shall take you to a certain

brilliant
successful
poetical
cultivated
aristocratic
elegant
delectable
luxurious
opulent
locality on a little trip."

The stone was delighted.

"What words will you cut? Where is this place you will take me to? I beg to be enlightened."

"Do not ask," replied the monk with a laugh. "You will know soon enough when the time comes."

And with that he slipped the stone into his sleeve and set off at a great pace with the Taoist. But where they both went to I have no idea.

Countless aeons went by and a certain Taoist called Vanitas in quest of the secret of immortality chanced to be passing below that same Greensickness Peak in the Incredible Crags of the Great Fable Mountains when he caught sight of a large stone standing there, on which the characters of a long inscription were clearly discernible.

Vanitas read the inscription through from beginning to end and learned that this was a once lifeless stone block which had been found unworthy to repair the sky, but which had magically transformed its shape and been taken down by the Buddhist mahasattva Impervioso and the Taoist illuminate Mysterioso into the world of mortals, where it had lived out the life of a man before finally attaining nirvana and returning to the other shore. The inscription named the country where it had been born, and went into considerable detail about its domestic life, youthful amours, and even the verses, mottoes and riddles it had written. All it lacked was the authentication of a dynasty and date. On the back of the stone was inscribed the following quatrain:

Found unfit to repair the azure sky
Long years a foolish mortal man was I.
My life in both worlds on this stone is writ:
Pray who will copy out and publish it?

练习题：

1. 将下面这段文学作品翻译为英语。（摘自余华的小说《在细雨中呐喊》）

1965年的时候，一个孩子开始了对黑夜不可名状的恐惧。我回想起了那个细雨飘扬的夜晚，当时我已经睡了，我是那么的小巧，就像玩具似的被放在床上。屋檐滴水所显示的，是寂静的存在，我的逐渐入睡，是对雨中水滴的逐渐遗忘。应该是在这时候，在我安全而又平静地进入睡眠时，仿佛呈现了一条幽静的道路，树木和草丛依次闪开。一个女人哭泣般的呼喊声从远处传来，嘶哑的声音在当初寂静无比的黑夜里突然响起，使我此刻回想中的童年颤抖不已。

我看到了自己，一个受惊的孩子睁大恐惧的眼睛，他的脸型在黑暗里模糊不清。那个女人的呼喊声持续了很久，我是那么急切和害怕地期待着另一个声音的来到，一个出来回答女人的呼喊，能够平息她哭泣的声音，可是没有出现。现在我能够意识到当初自己惊恐的原因，那就是我一直没有听到一个出来回答的声音。再也没有比孤独的无依无靠的呼喊声更让人战栗了，在雨中空旷的黑夜里。

紧随而来的另一个记忆，是几只白色的羊羔从河边青草上走过来。显然这是对白昼的印象，是对前一个记忆造成的不安进行抚摸。只是我难以确定自己获得这个印象时所处的位置。

可能是几天以后，我似乎听到了回答这个女人呼喊的声音。那时候是傍晚，一场暴雨刚刚过去，天空里的黑云犹如滚滚浓烟。我坐在屋后的池塘旁，在潮湿的景色里，一个陌生的男人向我走来。他穿着一身黑色的衣服，走来时黑衣在阴沉的天空下如旗帜一样飘荡着。正在接近的这个景象，使我心里蓦然重现了那个女人清晰的呼喊声。陌生男人犀利的目光从远处开始，到走近一直注视着我。就在我惊恐万分的时候，他转身走上了一条田埂，逐渐离我远去。宽大的黑衣由于风的掀动，发出哗哗的响声。

我成年以后回顾往事时，总要长久地停留在这个地方，惊诧自己当初为何会将这哗哗的衣服声响，理解成是对那个女人黑夜雨中呼喊的回答。

2. 分析并总结中文文学作品的文体特点及其英译对策。

下 编

- 第四章　汉英翻译的主要策略
- 第五章　汉英翻译常见错误例析
- 第六章　汉英翻译名家经验谈

第四章 汉英翻译的主要策略

与传统的汉英翻译的教程不同，本章讲解的主要内容是汉英翻译策略，而不是汉英翻译技巧。这主要是因为传统的汉英翻译技巧过于繁杂，不适合教师的教和学生的学，不符合人脑的认知规律。根据作者本人汉译英的教学经验，在具体讲解某一翻译技巧时，如增词法，学生听完老师讲解后，感觉清楚了，也觉得有用。但学期结束时，问问学生学过哪些翻译技巧，学生往往摇头。在学生的翻译实践中，他们也很少联想到这些翻译技巧的运用。因此，我们认为翻译学习的目标应是策略，而不是技巧。本章讲解的翻译策略主要是基于英汉对比的知识与英语写作的知识。

在进行汉英翻译时，我们首先必须提醒自己的一点是：汉语和英语存在着相当大的差异。英汉语属于不同的语系，汉语属汉藏语系（Sino-Tibetan Language Family），英语属印欧语系（Indo-European Language Family）。

从文字来说，汉语属表意（ideographic ）文字，英语属拼音（alphabetic）文字。由于两种文字的不同，在汉译英时就无法再现汉字象形和指示会意带来的美感以及它们给读者带来的联想，尤其是汉字书法之美，更是丧失殆尽。不过，汉语拼音的发明，给汉字音译带来了极大方便。英语虽是拼音文字，但单词的读音和拼写常常不一致，有些词甚至拼写相同，读音却不同，意思也不一样，译者应该特别注意。

从语音来看，汉语属声调语言（tone language），英语属语调语言（intonation language）。汉语的四声起着区别或改变字义的重要作用。如：吗 mā、麻 má、马 mǎ、骂 mà。英语的单词则没有固定的声调，一个单词可以读成不同的声调而不会改变其词义。但英语的句子必须有语调，语调对于表达思想感情起着非常重要的作用。汉语的句子虽然也有语调，但由于汉语每个字都有固定的声调，语调就必然受到相当大的限制，实际上是在字调上加语调。

从词汇来看，汉英都有名词、代词、动词、形容词、数词、副词、介词、连词和叹词。这是汉英词汇的相似之处，但汉英词汇之间也有许多区别。如汉语有助词，英语没有；汉语有量词，英语没有量词；英语有冠词，汉语没有。由于词类划分标准不同，相同词类之间也有区别。汉英两种语言在词汇方面相应的词所包含的词义范围不同，词的搭配也不同。

英汉互译时，英语冠词容易被译者忽略，而汉语的量词在英译时则常被省略，无法再现汉语量词的生动性。汉英词汇的构词法也有异同。

在节奏和韵律方面，汉语和英语也有很大差别，汉语是以音节计时的（syllable-timed），而英语是以重音计时的（stress-timed）。汉语古诗是按照音节的数目来决定它的韵律和节奏的，英语诗歌则是按重音和轻音交替出现的模式安排节奏的，但占主导地位的是重音。由于汉、英两种语言在声调、语调、韵律和节奏上的不同特征，在翻译音美特征明显的文本如诗歌、散文、戏剧等时，就很难再现原文的音美特征。

第一节 汉英词汇差异及汉译英策略

翻译教学和研究的经验表明：翻译策略的学习必须建立在不同语言和文化的对比分析基础上。因此，源语和目的语语言对比知识的学习与掌握是翻译学习的重要前提基础，不可或缺。

1. 汉英词汇异同比较

词是语言的最基本的组织单位。“词”这一概念在汉语中造成的困惑比在西方语言中大得多。这首先是由于汉语学者直接借用了英语等西方语言中“词”的定义，以此为标准在汉语中确定词。王力（1984）在说明“我们对于中国的词，更感觉确当的定义实在不容易想出”之后，暂时把“词”定义为“语言中最小的意义单位”。孙常叙（1956）指出“词是一个形式和内容统一起来的语言最小单位。”北京大学中文系编写的教材《现代汉语》（1993）则将“词”定义为“最小的能够独立运用的有意义的语言单位”。英语属于印欧语系，由字母组成，而汉语属于汉藏语系，其书写形式为方块字。英语和汉语中词的书写形式存在本质上的差别：从音韵的角度出发，英语是“元辅音体系”，汉语则属于“调韵声体系”。英语的音节由一个一个字母组成，而音节和单词间的界限不清楚，因此，英语在书写时音节之间相互连接在一起，而词与词之间则留有空格。汉语音节间比较清晰，因此汉语在书写时是没有间隙的。

整体来看，汉英词汇的大部分是对应的，这是汉英翻译的语言基础。但同时，汉语和英语词汇之间也存在很大的差异，这也是汉英翻译的难点。

1.1 汉英词汇量的差异

汉语和英语都有丰富的词汇，汉语词汇和英语词汇的总量至今没有一个确切的统计，但英语词汇量远远高于汉语是无疑的。《中华大字典》收词 48 000 条、《汉语大字典》54 678 条、《现代汉语词典》56 000 条。但英语词汇以最保守的估计，也有 50 万。如

Webster' Third International Dictionary 大约收词 450 000 个，*Oxford English Dictionary* 收词约 600 000 个。根据 Jackson & Amvela（2000），这两部词典出现的词项约有 75 万，如加上词典中未出现的缩略词和动植物名字等，英语词汇可达 100 万。根据在美国圣迭戈市的全球语言监测组织说，截至 2006 年 3 月 21 日，英语单词总量为 988 968 个。如加上各种科学术语，词汇数量很可能还要翻倍。汪榕培（1997）认为英语词汇总量远远超过 200 万。

通过词汇量的比较，我们就可以看出，英语词汇量巨大，这是我们英语学习的一大难点。同样，这也是我们进行汉译英时的一大难点。在进行汉译英时，由于我们英语词汇掌握不足或不深，就会导致我们所使用的词汇不够精细，不够准确，不够地道。

下面是美国 *Heritage* 的编辑们精心编辑的 100 个单词，用来检测美国高中生的英语词汇水平。此检测虽然无法做到完全翔实地反映语言水平，但仍然是检测词汇量的 一个很好的参考。可按 100 分计算，测测你的词汇量。

1. abjure 2. abrogate 3. abstemious 4. acumen 5. antebellum 6. auspicious 7. belie 8. bellicose 9. bowdlerize 10. chicanery 11. chromosome 12. churlish 13. circumlocution 14. circumnavigate 15. deciduous 16. deleterious 17. diffident 18. enervate 19. enfranchise 20. epiphany 21. equinox 22. euro 23. evanescent 24. expurgate 25. fatuous 26. feckless 27. fiduciary 28. filibuster 29. gamete 30. gauche 31. gerrymander 32. hegemony 33. hemoglobin 34. homogeneous 35. hoist 36. hubris 37. hypotenuse 38. impeach 39. incognito 40. incontrovertible 41. inculcate 42. infrastructure 43. interpolate 44. irony 45. jejune 46. kinetic 47. kowtow 48. laissez faire 49. lexicon 50. loquacious 51. lugubrious 52. metamorphosis 53. mitosis 54. moiety 55. nanotechnology 56. nihilism 57. nomenclature 58. nonsectarian 59. notarize 60. obsequious 61. oligarchy 62. omnipotent 63. orthography 64. oxidize 65. parabola 66. paradigm 67. parameter 68. pecuniary 69. photosynthesis 70. plagiarize 71. plasma 72. polymer 73. precipitous 74. quasar 75. quotidian 76. recapitulate 77. reciprocal 78. reparation 79. respiration 80. sanguine 81. soliloquy 82. subjugate 83. suffragist 84. supercilious 85. tautology 86. taxonomy 87. tectonic 88. tempestuous 89. thermodynamics 90. totalitarian 91. unctuous 92. usurp 93. vacuous 94. vehement 95. vortex 96. winnow 97. wrought 98. xenophobe 99. yeoman 100. ziggurat

（参考答案：1. abjure 发誓放弃 2. abrogate 废除 3. abstemious 节省的 / 有节制的 4. acumen 聪明 / 敏锐 5. antebellum 战争前的 6. auspicious 吉利的 7. belie 掩饰 / 证明为假 / 使失望 8. bellicose 好战的 9. bowdlerize 删除文句 / 删改 10. chicanery 欺诈 / 狡辩 11. chromosome 染色体 12. churlish 无礼的 / 脾气暴躁的 13. circumlocution 迂回之辞 14. circumnavigate 环航 15. deciduous 落叶的 16. deleterious 有毒的 17. diffident 羞怯的 / 缺乏自信的 18. enervate 衰弱 / 无力 19. enfranchise 给予选举权 20. epiphany 顿悟 / 主显节 21. equinox 春分 / 秋分 22. euro 欧元 23. evanescent 易逝的 24. expurgate 删除 25. fatuous 昏庸的 26. feckless 无力气

的 / 软弱的 27. fiduciary 受托人 28. filibuster 阻碍议案通过的人 / 发言等 29. gamete 生殖细胞 30. gauche 笨拙的 31. gerrymander 不公平地重新划分选区 32. hegemony 霸权 33. hemoglobin 血红蛋白 34. homogeneous 同一的 / 均匀的 35. hoist 升起 36. hubris 傲慢 37. hypotenuse 直角三角形的斜边 38. impeach 弹劾 39. incognito 匿名 / 隐身 40. incontrovertible 无可争议的 41. inculcate 教育 / 灌输 42. infrastructure 基础设施 43. interpolate 篡改 44. irony 讽刺 45. jejune 枯燥无味的 / 缺乏营养的 46. kinetic 运动的 47. kowtow 叩头 / 磕头 48. laissez faire 自由放任 49. lexicon 词典 / 辞典 50. loquacious 饶舌的 / 多话的 51. lugubrious 悲惨的 / 悲哀的 / 阴郁的 52. metamorphosis 变形 53. mitosis 有丝分裂 54. moiety 一部分 55. nanotechnology 纳米技术 56. nihilism 虚无主义 57. nomenclature 术语 / 命名法 58. nonsectarian 无宗派的 59. notarize 确认 / 证明 60. obsequious 谄媚的 61. oligarchy 寡头政治 62. omnipotent 无所不能的 63. orthography 正字法 64. oxidize 氧化 65. parabola 抛物线 66. paradigm 范例 / 典范 67. parameter 参数 68. pecuniary 金钱的 69. photosynthesis 光合作用 70. plagiarize 剽窃 71. plasma 等离子 / 血浆 72. polymer 聚合物 73. precipitous 鲁莽的 / 险峻的 74. quasar 类星体 75. quotidian 每天的 / 司空见惯的 76. recapitulate 概括 / 重述要点 77. reciprocal 互惠的 / 相互的 78. reparation 赔偿 / 修理 79. respiration 呼吸 80. sanguine 乐观的 / 血红色的 / 面色红润的 81. soliloquy 独白 82. subjugate 征服 83. suffragist 主张妇女参政权者 84. supercilious 目空一切的 85. tautology 同义重复 86. taxonomy 分类学 87. tectonic 构造的 / 建筑的 88. tempestuous 暴风雨的 / 暴乱的 89. thermodynamics 热力学 90. totalitarian 集权主义的 / 者 91. unctuous 虚情假意的 / 油性的 92. usurp 篡夺 93. vacuous 空虚的 / 空的 94. vehement 激烈的 95. vortex 涡流 96. winnow 扬谷 / 筛选 97. wrought 加工的 / 锻造的 / 工作 98. xenophobe 仇外 99. yeoman 自耕农 100. ziggurat 塔庙 / 金字形神塔）

1.2 词的形态对比

词是由语素构成的。语素是最小的语音语义结合体，是构成词的语言单位。例如：

钢 + 笔→钢笔　　计算 + 机→计算机

super+market→supermarket　　de+code→decode

语素一般可以分为两类：一类是自由语素、一类是黏着语素。自由语素能够独立构成一个词，也可以和其他语素一起组合构词。例如：电→电灯、电话、电视、闪电、静电；人→人类、人们、人生、生人、亲人；air → airmail、airconditioner、airline；house → housemaid、housekeeping、inhouse。黏着语素一般不能够独立构成一个词、需与其他语素一起组合构词。例如：初→初一、初二、初级、初中；第→第一、第二、门第；de → devalue、decentralize、decode; able → desirable、manageable、drinkable。

英语词素在构词时具有一定的固定性，其排列顺序不能随意改变。但在汉语中，语素的位置较为灵活，一般情况下，词素位置的变化对其含义的表达影响不大。例如：

anti-, mono-, un-

-tion，-let，-er

补贴—贴补

互相—相互

代替—替代

斗争—争斗

英语词素与汉语语素的位置差异还体现在其位置的稳定性上。英语的大多数词素是不能添加其他成分的，例如：extra- 正确、exxtra- 错误、trans- 正确、trrans- 错误。而汉语中的词素之间可以插入其他成分。例如：

撒谎—撒弥天大谎

倒霉—倒八辈子霉

出差—出了两次差

以语言词汇的形态特征来看，汉语属于孤立语，每个词只由一个语素构成；英语则偏向屈折语，每个词可以通过词形的变化或语法功能的变化来表示意义。屈折语中词汇的一个重要特征是词缀丰富，所以英语中派生词比例高，而汉语中复合词比例高。

汉语的词汇可分为单纯词和复合词。复合词的构词方式主要有以下两种：

1）缀合法

这种方法一般将表示实际意义的词根加上意义虚化后的词缀。例如：

老：老师　　老虎　　老乡

子：桌子　　骗子　　胖子

化：美化　　深化　　风化

然：坦然　　安然　　果然

词缀“老”“子”“化”“然”已不再表示具体的词汇意义，只起到语法作用。“老”表示感情色彩，“子”是名词的标志，“化”是动词的标志，“然”是形容词和副词的标志。但在汉语中，这类意义虚化的词缀数量有限，因此缀合法并不是汉语的主要构词方法。

2）复合法

这是汉语的主要构词方法，形式多样，功能多样，且含有类似句法的关系。主要有以下几种形式：

并列式

汉语复合词中大量的是并列关系，与英语复合词相比，这是其显著特征。

① 同一并列：道路　语言　脱离　贸易　猛烈

② 反义并列：首尾　早晚　方圆　褒贬　得失

③ 类义并列：领袖　手足　骨肉　笔墨　国家

偏正式

汽车 红茶 红楼 坏人 春耕 牛肉 木盆 公路 黄河

补充式

推翻 揭穿 说服 阐明 振兴 拉长 增加

动宾式

讲课 动员 称心 喝茶 玩电脑 放下包袱

重叠式

重叠式则是汉语中独有的构词法，在汉语中是一个能产的构词法，名词、动词、形容词、量词等不同词类的词中都有一部分重叠。而英语里则很少利用重叠法构词，个别的例子有 so so（一般的）等。除了文学作品的需要，一般来说，重叠在英语是比较忌讳的。汉语中重叠法的使用都是按照一定规则进行的，最常见的几种是如下所示（王安、王桂芝，2013：116）：

AA 式：人人、笑笑、听听、呜呜、看看

AABB 式：风风雨雨、世世代代、花花绿绿

ABAB 式：雪白雪白、琢磨琢磨

AAB 式：毛毛雨、悄悄话、绿油油

ABB 式：轰隆隆、亮晶晶

运用重叠法，词语音节匀称，形式整齐，使表达更加形象生动，感情更加充分。

此外，汉语中还有一种独特的复合构词法，与英语构成了明显的区别。表示属概念的词加上修饰语素就可以形成一个词族，如花、树、草、虫、车、房、船、药等。

蝴蝶花	iris	杜鹃花	azalea
鸡冠花	cockscomb	百合花	lily
金银花	honeysuckle	牵牛花	morning glory
菊花	chrysanthemum	凌霄花	creeper
兰花	orchid	荷花	lotus
茉莉花	jasmine	昙花	epiphyllum
水仙花	daffodil	茶花	camellia
牡丹花	peony	玉兰花	mangnolia
梅花	plum	丁香花	lilac
报春花	polyanthus	栀子花	gardenia

英语的构词方式也主要有以上两种：

1）缀合法

这是英语主要的构词法。英语中有不少构词能力很强的词根，而且构词的前缀和后缀也十分丰富，形式多样，功能多样。现例举如下：

名词性后缀：

-age 为抽象名词后缀，表示行为、状态和全体总称：percentage, shortage

-cy 表示抽象名词：accuracy、infancy

-ence、-ance 表示性质和动作：interference、significance

-ency、-ancy 为抽象名词后缀：dificiency、tendency、sufficiency

-ics 表示科学：psdiatrics、psychiatrics、obstetrics、orthopedics、auristrics、gnathostomatics、andriatrics

-ian 表示人称名词：physician、technician

-ication 表示由动词变化而来的抽象名词，常译为“化”：simplification、classification

形容词性后缀：

-able 表示“可能的”“可以的”：acceptable、movable、alterable

-al 表示具备某种属性的：regional、natural、special、spinal、cervical、mural、terminal

-ant 表示是从动词派生来的：significant、resistant

-ent 与 -ant: consistent、sufficient、convenient

-ful: useful、successful、plentiful

-ible 与 -able: visible、irreversible、impossible

动词性后缀：

-ate: deviate、decelerate、accelerate、degenerate

-en: weaken、soften、strengthen、shorten、sharpen

-ize: neutralize、standardize、mineralize、repolarize、depolarize

副词性后缀：

-ly: simultaneously、concurrently、widely、exclusively、scarcely

-wise: moneywise、clockwise、weatherwise

表示否定意义的前缀

a- 与 an-: asymmetry、anhydrous

dis: dishonest、dislike

in-、ig-、il-、im-、ir-: incapable、inability、ignoble、impossible、immoral、illegal、irregular non-: nonsense

un-: unable、unemployment

表示错误意义的前缀：

male-、mal-: malfunction、maladjustment

mis-: misrepresent、mislead

表示反动作意思的前缀；

dis-: disarm、disconnect

un-: unload、uncover

2）复合法

把两个或两个以上独立的词结合在一起，构成新词的方法。如 care-free、deaf-mute、slip-up、backrest、scarecrow。

因此，总体来说，复合构词是汉语的主要构词方式，缀合构词是英语的主要构词方式。古汉语以单字为本，但现代汉语以复合的双音节词居多，也有丰富的合成的四字成语。这主要是因为汉语中单字的搭配能力较强。由于缀合构词是英语的主要构词方式，汉译英时我们要注意英语缀合词，即派生词的使用。

1.3 词义对比

汉语词汇意义的主要特征是表意准确、言简意赅、意义相对固定。但英语词汇常常一词多义、受上下文影响大、词义灵活。因此，汉英翻译中，词义的对应很重要。

词的意义大体可分为两种：指称意义和联想意义。由于文化的差异，英汉词汇的指称意义对应主要有三种情况：基本对应、部分对应和不对应。

指称意义基本对应：

英汉词汇的指称意义基本对应是存在的，多见于专有名词、科技术语等，举例如下：

China— 中国

radar—雷达

microbiology—微生物学

speciology—物种学

指称意义部分对应：

英汉词汇的指称意义部分对应是较为普遍的现象。部分对应，就是词语在各自语言中所涵盖的意义不尽相同，其中只有一个或若干个词义对应，而其他方面的意义不同。举例如下：

uncle—叔叔、伯伯、姑父、伯父

公司—company、corporation

由部分对应衍生出的一词多义（polysemy）是语言的普遍现象，但在英语中这一现象尤为普遍，而且在名词、动词、形容词、副词中，往往词的使用频率越高，词义就越多。“词本无义，义随人生”。（Words do not have meanings, people have meanings for words.）这也体现出英语一词多义的特征。

与汉语相比，英语词义最显著的一个特征是意义灵活多变，对上下文依赖较大。下面，我们以一个最普通的英语单词 good 为例进行说明：

1) It is essential to do a *good* deal of explanatory work among them.
像他们多作解释工作是完全必要的。

2) This will not bring them much *good*.
这对他们没有什么好处。

3) He will act in *good* faith and carry out the terms he has accepted.
他将确守信义，践行他承诺的条件。

4) All things are determined from above; no one can be sure whether they will turn out *good* or bad.
凡事都由天命，是吉是凶，谁也保不定。

5) Jack had a *good* sleep.
杰克美美地睡了一觉。

6) She was praising your *good* service。
她夸你勤快。

7) They have such *good* manners。
他们仪态端庄。

8) According to the philosophy of fortune telling, that fatness meant *good* temper and therefore meant luck as a general principle.
按算命哲理说，胖就是和气，一般说也就是福气。

9) It will do you *good* to make friends with him and learn something serious from him.
同他交朋友对你有好处，可以向他学点正经东西。

10) He was a *good* climber.
他是个爬山能手。

11) Smith was a *good* drinker.
史密斯酒量很大。

12) I know your *good* intentions.
我知道你的善心。

13) He couldn't show a *good* reason for it.
他说不出一个站得住脚的理由。

14) This is too *good* to be true.
这太完美了，不太现实。
15) She is a *good* wife and helpful mother.
她是一位贤妻良母。
16) Tom is a very *good* servant.
汤姆是个非常能干的用人。
17) The weather was *good* and there had been large crops and prosperous trade.
风调雨顺，五谷丰登，生意兴隆。

从上面的17句话中，我们可以看出，good没有一个是直接翻译为“好”的，而是根据不同的语境进行了相应的变化处理。在专业领域，还会有专业性的特点。

a good contract指“有效合同”，复合词goodwill不表示“善意”，而是“公司或企业的商誉”。我们再看几个法律英语的例句：

1) Neglect of duty is *good* cause for removal of a trustee.
理事玩忽职守，理应废除其职务。
good在此表示“正当的，充分的”。
2) The warranty is good for two years.
此担保有效期为两年。
good在此表示“有效”。
3) Party A is a company duly organized, validly existing and in good standing as a legal person under the laws of the PRC.
甲方是依据中国法律正式成立、有效存续和资格完备的法人公司。
in good standing表示“符合法律法规要求的，有资格的”。
4) Now therefore, in consideration of the premises, and the representations, warranties, covenants, and undertakings of the parties hereinafter set forth, and for other *good* and valuable consideration, the parties agree among themselves as follows.
鉴于上述事实和各方在下文所作的陈述、保证、立约和承诺，及其他有效的有价约因，现各方达成协议如下。
good consideration指consideration that is valid under the law（法律上有效的约因或对价）。
5) If any term or provision of this Agreement shall become or be declared illegal, invalid or unenforceable for any reason whatsoever, such term or provision shall be severed from this Agreement shall be deemed to be deleted from this Agreement, provided that if such deletion materially affects or alters the basis of this Agreement, the parties shall negotiate in *good* faith to amend and modify the provisions and terms of this Agreement as may be necessary or desirable in the circumstances.

如果因任何原因本协议的任一条款或规定变为或被宣布为不合法、无效或不可执行，该条款或规定须与本协议分离，且被视为从本协议中删除，但如果删除该条款或规定会实质性影响或改变本协议的基础，双方应以诚信的态度进行谈判，以期在必要或可取的情况下对本协议的规定和条款进行修改和变更。

good faith 中 good 的意思是表示 thorough。

指称意义不对应：

由于两种语言文化上的差异，有时一种语言中的词语在另一种语言中找不到对应词，这也叫作词汇空缺现象。汉语和英语间也存在这种词汇空缺现象，但比例并不是太大。当出现这种词汇空缺现象时，我们采用的翻译方法通常有释译、近译、意译、音译等。

“笏”是古代大臣朝见皇帝时手持胸前的一块狭长板子，英语民族没有这种东西，只好释译为 a tablet held before the breast by officials when received in audience by the emperor。再如今天我国的“包产到户”，西方没有此概念和说法，就释译成 fixing of farm output quotas for each household。“气”在中国文化中是个十分重要的概念，而在西方文化中不存在对应的概念，先后被译作 quintessence、vital energies 等，难尽其意，后来就干脆音译成 qi。“道”被译作 the Way，实也不准确。“京剧”译作 Peking Opera 也不准确，音译可能更好。

汉英词汇联想意义的差异

联想意义就是词汇在不同的上下文或不同语篇，或为不同身份的说话者使用时所表现出的特殊信息、价值或情感态度等。联想意义又称内涵意义。

其中较为典型的例子是 dog（狗），dog 在英语中为褒义词，如 a luck dog（幸运儿），“Fight dog, fight bear.”（不获全胜不收兵）。在汉语中，一般情况下，“狗”多表达贬义，如“猪狗不如”“狗急跳墙”“狗眼看人低”等。

英汉颜色词所引起的联想意义也不同，例如 red（红色），在汉语中表示“喜庆，欢乐”，如“红红火火”“开门红”“走红”“红墙碧瓦”等，在英语中 red 使人联想到的是“粗俗”“亏损”“暴力”“流血”。例如：

red-necked　粗俗的乡巴佬

the Red May　1968 年 5 月巴黎学生动乱

catch somebody red-handed　抓住某人正在干坏事

此外，还存在联想意义空缺的情况，例如：

六—顺利、牛

八—发财

九—尊贵、长久

这些词在英语中并没有这些联想意义，只是单纯地代表数字。联想意义在英语中出现了空缺。

1.4 词类的对比

词类的对比就是指一种语言与另一种语言中各类实词和各类虚词使用的比例、使用的特征等差异情况。要了解两种语言间的词类对比情况，就要首先了解两种语言的词类系统的整体情况。下面，我们先看下汉语和英语的词类系统的整体情况。

汉语和英语的词类系统如下：

汉语词类系统

实词	名词 数词 量词 代词 动词 形容词 副词
象声词	感叹词、拟声词
虚词	介词 连词 助词

英语词类系统

实词	名词 数词 代词 动词 形容词 副词
象声词	感叹词、拟声词
虚词	介词 连词 冠词

从表面来看，整体上汉语和英语的词类系统基本相同，这是汉英翻译的共同基础。但也有一个大的不同点：英语的冠词和汉语的助词分别为各自所独有，没有直接对应。汉译英时要注意冠词的添加，英译汉时要注意助词的添加。但从内部而言，汉语和英语间差异较大。就副词而言，副词在汉语中数量相对较少，英语中副词为实义词，数量众多且较复杂，

只有一小部分与汉语的副词相当（程度、疑问、时间、范围、连接副词等）。就代词而言，汉语中没有英语中的关系代词。就介词与连词而言，英语多汉语少。从词类使用频率上来看，汉英词类有如下不同点：汉语多用动词，英语多用名词。汉语的动词在使用频率上远远高于英语，因为英语动词的使用要受限制，一句话只要一个谓语动词，而汉语的动词无此限制。英语中代词、介词、连词的使用频率比汉语高。

汉语和英语的词类是相对固定的，但有时又能转化。"报告上级机关"中的"报告"是动词；"写个报告"中的"报告"是名词。Report the progress 中的 report 是动词；a report on the work 中的 report 是名词。但这类转化词的比例并不是很高。

1）英语的名词比例大

作为形态变化丰富的综合型语言，英语句子中的谓语动词要受到很多形态变化规则的约束，因而使用时有很多不便，所以一般每个句子只有一个谓语动词。因此，英语中动词的使用较少。名词化（nominalization）是英语的一大特点，这还包括对大量抽象名词的使用。这一特点在外交、法律、科技、学术等文体中表现得更为突出，构成了以静态化为主的英语语言特征，主要目的是为了表达的客观化和正式性。

例 1　原文：Aggression took many forms, the unilateral denunciation of treaties and international commitments, interference in the internal affairs of other states, the use of threats against weaker neighbours, the imposition of unequal relationships, outright armed attack against the territories of other states and their dismemberment, the subjugation of colonial peoples and the denial of the right of self-determination and fundamental human rights.

译文：侵略有多种形式：单方面废除条约与国际义务，干涉别国内政，对较弱邻国实施威胁，强迫实行不平等关系，赤裸裸武装进攻别国领土核肢解别国，征服殖民地民族，否认自决权和基本人权。

例 2　原文：Each State Party undertakes to cooperate with the Organization and with other States Parties in the improvement of the verification regime, and in the examination of the verification potential of additional monitoring technologies such as electromagnetic pulse monitoring or satellite monitoring, with a view to developing, when appropriate, specific measures to enhance the efficient and cost-effective verification of this Treaty.

译文：每一缔约国承诺与本组织和其他缔约国合作，设法改进核查机制并审查电磁脉冲监测或卫星监测等另外的监测技术的核查潜力，以期在适当时制订具体的措施，提高条约核查的效率和效费比。

例 3　原文：There is no pollution of the melted product. In vacuum induction furnaces in particular the cleaniess of the metal can be maintained by direct casting in the furnaces under the protective vacuum atmosphere. Distillation and the recovery of distillates is also performed in the vacuum unit.

译文：这种熔炼产品无污染。由于在炉内真空保护气氛下直接浇铸，真空感应炉尤能保持金属净度。蒸馏与蒸馏物的回收也在真空设备内完成。

这个英语小段共 42 个词，名词 16 个，占近 40%，充分说明了英语的名词化主导。

例 4　原文：可以使用超热蒸汽改进其性能。

译文 1：We can improve its performance when we use superheated steam.

译文 2：An improvement of its performance can be effected by the use of superheated steam.

两个译文相比，很明显，译文 2 更正式、更客观。

2）英语的介词功能多

由于名词之间的衔接需要介词，英语的名词优势带来的是英语中介词的广泛使用。介词置于名词或名词短语前，英语中的介词有四类：简单介词（in、at、between、through 等）；合成介词（onto、outside、without 等）；双重介词（from under、until after、in between 等）；成语介词（apart from、in front of、in spite of 等）。

英语介词虽然数量有限，但用法灵活，使用广泛，表意功能强。例如：

to be+ 介词短语可替代动词：

例 1　原文：机器正在运行。

译文：The machine is in operation.

例 2　原文：尽管我们努力推进素质教育，许多老师和家长还是热衷于分数。

译文：Despite our efforts at quality-oriented education, many teachers and parents are still keen on marks.

例 3　原文：他最近忙着写毕业论文。

译文：He has been on his dissertation these days.

介词一词多义（polysemy）：

下面以介词 in 为例进行说明。in good health（处于某种状态），in a minute（在一段时间后），in the evening（在某段时间内），in a new style（具有某种特征），in a black coat（穿着某种衣服）。由此可见，介词 in 具有多种意义。

3）英语形容词的动态性

汉语中形容词的主要功能是用来修饰名词，作定语表示事物的性状。就语法功能而言，在英语中，形容词除作定语外，在很多情况下可作表语，而表语相当于汉语的谓语成分。因此，英语的形容词与汉语的形容词的一个重大区别就是其具有动态性。也就是说，汉语中的动作概念，在英语中有时可用形容词来表达。

例 1　原文：为执行发展经济的政策，中国需要和平。

译文：In order to carry through its policies of economic development, peace is necessary for China.

例 2　原文：消息传来，全村轰动。

译文：The whole village was astir with the news.

例 3　原文：这些设计计算可用来说明半导体器件理论的实际应用。

译文：The design calculations will serve as an illustrious application of the theory of semi-conductor devices.

4）汉语的动词频率高

动词对任何语言来讲都很重要，在汉语中的作用尤为突出，使用频率超过英语。

武松走了一阵，酒力发作，焦热起来，一只手提哨棒，一只手把胸膛前袒开，踉踉跄跄，直奔过乱树林来；见一块光挞挞大青石，把那哨棒倚在一边，放翻身体，却待要睡，只见发起一阵狂风。那一阵风过了，只听得乱树背后扑地一声响，跳出一只吊睛白额大虫来。武松见了，叫声“阿呀”，从青石上翻将下来，便拿那条哨棒在手里，闪在青石边。那大虫又饿，又渴，把两只爪在地上略按一按，和身望上一扑，从半空里撺将下来。（《水浒传》）

由上面《水浒传》中这段武松打虎的文字可以看出，汉语中使用了大量的动词。汉语中大量使用动词的原因之一是，与英语的动词相比，汉语的动词没有形态的屈折变化，使用较为方便。另外一个原因可能是，与英语相比，汉语是重过程的语言，具有动态性，自然动词使用的就多（王建国、何自然，2014）。英译汉时，英语中除了动词外，许多名词、形容词和介词也都可以转换为汉语中的动词。

例 1　原文：Let me be your banker.

译文：你需要钱，我可以借给你。

例 2　原文：He was a clever man; a pleasant companion; a careless student; with a great propensity for running into debt, and a partiality for the tavern.

译文：他是个聪明人，谈吐非常风趣，可是学习又不肯用苦功，他老是东挪西借，又喜欢下酒馆喝酒。

例 3　原文：They were suspicious and resentful of him.

译文：他们不信任他，讨厌他。

例 4　原文：“Coming!” Away she skimmed over the lawn, up the path, up the steps, across the veranda, and into the porch.

译文：“来啦！”她蹦着跳着跑了，越过草地，跑上小路，跨上台阶，穿过凉台，进了门廊。

例 5　原文：Through the airport, into the cab and then into the client’s office, Pyles struggle while the men forged ahead.

译文：其他人轻松地走在前面，而派尔却吃力地穿过机场，钻入出租车，走进客户办公室。

2. 汉英词汇翻译策略

根据上述汉英词类的对比特征，总体来看，在词汇方面，汉译英时要变汉语的动词主导为英语的名词主导，发挥英语中形容词和介词的多态性，注意英语副词和冠词的添加和使用。这是汉译英时词汇翻译的总体策略。

1）将汉语动词转化为英语名词、形容词和介词

例 1　原文：看到我们的喷气式飞机，听见隆隆的机声，令我特别神往。

译文：The sight and sound of our jet planes filled me with special longing.

例 2　原文：桥窄，请当心。

译文：Narrow bridge.

例 3　原文：总统先生，我支持您，效忠您。

译文：Mr President, you have my support and my loyalty.

例 4　原文：如果我们不知道原子的结构，我们就不能研究核物理学。

译文：If we were ignorant of the structure of the atom, it would be impossible for us to study nuclear physics.

例 5　原文：同时，我们希望将能继续与这些人会晤，与这些个人会晤。

译文：At the same time, we are hopeful that we are going to be able to continue our meetings with these people, these individuals.

例 6　原文：要是一个人不能在一上任就看出谁支持他，谁反对他，那他就不配搞政治。

译文：If a man couldn't walk into a room and tell who was for him and who was against him, then he was not much of a politician.

例 7　原文：正义战胜了专断，理智战胜了堕落和盲目，民主战胜了帝国主义，善战胜了恶。我们在 10 月 25 日取得的胜利将在历史上写下光辉的一页，我们将把它传之于子孙后代。

译文：The victory of justice over arbitrary acts, of reason over decadence and blindness, of democracy over imperialism, of good over evil, our victory of October 25 will represent one of the glorious pages of our history, and we shall be able to leave it to our heirs.

2）添加冠词和副词（特别是连词）

例 1　原文：各国社会制度不同，但不应妨碍彼此接近与相互合作。

译文：Differences between <u>the</u> social systems of states shall not be <u>an</u> obstacle to their approachment and cooperation.

例 2　原文：科学家因潜心科学研究，所以没有兴趣关心外界的事情。

译文：<u>The</u> pursuit of science withdraws a scientist's interest from external things.

例 3　原文：弟子入则孝，出则悌，谨而信，泛爱众，而亲仁，行有余力，则以学文。

译文：A young man, <u>when</u> at home, should be a good son; <u>when</u> out in the world, a good citizen. He should be circumspect and truthful. He should be in sympathy with all men, <u>but</u> intimate with men of moral character. <u>If</u> he has time and opportunity to spare, <u>after</u> the performance of those duties, he should then employ them in literary pursuits.

例 4　原文：真正的经济学理论，绝不会同最高的伦理道德准则产生冲突。经济学说

应该代表公正和诚信，平等地促进所有人，包括最弱势人群的福祉。

译文：True economic theories will never come into conflict with the highest moral and ethical standards. Instead, they should stand for justice and integrity, and contribute in an equal way to the well-being of all people, including the most vulnerable ones.

例 5　原文：中国曾长期实行高度集中的计划经济，把计划看成是绝对的，束缚了生产力的发展。这场金融危机使我们看到，市场也不是万能的，

译文：For many years in the past, China practiced a highly centralized planned economy and regarded planning as being absolute. This hampered the development of productivity. The ongoing financial crisis has made it clear to us, however, that the market is not a cure-all, either.

至于具体的词汇翻译，汉译英时一定要切记不要思维固化，一一对应。下面是庄绎传（1980）举过的很普通的一个汉语词“历史”的英译的例子。

例 1　原文：民主自由都是相对的，不是绝对的，都是历史上发生和发展的。

译文：Both democracy and freedom are relative, not absolute, and they come into being and develop in specific historical conditions.

此句中“历史”仅是字面意义，实际意义是“在一定的历史条件下”，因此译为 in specific historic conditions。

例 2　原文：历史上的战争分为两类，一类是正义的，一类是非正义的。

译文：History shows that wars are divided into two kinds, just and unjust.

如果将这句话译为“Wars in history can be divided into two kinds, just and unjust.”, 就可能被曲解为不包括现代战争了。

例 3　原文：从他注意研究中国历史情况和当前社会情况方面——知道他是虚心的。

译文：From the way he applied himself to the study of both China's past and present — I knew he was a man with a receptive mind.

在英语里，当把历史和现状相提并论的时候，往往用的说法是 past and present，而不是 history and present。

例 4　原文：他们想问题做事情的方法，他们的历史习惯，跟我们不同。

译文：The way they think, the way they do things and their traditional habits are different from us.

这里所谓“历史习惯”，大概是指在历史上形成的沿袭已久的习惯。

例 5　原文：不但要看干部的一时一事，而且要看干部的全部历史和全部工作，这是认识干部的主要方法。

译文：We must not confine our judgment to a short period or a single incident in a cadre's life, but should consider his life and work as a whole. This is the principal method of judging cadres.

这个例子讲的是个人，自然是 life 和 work 连在一起较为通顺。

由以上的例子可以看出，即使最为普通的汉语词语在英语中都有多种对应翻译。因此，对于汉译英中词语的翻译，一要深入其实质意义，而不是仅仅停留在表面字义；二是翻译时要时刻考虑英语的语言组织原则和习惯。

其次，要注意汉语中的词语往往较为雅致，如果仅从字面直译，则往往束手无策，无法直接找到对应词，此时就应将其转换为较为平实的词语，再译为英语。例如：

汉语雅致表达	汉语平实表达	英语译文
栩栩如生	生动的	lively
风马牛不相及	无关的	irrelevant
千篇一律	相同的	identical
如胶似漆	厚的，稠的	thick
稳扎稳打	小心谨慎的	with discretion
娓娓动听	以雄辩的口才	with eloquence
丰功伟绩	巨大贡献	great contribution
固若金汤	无法攻破	invulnerability
粗茶淡饭	简单的食物	meager food
胆战心惊	害怕的	frightened

再者，要注意英语词语的精细化，汉译英时要尽量选择具体化的英语词语，而不要只是停留在表面上。

例如，汉语中的"说"在英语中可有如下多种表达法：

acknowledge 承认
add 接着说，又说
admit 承认
affirm 肯定，确认
allege 宣称
analyze 分析道
announce 宣布
argue 争辩
assert 断言
boast 夸口说
caution 告诫说
claim 声称
emphasize 强调
exclaim 大声说
explain 解释说
express 表示
go on 继续说
imply 暗示
insist 坚持说
joke 开玩笑地说
maintain 主张，认为
note 表明
object 提出异议，反对
observe 评述
stress 着重说，强调
suggest 建议
tell 告诉

complain 抱怨说	pledge 保证	urge 敦促，力劝
communicate 传达，沟通	proclaim 宣告，声明	voice 表达，吐露
concede 承认	protest 抗议	warn 告诫
conclude 断定，下结论	reaffirm 重申	
confess 供认，承认	recite 讲述	
contend 争辩	reiterate 重申	
continue 接着说	remark 议论	
contradict 反驳，否定	reply 回答	
declare 声明，声称	refute 反驳	
deliver 发表，宣布	report 据报道	
drive (drive at) 说，用意	reveal 透露	
deny 否认	say 说	
disclose 透露	speak 说	
elaborate 详细述说	state 声明，声称	

汉语中的“笑”在英语中有如下多种表达法：

1）smile 微笑

Gradually a smile appeared on her face.

2）grin 露齿而笑

He was grinning with delight.

3）chuckle 轻笑

She does not laugh out loud; she only chuckles.

4）smirk 傻笑

He could not help smirking on seeing his bride in his dream.

5）simper 痴笑

She couldn't stop simpering when she saw the handsome man.

6）snicker 坏笑

After making practical joke, he snickered.

7）giggle 咯咯地笑

The little boy started to giggle and ate his breakfast and went out to play.

8）guffaw 狂笑

We got a fright when he suddenly guffawed.

9）ridicule 嘲笑，奚落，或善意或恶意地用语言戏弄某人，使之出洋相

Her brothers poured ridicule on her boyfriend.

10）mock 嘲弄，用语言、手势等模仿某人的行为举止以讥笑他人

The children mocked their classmate's sore foot by pretending to walk with a limp.

11）deride 讥笑，用轻蔑的语言讥讽某人的缺点

The boys derided him for his fear of the snake.

汉语中的“走”在英语中有如下多种表达法：

1）creep 爬行；蹑手蹑脚地走

We take off our shoes and creep cautiously along the passage.

2）loiter 闲荡

The girl loitered on her way home.

3）march 游行

The troops marched on.

4）meander 漫步

I liked to meander through familiar streets.

5）wander 漫步

He likes to wander over the countryside.

6）ramble 漫游

I like rambling around in the country.

7）roam 漫步

They loved to roam the hills of west Virginia.

8）saunter 漫步

He sauntered by with his hands in his pockets.

9）stroll 漫步

A stroll round the garden hardly qualifies as exercise!

10）pace 踱步

The lion paced the floor of his cage restlessly.

11）patrol 巡逻

Guards patrol the perimeter of the estate.

12）plod 沉重地走

They had to plod wearily on up the hill.

13）prowl 潜行（觅食）

Many wild animals prowl at night.

14）shuffle 慢吞吞地走

The prisoners shuffled along the corridor and into their cells.

15）stagger 蹒跚

The drunk man staggered across the room.

16）stalk 阔步走；偷偷接近

He moved like a tiger stalking its prey.

17）step 迈步

She stepped on a loose stone and twisted her ankle.

18）tread 踏，踩

The cattle had trodden a path to the pond.

19）stride 大步走

The boy is too young to stride the ditch.

20）strut 趾高气扬地走

He strutted up and down before the manager.

21）toddle（幼儿等）东倒西歪地走

Her two-year-old son toddled into the room.

22）tramp 脚步沉重地走 / 徒步走

The boys took a tramp together over the hills.

23）trudge 跋涉

The old man trudged home through the deep snow.

汉语中动物的“叫”在英语中有多种不同的译法：

猿：call; chatter; howl; gibber; wail

驴：bray; hee-haw; neigh

蜜蜂：buzz; hum; drone

公牛：bellow

青蛙：croak

猫：mew; purr; caterwaul

蝉：sing

母牛：low; moo; bellow

蟋蟀：chirp; chirr; chirrup; cry

鹿：bell

狗：bark; bay; yap; yowl

象：trumpet

苍蝇：buzz; drone

马：neigh; whicker; whinny

狮：roar

猎犬：bark; bay; ululate; yap; yowl

猴：call; snarl

蚊：buzz; hum

鼠：peep; squeak

猪：grunt; squeak

绵羊：blat; bleat

虎：howl

狼：howl; ululate

最后，由于语义的不对应，有些汉语范畴词在英译时可省略。例如：

例 1　原文：有些国家失业现象普遍。

译文：Unemployment is widespread in some countries.

例 2　原文：那里的雇主使用了暴力手段。

译文：The employers there used violence.

例 3　原文：她说话时脸上露出了拘谨的神色。

译文：She spoke with restraint in her face.

例 4　原文：他听见了家庭的困难情况后，同意去找工作。

译文：After he had heard about the family trouble, she agreed to look for a job.

练习题：

一、请将以下词汇或短语译为英语，有下划线的句子或短语中只翻译下画线部分。

1. 在世界率先实现经济回升向好
2. 实际增长 9.8% 和 8.5%
3. 保障性住房
4. 社会正常秩序
5. 物联网
6. 建设中华民族共有精神家园
7. 国际关系民主化
8. 他昨天擦破了皮，现在到医院换药去了。
9. 积极的财政政策

   积极利用国外资源
10. 逝世、与世长辞、寿终、断气、归西天、了结尘缘、命归黄泉、见阎王、翘辫子、蹬腿
11. 他们讲索取，我们讲奉献。
12. 其实中年是人生盛华的开始，不应贪懒，不应享受。
13. 浓茶，浓汤，浓烟
14. 拆东墙，补西墙
15. 安居工程

16. 八个坚持，八个反对
17. 当务之急
18. 抵抗全球经济衰退
19. 打白条，打假，打卡机，打开天窗说亮话，打小报告的人，打出王牌

二、分析并总结你自己汉译英实践中的词汇翻译与短语翻译策略。

第二节 汉英词汇搭配对比与汉译英策略

英汉词汇在使用方面的另一个重要的差异是搭配的差异。现代语言习得研究已经表明，搭配能力是语言高级阶段重要的标志性能力。搭配既包括常见的语法搭配，也包括习惯性搭配，特别是习惯性搭配较难掌握，也是汉英翻译的一大难点。

根据我们的观察，中国学生翻译中最常见的搭配错误主要包括：主谓搭配、动宾搭配、修饰语与中心词的搭配。

1）主谓搭配

英语和汉语存在类型上的差异：汉语是主题突出语言，英语是主语突出语言。实际上，汉语中的主语有许多情况下是话题，而不是主语，因此和谓语的关系较为松散，语义、语法限制较少。但英语中话题句较少，主语和谓语的关系紧密，语义、语法限制较为严格。

例 1　我们国家的建设事业不仅仅需要的是工程师和科学家，同样需要各行各业的能工巧匠。

* The **building cause** of our country **needs** not only engineers and scientists, but talents of various kinds.

Our **country** in her development **needs** not only engineers and scientists, but talents of various kinds.

例 2　这个战略思想现在已经有了实施的机遇。

* The **strategy** now **has** an opportunity to implement.

We now **have** an opportunity to implement the strategy.

The opportunity now has arisen to implement the strategy.

上述两句在英语中的 need 和 has 都需要有灵主语，而汉语则无此要求。因此，不知道这种主谓搭配的限制，就会在汉译英时出错。

2）动宾搭配

例 1　有必要教给学生一些美国历史的知识。

* It is necessary to **teach** students a little **knowledge** of American history.

It is necessary to **impart** students a little **knowledge** of American history.

例 2　帝国主义和国民党反动派的长期统治，造成了社会经济的不正常状态，造成了广大的失业群。

* Long years of imperialist and reactionary Kuomintang rule **caused** our economy in a chaotic **state** and widespread **unemployment**.

Long years of imperialist and reactionary Kuomintang rule **left** our economy in a chaotic **state** and **caused** widespread **unemployment**.

例 1 中的 teach 的宾语应为人。在例 2 中，cause 一般表示造成某种结果，不能表示造成某种状态，所以表示造成某种状态时就需将动词换为 left。

3）修饰语与中心词的搭配

例 1　我是超市的老顾客，所以也不抱怨什么。

* As an **old customer** of the supermarket, I did not make a complaint.

As a **regular customer** of the supermarket, I did not make a complaint.

例 2　我们要广泛普及科学文化知识。

* We need to **extensively popularize** science and culture.

We need to **popularize** science and culture.

例 1 中的 old 在英语中并无"频繁"之义，因此和汉语原文不对应。在例 2 中，popularize 本身就已包含"广泛的"之义，因此在英语中无须再加 extensively。

下面，我们再具体分析"克服"这一概念的英汉搭配差异。例句均来自《毛泽东选集》及其英译本。

	常见搭配词
克服	现象，困难，矛盾，阻力，观念，官僚主义，危险，不平衡，风气，逆转，思想，旧毒，污浊，波折，回头路，意见，缺点，贪污，行贿，盗窃，东西，错误

	常见搭配词
overcome	problem, obstacle, shyness, difficulty, resistance, shortcoming, weakness, friction, disadvantage, temptation, prejudice, barrier, hardship, jealousy

1. 克服现象

1）共产党员应和党外一切先进分子协同一致，为着团结全国人民克服各种不良现象而努力。

2）但是我们有信心，我们的党、我们的国家有能力逐步克服并最终消除这些消极现象。

2. 克服矛盾

克服了矛盾，暂时归于一律了；但不久又会产生新矛盾，又不一律，又须要克服。

3. 克服阻力

抓住典型，处理了，效果也大，表明我们下决心克服一切阻力抓法制建设和精神文明建设。

4. 克服观念

首先，是由于历史上“好子不当兵”的传统观念我们还未能给以有力的克服。

5. 克服官僚主义

提高效率，克服官僚主义，包括精简机构，还包括其他许多内容。

6. 克服危险

它能够使我们党得到群众的监督，克服党员堕落腐化的危险，及时发现投机分子以及破坏分子而清洗出党。

7. 克服风气

上述两个运动的后期，事前不请示，事后不报告，不按章程办事的无政府无纪律的风气，又在抬头，（请中南、华东各省严密注意这些教训，坚决执行请示报告制度，绝对不容许此种坏作风抬头。毛注。）我们已告各地注意克服。

8. 克服逆转

在这种形势下，争取时局好转，克服时局逆转的可能性，还是存在的，中央二月一日的决定是完全正确的。

9. 克服思想

党内要分清理论是非、路线是非，要开展批评和自我批评，互相帮助，互相监督，克服各种错误思想。

10. 克服旧毒、 污浊、 波折、 回头路

旧毒，污浊，革命进程中的某些波折，以及可能的回头路，只有斗争和努力才能够克服，而且需要长期的斗争和努力。

11. 克服贪污、行贿、盗窃、其他的东西

对贪污、行贿、盗窃以及其他乌七八糟的东西，人民是非常反感的，我们依靠人民的力量，一定能够逐步加以克服。

参考译文：

1. 1) Communists should work in harmony with all progressives outside the Party and endeavour to unite the entire people to **do away with whatever is undesirable**.

   2) But we are confident that our Party and our country are capable of gradually **reducing** these negative **phenomena** and eventually eliminating them.

2. The resolution of contradictions results in temporary uniformity, but new **contradictions**

soon emerge, which means non-uniformity, and they, in turn, have to be **resolved**.

3. Dealing with these cases will have the most effect; it will show our determination to **surmount** all **obstacles** in strengthening the legal system and promoting ethical progress.

4. First of all, we have not **exploded** the traditional **myth** that " a good man does not join the army."

5. Increasing efficiency and **eliminating bureaucratism** include, among other things, streamlining Party and government organs.

6. It can keep the Party under the supervision of the masses, so that Party members can **avoid** the **danger** of becoming degenerate and so that careerists and saboteurs can be uncovered and expelled from the Party before it is too late.

7. In the later stages of the two movements, anarchy and indiscipline began to gain ground when people concerned did not ask higher authorities for instructions or submitting reports afterwards and violated rules and regulations. (Mao's comment: Comrades working in the provinces in south-central and east China are expected to pay close attention to this lesson and see to it that the system of asking for instructions from above and submitting reports afterwards is applied rigorously and that no practices of this undesirable type shall be tolerated.) We have already notified all localities to **check** this **tendency**.

8. In these circumstances the possibility still exists of **preventing** the situation from **deteriorating** and of changing it for the better; the Central Committee's resolutions of February 1 are entirely correct.

9. Inside the Party we should distinguish right from wrong in terms of theory and of the Party line, conduct criticism and self-criticism and help and supervise each other in **correcting** wrong **ideas**.

10. It is only through struggle and hard work, and over a long period too, that we can **eliminate** the old **evils** , the old **filth**, and **prevent setbacks** or even **reversals** in the revolution.

11. The people detest **graft, bribery, theft** and other dirty **practices**. I have no doubt that if we rely on the strength of the people, we shall be able to gradually **eliminate** those practices.

实际上，“克服” 在英语中还可有如下表达方式：

1) Fortunately Scarlett had come into contact with the two men very little, for Will had persuaded her to let him handle the trading while she managed the plantation. In his mild-tempered way, Will had **straightened out** several difficulties of this kind and said nothing to her about them.

幸好思嘉很少同这两个人发生什么联系，因为威尔早已说服她让他来管理买卖上的事，而她自己只管理农场。威尔用他那种温和的办法克服了好几种这一类的困难。并对她什么也没有说。

2) Greater things than the Doctor had at that time to **contend with**, would have yielded before his persevering purpose.

即使当时医生要克服的困难比现在还要大得多，在他那坚持不懈的努力之下困难也是会退让的。

3) If I do, she'll **outgrow** it and forget about it.

只要我这样做，她就会逐渐克服它，把它忘了。

4) Knowing your natural temper better than I, he could the better judge what arguments to use, whether of tenderness or terror, such as might **prevail over** your hardness and obstinacy, insomuch that you should no longer hide the name of him who tempted you to this grievous fall.

由于他比我更了解你的秉性，他应该是个更合格的法官，他更清楚应该选用什么样的刚柔相济的辞令，来克服你的桀骜不驯；以使你不再隐瞒那个诱惑你如此堕落的人的姓名。

5) Mapping the position of genes on chromosomes gives today's biotechnology researchers a huge advantage over their predecessors in discovering the molecular activities involved in diseases and devising new, more effective therapeutic interventions to **counteract** them.

确定染色体上的基因位置，给今天的生物技术研究者比他们前辈更大的便利，例如发现疾病的分子活动和设计新的更有效的治疗介入方法克服疾病。

6) We know now, the natural antipathy you strove against, and **conquered**, for her dear sake.

现在我才明白你为她的缘故跟发自天性的憎恶作了多少年斗争，并且克服了它。

7) But, few cared enough for that to think of it a second time, and, in this matter, as in all others, the common wretches were left to **get out of** their difficulties as they could.

可是注意到这类事件并加以考虑的人却很少。因而在这件事上也跟在别的事上一样，普通的穷苦百姓便只有自行努力去克服困难了。

8) He, on this part, had pretty well **fought** his weakness **down**.

至于希尔弗，他已经比较成功地克服了自己一时的怯懦。

下面是我们对 eyes 一词在英国国家语料库（BNC）中进行检索得到的部分主谓和定中搭配。

主谓搭配

Their mouths fell open and their eyes **popped** with astonishment.
Sladen's eyes **searched** for comfort.
his strong dark face and amber eyes **danced** between her and the
shoulders like a caress. Blue eyes **smiled** from a face that,
the ice in his tone and his eyes **surpassed** it.
she said automatically, but then her eyes **flicked** to his in alarm
she said, anger making her eyes **flash**.

His eyes **crinkled** with amusement.
he asked, his eyes **laughing** at her.
impossible in any dream. Her eyes **flew open** as Roman kissed
and he went very still, his eyes **leaping** with fire
Claudia said, her eyes **darting,** from one single
About time; he said, his eyes **taking in** the picture
under the flimsy nightgown, his eyes **caressing** her as blatantly as
He smiled again, his eyes **hooding** as he looked at he
Luke' eyes **devoured** her.
Her eyes **strayed** involuntarily to the
His eyes **glazed** on the swaying barley
from the way his amber eyes **lingered** on every inch of
定中搭配
of brown dust, and their **yellow** eyes a slightly inebriated, glazed
with big **golden-brown** eyes that saw everything as wildly
for a glance from his **magnificent** eyes.
bright **aqua-marine** eyes that looked out from her
the watery **bad-tempered** eyes.
she insisted, her eyes still **stormy**.
Not cocky young men with **roving** eyes and a nice taste in girls
His **lazy, supercilious** eyes, too, managed their affect
features and long, **indifferent lapis** eyes, belonged to a statue
white-faced with huge **puffy red-rimmed** eyes, his thin hair plastered
His little eyes are completely **raw**, he can
the gown round her roughly, his eyes as **cold** as stones.

由此可见，汉英两种语言在搭配模式上存在较大的差异。汉译英中，词汇搭配的翻译是一个大问题，应引起重视。

练习题：

一、将以下词汇或短语译为英语，是句子的仅翻译下画线部分，注意搭配。

1. 个人演唱会
2. 环保电池
3. 基层民主
4. 化解分歧
5. 建筑面积

6. 开小灶
7. 破坏
   1）中国人民和中国人民解放军战胜了帝国主义、霸权主义的侵略、破坏和武装挑衅，维护了国家的独立和安全，增强了国防。
   2）这起事件严重破坏了拉萨正常的社会秩序，给拉萨市人民群众的生命财产带来了极大的损失。
   3）他们极力破坏国内社会稳定，诬蔑损害国家形象，干扰我国国家领导人出访，损害我国国家领土和主权安全。
   4）社会主义制度是中华人民共和国的根本制度。禁止任何组织或者个人破坏社会主义制度。
   5）美国领导人如果选择在这个时候会见达赖，就是破坏两国的信任和合作。
   6）国家保障自然资源的合理利用，保护珍贵的动物和植物。禁止任何组织或者个人用任何手段侵占或者破坏自然资源。
   7）越来越多的包括我自己在内的藏民，认为达赖喇嘛不仅仅是一个宗教人士，他是一个打着宗教的幌子，长期搞分裂祖国、破坏民族团结的政治集团的头子。
8. 精神
   1）具有不屈不挠精神的男子汉
   2）他是一个充满冒险精神的人。
   3）汤姆很有进取精神。
   4）她既没有克莱德那股毅力，又没有他那种反抗精神。
   5）他献身科学的精神令人敬佩。
   6）一位医生证明他精神不正常。
   7）度假之后，他的身体状况和精神状况都很好。
   8）撞车事故后，她好像精神崩溃了。
9. 发财，发脾气，发车，发电，发球，发难，发问
10. 白菜，密码，救火，早恋，买一赠一，青春痘，长镜头，方便面，隐形眼镜
11. 假花，假唱，假钞，假酒，假新闻
12. 创造奇迹
    接电话
    拉动消费
    听取意见
13. 他们是我们现在工作重要的基础。
    我们完全可以预言。
    我们必须防止急躁情绪。

14.

鸡啼

鹿鸣

犬吠

羊咩

狮吼

虎啸

狼嚎

马嘶

象吼

鹤唳

熊 / 公牛吼

蛇咝咝

青蛙“呱呱”叫

喜鹊“喊喊喳喳”叫

鹅“嘎嘎”叫

夜莺啭鸣

小鸡“叽叽”叫

老鼠“吱吱”叫

驴叫

麻雀“唧唧喳喳”叫

猫“喵喵”叫

15. 我看出了他的心事。

他看出了她的破绽。

16. 不冻港

冷餐会

流动资金

江洋大盗

17. 江湖骗子

江河日下

18. 厚颜无耻

提高人们的生活水平

19. 馆

博物馆 图书馆 宾馆 大使馆 领事馆 茶馆 饭馆 理发馆 体育馆 展览馆 文化馆 美术馆 科技馆 天文馆 照相馆

二、分析并总结你自己汉译英实践中的词汇搭配策略。

第三节 汉英句法差异及汉译英策略

依据美国学者 Li & Thompson (1984) 的研究，语言有四种基本类型：注重主语（subject-prominent）的语言；注重主题（topic-prominent）的语言；主语和主题都注重的语言；主语和主题都不注重的语言。

在注重主语的语言中，句子结构便于主要用主语－谓语这种语法关系进行描写；在注重主题的语言中，基本句子结构便于主要用主题－述题这种语法关系进行描写。下面以两个英语句式分别说明主语－谓语结构和主题－述题结构。

（1）John hit Mary.
主语　谓语

（2）As for education, John prefers Betrand Russell's ideas.
主题　述题

四种类型语言的举例如下：

注重主语的语言
印欧语
尼日尔－刚果语
芬兰－乌戈尔语

注重主题的语言
汉语
拉祜语
缅甸语

主语和主题都注重的语言
日语
朝鲜语

主语和主题都不注重的语言
他加禄语
伊洛干诺语

由以上可以看出，英语是属于注重主语的语言，汉语是属于注重主题的语言。这是英汉两种语言在句子结构方面的最大差异。汉语句子的基本结构是“主题＋述题”，而英语句子结构是“主语＋谓语”，主语在句中处于不可或缺的地位，要求意足形完。赵元任先生在《汉语口语语法》一书中指出：“在汉语里把主语、谓语当作话题和说明来看待，比较合适。”注重主题的语言还有如下特征：（1）在主题突出的语言中，主题有表层标志，主语则不一定有表层标志。例如，汉语的主题总是在句首，在傈僳语和拉祜语中，主题带有形态标志。（2）被动结构。在主语突出的语言中，被动结构很普遍。但在主题突出的语言中，被动化或者根本看不到，或者看起来是一种边缘结构，在讲话中几乎不用。（3）“假位”主语。

主语突出的语言可以有假位或虚位主语，比如英语的 it 和 there；德语的 es, 法语的 il 和 ce，而主题突出的语言则没有。(4)“双重主语结构。“双重主语”句子是最典型的主题－述题句，广泛见于汉语、日语、朝鲜语、傈僳语和拉枯语。例如：

1）象鼻子长。

2）那种豆子一斤三十块钱。

主题句由“主题”和“述题”两大部分组成，结构简单，语义关联。没有语义和语法规则的强制要求，也没有主谓一致的要求，词性和句子成分之间未必要保持一一对应的关系。主谓句则恰恰相反，主语和动词之间必须保持语义上的选择关系、形式上的一致性以及词性和句子成分的对应关系。总之，主谓句对语义和语形都有严格的要求。主谓句是强制性、封闭性的语言结构，句子结构是立体的，主次分明，逻辑清晰，而主题句则是开放性的，在主题限定的范畴内，述题顺序而出，恰如竹节，不分主次。控制这种结构的主要是主题链而非句法成分和一致性原则。这是开放式和封闭式语言结构的一个重要区别。英语以主谓为纲，衍生出树型句子结构，汉语以主题为起点衍生出竹节式句子结构。这两种类型的句子结构用图来表示，其间差异一目了然。

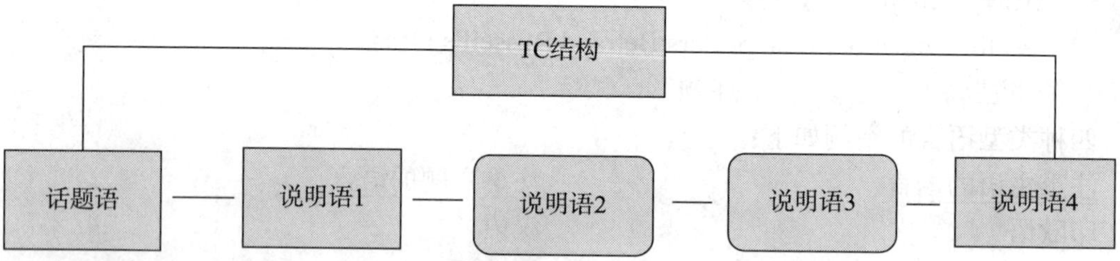

（徐莉娜．英译汉话题句取向翻译模式研究．中国翻译，2010（3））

由于汉语句子和英语句子存在以上结构上的根本差异，因此汉语句子英译时的主要策略就是跳出汉语原文的句法制约，将句子层面汉语的二维平面结构（并列结构）转化为英语的三维立体结构（从属结构）。

换言之，汉译英时句法层面的主要困难是句式结构转换的困难。如上图所示，英语是双轨制，一轨是以“主语－谓语”结构为框架的句法，一轨是与句子结构成分有对应关系的名词、动词、形容词的词类划分，一致关系是支撑这两轨的大梁。这就是英语作为注重主语语言的主要特征。汉语作为主题突出的语言，既没有主谓的一致关系，也不强求句子成分和词性的对应，汉语的句子结构经常表现为一种以主题语为出发点、以说明语为展开成分的开放式句子结构。

英语的立体性主要是依靠结构词使从属结构（subordination）与主句相连接。汉语的平面性主要是借助词序和助动词，按动作发生的时间顺序和事理的逻辑顺序呈线性递进，使语句呈并列样态（coordination）。因此，从另一个角度来说，在句法层面，英语的主要特征是从属（subordination），汉语的主要特征是并列（coordination）。

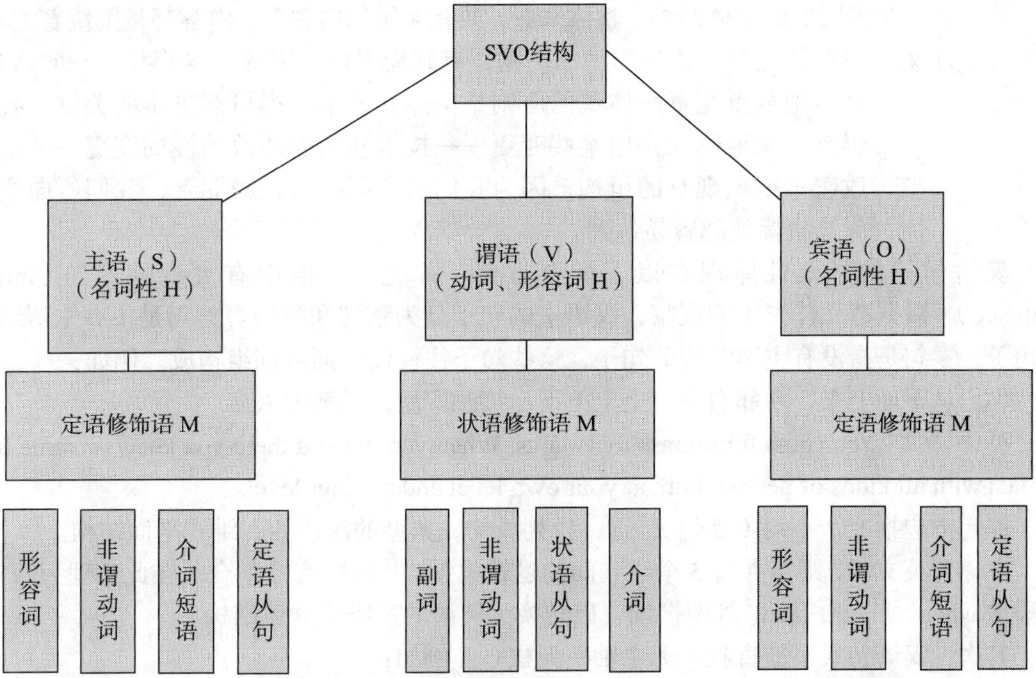

（徐莉娜．英译汉话题句取向翻译模式研究．中国翻译，2010（3））

英语句子结构的立体性体现在两方面：首先是句子有个主干结构，而且许多时候主干结构较短。例如：

The assertion that it was difficult, if not impossible, for a people to enjoy its basic rights unless it was able to determine freely its political status and to ensure freely its economic, social and cultural development was now scarcely contested.

该句英文很长，但主干很短，为：The assertion was now scarcely contested。

汉语译文：如果一个民族不能自由地决定其政治地位，不能自由地保证其经济、社会和文化的发展，要享受其基本权利，即使不是不可能，也是不容易的。这一论断，几乎是无可置辩的了。

其次是，英语句子中的从属成分都与主干结构紧密相连。例如：

Our Charter, being a historical product, has its limitations, Ⅰ and although we have always considered that strict respect for the principles it embodies is the key to considerable progress in international coexistence, Ⅱ we now venture to suggest certain changes, Ⅳ which are technical rather than political, to improve the machinery available to the Organization, Ⅲ since the lofty aims to which we aspire will be the more readily attainable the better the machinery at our disposal.

该句是一个多层次的立体结构，整体来看，共有 4 层句内关系，内容都是围绕着宪章。

汉语译文：我们的宪章，作为历史的产物，有其局限性。因此，尽管我们一向认为，严格地尊重宪章所体现的原则是国际共处中取得可观进步的关键，我们仍然冒昧地建议作出某些变更——技术性的而非政治性的变更——借以改善本组织现有的机构，因为我们所掌握的机构越完善，我们所向往的崇高目标就越容易达到。

汉语句子的平面性体现在以下两个方面。首先，汉语中有大量的零句（minor sentence）。根据赵元任先生的观察，汉语中的句子分为整句和零句。整句是指有主谓结构的句子，零句是指没有主谓结构的句子，这些句子往往仅由词或词组构成。例如：

你们从下面上来，左邻右舍，上上下下，接触广泛，了解的人多。

英语译文：You come from grass-roots units. When you worked there you knew or came into contact with all kinds of people, both at your own level and at other levels.

原句中包括 5 个小句（零句），逐一排列成句，典型的汉语的二维式平面结构。

在译为英文时，则需弄清 5 个小句间的逻辑关系，并进行有效整合。在此整理为两句，并添加 when、"both…and" 等衔接词，以转换为英语的三维式立体结构。

其次，汉语句式平铺直叙，无主轴，无核心。例如：

原文：知己知彼，百战不殆；不知己而知彼，一胜一负；不知己不知彼，每战必殆。

译文：You can fight a hundred battles without defeat if you know the enemy as well as yourself. You will win one battle and lose one battle if you know the enemy but yourself in the dark. You will lose every battle if you leave both the enemy and yourself in the dark.

汉语原句分三个部分，每个部分，自因至果，平铺直叙。但在英语译文中，三个部分则主次分明，先主句，后从句。

由于汉语和英语这种句法结构上的差异，所以对于汉译英来说，就必须有效地把主题－述题结构转换为主语－谓语结构，变汉语的并列句式结构为英语的从属句式结构，变汉语的平面句式结构为英语的立体句式结构。我国著名翻译家程镇球先生指出：

Unfortunately for translators, subordination is not so plainly marked in Chinese. Chinese tends to juxtapose phrases and clauses without any connecting words to indicate the relationship between them. The various parts of a Chinese sentence often appear to be coordinate with one another without any grammatical indication of their relative importance.

将汉语的平面句式结构转换为英语的立体句式结构，关键步骤有以下两点：

1）确定汉语小句之间的逻辑关系。

例 1　原文：我又冷又生气，浑身发抖，登上了列车。

译文：Shaking with cold and anger, I climb inside the train.

通过分析，我们发现这句话中的三个分句间存在一定的逻辑关系，即"登上列车"是主要动作，而"又冷又生气，浑身发抖"则是伴随的次要动作。因此，在英译文中将

climb 处理为了限定动词，而将另两个动词处理为了非限定动词。

例 2　原文：这药吃了准好。

译文：If you take this medicine, your illness will surely be cured.

通过分析，我们发现"吃药"和"好"之间存在条件句的逻辑关系，因此在译文中改为了条件句。

例 3　原文：中国的特点是又大又落后，办起事情来不容易。

译文：It is difficult for us to get things done, because China is a big and backward country.

这句话实际上是由两部分组成，第一部分讲结果，第二部分讲原因，所以这句话的两部分间是有内部逻辑关系的。英译时就可根据这种内部的逻辑关系将汉语的并列结构转换为英语的从属结构。

2）建立"合"的概念，善于运用衔接词把两个在意义上有联系的简单句连接起来。

例 1　原文：我们常听到人们谈论"过去的好时光"。那个时候，美国人更善良，幸福，而且待人也更诚实。

译文 1：We often hear about "the good old days." At that time Americans were better, happier and more honest.

译文 2：We frequently hear about "the good old days" when Americans were better, happier and more honest.

汉语原文实际上是由两个从句组成，且意义联系紧密。对比两个译文后，我们发现译文 1 基本上是达意的，但在结构上被汉语原文束缚了手脚，过于机械，两个并列分句也使英译文显得松散。相比之下，译文 2 有"合"的意识，运用连词 when 将两个从句衔接起来。这样就使英译文不仅联系紧密还体现了层次。

例 2　原文：中方坚决反对喊着法治反法治的做法，要求欧方不要一而再再而三地犯同样的错误，切实遵守平等和相互尊重的原则，多为中欧关系健康稳定发展做点有益的事情。

译文：China strongly opposes the practice of breaking the rule of law under the pretext of rule of law, and urges the EU to earnestly abide by the principle of equality and mutual respect rather than make the same mistakes over and over again, with a view to contributing to the healthy and stable development of China-EU relations.

该英译文通过 rather than 和 with a view to 两个衔接词将四个从句合在了一起，既结构紧凑又体现了层次，是一个典型的英语句式。

例 3　原文：最令女主人失望的是，她花了许多心神或费用来招待客人，可是这位客人只顾津津有味地与她的丈夫论政治、谈生意，丝毫也没有注意到咖啡的浓香、糕点的松软或房间内讲究的陈设，而这些却可能是她最感兴趣、最为自豪的东西。

译文：There is nothing more disappointing to a hostess who has gone to a lot of trouble or expense than to have her guest so interested in talking politics or business with her husband that he fails to notice the flavor of the coffee, the lightness of the cake, or the attractiveness of the house, which may be her chief interest and pride.

该译文通过运用 who 和 which 引导的两个定语从句以及 so...that 结构，很好地将原文进行了整合。

此外，在汉译英句子翻译中，除了上述主要策略外，还要注意以下次要策略。

1）增补与选择主语

汉译英时首先要确立英语句子的主语，主语的选择很重要，主要是因为汉语中的句子往往没有主语，但在英语句子中主语是必要成分。王力先生曾指出："西洋的语法通则是需求每一个句子有一个主语，没有主语就是例外，是省略。中国的语法通则是，凡主语显然可知时，以不用为常，故没有主语则是常例，是隐去，不是省略。"

例 1　原文：话说天下大势，分久必合，合久必分。

译文：They say that the momentum of history was ever thus: the empire, long divided, must unite; long united, must divide.

汉语句子原文中并没有交代"什么分，什么合，"但英译文中添加了主语 the empire。

例 2　原文：要全面深化各领域改革，加快推进基础性、关键性改革，增强内生发展动力。

译文：Full reform will be deepened in all areas. We will move faster to advance fundamental and critical reforms to boost the internal forces driving development.

汉语句子原文中的各个动作并没有交代主语，但在英译文中添加了两个主语 full reform 和 we。

从句子主语来看，汉语中主语或隐含的主语通常是有生命的名词，作主语的常常是具体的成分，称为有灵主语。英语较多使用无生命的名词作主语，称为无灵主语。这可能是由于以孔子为代表的中国传统文化以人本为主，而以亚里士多德为代表的西方传统文化则注重对自然客体的观察与研究。因此，汉译英中，有时需将人称主语转换为物称主语。

例 1　原文：他家起火了。

原译：His home broke out a fire.

改译：A fire broke out in his house.

例 2　原文：他出什么事了？

原译：Has he happened anything?

改译：What has happened to him?

例 3　原文：儿子考试不及格，他非常生气，结果就和妻子吵了起来。

译文：His anger over the boy's failure in the exam led him to quarrel with his wife.

例 4　原文：望着眼前晃来晃去的各色面孔，我时常生出时间错觉，似乎明天就是周末。

译文：The swinging countenances before me always put me under a time illusion that it would be weekend tomorrow.

例 5　原文：我们在分析破损材料时，通常需要先做直观判断，再做实际试验。

译文：Analysis of a damaged material usually requires intuitive judgment followed by real-life testing.

有时，汉语句子开头的成分并不能成为英语句子的主语，需将句中的其他成分转换为主语。

例 1　原文：在历史上，由于长江不断改道，在武汉地区形成了众多的湖泊。

译文：The constant change of the course of the Yangtze River in history helped form a great many lakes in the areas around Wuhan.

例 2　原文：沉默了很长时间的丈夫，突然说出这样的话来，而且在声音中还带着一丝藏不住的伤感。

译文：A tinge of melancholy was tangible in my husband's voice which broke the long silence.

例 3　原文：多种东南亚热带蝴蝶在台湾落脚，也被怀疑与全球变暖有关。

译文：The arrival in Taiwan of many varieties of tropical butterflies from Southeast Asia may also be linked to global warming.

例 4　原文：他疲惫不堪，天气也越来越热，他于是下了决心，一碰到舒适的阴凉处，就坐下休息。

译文：His weariness and the increasing heat determined him to sit down in the first convenient shade.

有时，汉译英时需利用形式主语 it 或 there be 作主语。

例 1　原文：回信，固然可畏，不回信，也绝非什么乐事。

译文：If it is conceded that replying to letters is to be dreaded, on the other hand, not replying to letters is by no means a matter of unalloyed bliss.

例 2　原文：去年冬天连一片雪花也没下过。

译文：There wasn't a single flake of snow last winter.

在这一句型中，there 是引导词，根据语义需要，它后面可跟 exist、happen、occur、appear、come、go、live、rise、stand 等不及物动词作谓语，表示事物的存在、出现、发生或消失等意义。

有时采用拟人修辞格来选择主语。

例 1　原文：在东方拂晓的时候，他早已走了一大段路了，这次骑马旅行是很愉快的，没有碰到意外事件。

译文：Dawn met him well along the way. It was a pleasant uneventful ride.

例 2　原文：这几年，西欧的经济和工业不景气。

译文：The last few years have witnessed an economic and industrial depression in Western Europe.

2）将汉语的动态转化为英语的静态

从谓语来看，汉语呈动态，句中动词使用较多。相对而言，英语呈现静态，在汉语使用动词的地方，英语多由介词短语、现在分词、过去分词、不定式等形式来充当。这主要是由汉语和英语的语种特征决定的。英语属于曲折语，动词使用受到限制，动词的形式变化复杂；汉语属于独立语，动词没有词形的变化，使用限制少。在英语使用经过曲折变化的动词的地方，汉语多直接用动词。另外，英语的很多名词直接由动词变化而来，与动词属于同源词汇。比起同源动词，英语中使用其名词形式的频率更高。此外，介词的大量存在是英语的一大特点，并常与名词搭配使用。而汉语中的介词则相对较少。英语中使用介词的地方，在汉语中更倾向于使用动词来表达相应的意义。所有这些都使得汉语的动词使用更多，整体呈现动态，而英语整体呈现静态。

例 1　原文：教材不按时送到就会打乱我们的教学计划。

译文：Any delay in the delivery of the textbooks will disturb our teaching plan.

汉语原句中出现了“按时”、“送到”和“打乱”三个动词，英语译文句子中则只出现了一个限定动词，根据句子的逻辑关系，选择谓语“打乱”，其他的动词就要作相应的名词化。

例 2　原文：要在巩固成果基础上，针对新情况新问题，完善政策措施，努力取得更大成效。

译文：We should, on the basis of consolidating and building on what we have achieved, improve our policies and measures in light of new developments and new problems so as to make greater progress.

此句中，出现了“巩固”、“完善”、“努力”和“取得”四个动词，在译为英语句子时，需分析句子成分，将动词“巩固”和“努力取得”适当变形为 consolidating and building 和 so as to make，以符合英文句子的静态结构。

例 3　原文：中国成功地爆炸了第一颗原子弹，在全世界引起了巨大的反响。

译文：China's successful explosion of its first atomic bomb caused tremendous repercussions across the globe.

例 4　原文：他们怀疑他是否能负担得起。

译文：They are doubtful whether he can afford it.

在此句话中，汉语原文句子中的动词“怀疑”转换为了英语译文句子中的形容词 doubtful，进行了静态化处理。

例 5　原文：我们全体赞成他的建议。

译文：We were all in favor of his suggestions.

在此句话中，汉语原文句子中的动词“赞成”转换为了英语译文句子中的介词结构 in favor of。

3）将汉语的主动转换为英语的被动

就语态这一语法范畴而言，汉语与英语均有主动与被动。如前所述，汉语习惯用表示人或有生命的物体作主语，而在英语中，有生命名词和无生命名词都可以作主语，而且有多使用无生命名词作主语的倾向。这就使得汉语多主动，英语多被动。在表达被动含义时，汉语常使用词汇化手段。从这一层面来看，汉语中的被动多为“意义被动”。而且被动语态在汉语中使用时，常有消极色彩。在英语中，通过动词的曲折形式来表达被动含义，以陈述客观事理，定界分明，形式稳定，即“结构被动”，其使用频率比在汉语中频繁得多，而且英语中的被动语态通常不含消极意义。“在汉语的定式思维中，行为（动作）是（而且必然是）‘人’这个主体进行或完成的，‘事’或‘物’不可能自己去进行或完成任何动作，再加上汉语语言文字上并不具备语态形态标定手段，因而表现出广泛的‘受事施事化’”（刘宓庆，2006）。

例 1　原文：文章总算写完了。

译文：The article has been at last hammered.

在汉语原文中，“文章”为受事主语，汉语将其提前作主题，“写完”一词，用主动表达“意义被动”。在英译文中，需结合英语重客观，被动形式界定分明的特点，译为被动结构。

例 2　原文：据说第一座装有钟摆和齿轮的钟大约是在公元一千年左右发明的。但是这样的钟不便携带。又过了四百五十年，第一块表才在德国制造出来。

译文：The first clock with weights and wheels is said to have been invented about the year 1000 A. D. , but clocks of that kind could not be carried about from place to place. Another four hundred and fifty years passed before the first watch was made in Germany.

例 3　原文：决议一致通过。

译文：The resolution has been unanimously adopted.

例 4　原文：全体演职人员再一次返回台上，观众们给予热烈的鼓掌，以表示演出的成功。

译文：All the staff and actors returned to the stage, and were warmly applauded by the audience for the success of the performance.

4）将汉语的就近否定转换为英语的谓语否定

汉语和英语在否定句的构词方式上也有差异。汉语的否定句通常该否定哪一部分，就将哪一部分置于否定范围内。而“英语总的趋势是：只要可能，就把本应用特殊否定的地方改用谓语否定而不顾逻辑上是否合理，这种情况在口语里特别显著”（陈文伯，1978）。不能充分认识这一差异，将不仅在理解上造成差错，还给翻译带来困惑。分析其差异的根源，汉语注重从客观实际出发，习惯将否定词置于要否定的部分之前；而英语强调谓语动词的中心作用，以突出主语的动作和行为，因此习惯于将否定词置于谓语动词之前。

例 1　原文：发光的并不一定都是金子。

译文：All that glitters is not gold.

例 2　原文：他们我不全认识。

译文：I don't know any of them.

例 3　原文：我认为这个主意不好。

译文：I don't think it's a good idea.

5）汉语长句的断句与合句

由于英语句子结构相对较为复杂，英语句子相应的往往也较长。实际上汉语中也有很多的长句，英译时这也是一大困难。汉语长句的英译一般来说有两种方法。一种方法是利用英语的从属结构和并列结构将一个汉语长句译为一个英语长句。例如：

例 1　原文：中国是个大国，百分之八十的人口从事农业，但耕地只占土地面积的十分之一，其余为山脉、森林、城镇和其他用地。

译文：China is a large country with four fifths of the population engaged in agriculture, but only one tenth of the land is farmland, the rest being mountains, forests and places for urban and other uses.

例 2　原文：他才三十岁，正处在篮球事业和赚取金钱的鼎盛时期，因此大多数人认为他上周宣布退役为时过早，但是根据他的说法，这一决定完全出于自愿，并非是匆忙之举。

译文：He is thirty and at the height of his performing and earning power, and last week's announcement of retirement was premature in most people's opinions—but it was quite on his willingness, by his own account, not taken hastily.

另一种方法是断句。英译汉时往往需要对英语句子进行断句处理，实际上汉译英时也需要断句。但在何处断句、断为几句是汉译英时较大的难题。请试译以下各句：

例 1　原文：眉间尺刚和他的母亲睡下，老鼠便出来咬锅盖，使他听得发烦。

译文：Mei Jianchi had no sooner lain down beside his mother than rats came out to gnaw the wooden lid of the pan. The sound got on his nerves.

例 2　原文：中国政府充分认识到法律在维护正义与公平，促进和平与发展中的巨大作用，在推行改革开放政策的同时，非常重视法制建设。

译文：The Chinese government fully recognizes the importance of the law in safeguarding justice and fairness and in promoting peace and development. We are paying great attention to building a legal framework in the process of carrying out policies of reform and opening up.

例 3　原文：他们威胁着要开枪，但却没法挡住游行的人，手无寸铁的工人不断向前逼进，尽管警察掷着催泪弹，他们还是推进了整整一公里。

译文：They threatened to shoot, but the marchers could not be stopped. The armless workers press on and on. They sweep on for a kilometer, against police firing guns and throwing tear gas bombs.

例 4　原文：种子不落在肥土而落在瓦砾中，有生命力的种子绝不会悲观和叹气，因为有了阻力才有磨炼。

译文：The seed does not choose to fall on fertile land but among debris. If it is filled with life, it is never pessimistic or sad, for it is tempered by resistance and pressure.

例 5　原文：我从十二岁起，便在镇口的咸亨酒店里当伙计，掌柜说，样子太傻，怕侍候不了长衫主顾，就在外面做点事罢。

译文：At the age of twelve I started work as a pot-boy in Prosperity Tavern at the edge of the town. The boss put me to work in the outer room, saying that I looked too much of a fool to serve long-gowned customers.

例 6　原文：我在倒数上去的二十年中，只看过两回中国戏，前十年是绝不看，因为没看戏的意思和机会，那两回全在后十年，然而都没看出什么来就走了。

译文：In the past twenty years only twice have I been to see Chinese opera. During the first ten years I saw none, lacking both the wish and the opportunity. The two occasions on which I went were in the last ten years, but each time I left without seeing anything in it.

例 7　原文：大概是因为正在下午的缘故罢，这虽说是酒楼，却毫无酒楼气，我已经喝下三杯酒去了，而我以外还是四张空板桌。我看着废园，渐渐的感到孤独，但又不愿有别的酒客上来。偶然听得楼梯上脚步响，便不由的有些懊恼，待到看见堂倌，才又安了心，这样的又喝了两杯酒。

译文：Probably because it was the afternoon, the place had none of the atmosphere of a tavern. By the time I had drunk three cups, the four other tables were still unoccupied. A sense of loneliness stole over me as I stared at the deserted garden, yet I did not want other customers to come up. Thus I could not help being irritated by the occasional footsteps on the stairs, and was relieved to find it was only the waiter. And so I drank another two cups of wine.

例 8　原文：一九一一年，在一个小县城里边，我生在一个小地主的家里。那县城差不多就是中国的最东北部——黑龙江省——所以一年之中，倒有四个月飘着白雪。

译文：In 1911, I was born into a small landlord family in a small county town in Heilong-jiang—China's far northeastern province where it snowed for four months of the year.

从以上例子可以看出，汉语长句的英译是有一定规律的，并不是随意的。前面我们谈到了英语和汉语句子结构的差异，其核心是汉语是主题 – 述题结构，英语是主语 – 谓语结构。从以上例子的原文与译文的对比可以看出，汉语长句英译断句的基本规律是：主题转换后需换句，原因是英语一句话只有一个主题，汉语一句话可有多个主题。明显的外在标志是英译句子中断句后的句子都增添了新的主语。例如，第一句中加了主语 The sound，第二句中加了主语 We，第三句中加了主语 The armless workers 和 They。

练习题：

一、请将下列句子翻译为英语。

1. 这篇论文很不理想。

2. 洪水退了以后，有些恢复宁静的迹象。
3. 我们不能不顾及我们的邻邦。如果我们不顾及他们的安危，就只能自身难保。
4. 有些国家失业现象普遍。
5. 那里的雇主使用了暴力手段。
6. 玛丽说话时脸上露出了拘谨的神色。
7. 一切爱好和平的人民都要求全面禁止核武器，彻底销毁核武器。
8. 承诺尊重人权而不接受国际监督是不彻底的措施。
9. 看到我们的喷气式飞机，听见隆隆的机声，令我特别神往。
10. 一朵庞大的烟云随着一轮巨日从地面升起。它起初是个巨大的圆柱，很快形成了凌云架空的大蘑菇，一瞬间又变成了一座扩大了许多倍的自由女神像。
11. 侵略有多种形式：单方面废除条约与国际义务，干涉别国内政，对较弱邻国实施威胁，强迫实行不平等关系，赤裸裸武装进攻别国领土和肢解别国，征服殖民地民族，否认自决权和基本人权。
12. 我们看到并欢迎中国在处理同其他国家的关系中所持的原则——强调各国一律平等，强调尊重中小国家的权利和意见。
13. 资本主义国家建立自己的重工业，通常是利用从外国获得的资金：要么依靠掠夺殖民地，要么依靠勒索战败国人民的赔款，否则依靠外债。
14. 为此，通常使用的是校正电动机，但就目前的技术水平而言，这种电动机结构复杂、价格昂贵，且性能往往不能尽如人意。
15. 他们正在为实现一个理想而努力，这个理想是每个中国人所珍爱的，在过去，许多中国人曾为了这个理想而牺牲了自己的生命。
16. 一个国家，若想成为世贸组织的成员，须先呈递申请，而后由世贸组织成立一个工作小组对该国的具体条件进行审查。
17. 我们知道，由于猫的眼睛比我们人的眼睛能吸收更多的光线，所以猫在黑夜也能看得清楚。
18. 当然，事情发生后，我们还得尽力去补救。
19. 我又冷又生气，浑身发抖，登上了列车。
20. 有时我经过这种假想的对话后就真的改变了自己的看法。
21. 爱因斯坦的方程式表明，当一颗比太阳大几倍的星球耗尽其核燃料而塌缩时，其物质以极大的力量挤压聚集在星球中心，结果形成一个奇点，即是一个没有体积而密度无限大、具有不可抗拒的引力的点。
22. 虽然有经验的外交官对国际法并不抱有这种颇为流行的怀疑态度，但仍存在着如下的危险性：公众的怀疑也许会影响那些缺乏经验的官员和国内施加压力的集团。其结果是，国家或许会被迫违反国际法。
23. 这次选举你为本届大会主席，实是极为明智的选择，是对你的伟大国家的敬意。

贵国对自由国家的历史发展贡献了一种和平传统，这一传统是我们法治社会的榜样。全世界一贯对贵国表示尊重和敬佩。

二、分析并总结你自己汉译英实践中的句法翻译对策。

第四节 汉英语篇差异及汉译英策略

1. 汉英语序差异及翻译

语言是思维的外在形式。由于中西思维方式的不同，因此英语和汉语的语序存在重大差异。在时间顺序上，汉语往往按照动作或事件发生的前后顺序来安排其语序，而英语则可不受此限制，先发生的可后说，后发生的可先说。在逻辑顺序方面，汉语往往按照原因—结果、叙事—表态、条件—结果、假设—推论的顺序排列，而英语则不尽然，有时还与汉语顺序相反。因此，汉译英时需进行语序的调整，否则译文就不符合英文的语篇结构规则。

（1）时间顺序的调整

整体来说，现实世界中所发生的动作或事件的顺序就是汉语中的语序，而英语语序则往往与现实世界中的顺序不同。

例 1　原文：我吃过饭后去找你。

译文：I will visit you after dinner.

例 2　原文：半轮晓月正渐渐西沉，月光透过我小床边窄窄的窗户倾斜而入，我乘着月光穿上衣服。

译文：I put on my clothes by the light of a half moon just setting, where rays streamed through the narrow window near my crib.

（2）逻辑顺序的调整

当句子里既有叙事又有表态的部分时，汉语往往是叙事在前、表态在后，而英语往往则是表态在前、叙事在后。这是因为英美人认为表态的部分更为重要，重心在前，而汉语则是先交代事实，再亮出态度，重心在后。

例 1　原文：我们认为生活在不同政治和社会制度下的各国人民应该共处，不仅仅是消极共处，而且要积极地友好相处，这是正确，而且必要的。

译文：We believe that it is right and necessary that people with different political and social systems should live side by side—not just in a passive way but as active friends.

例 2　原文：考虑到上届政府遗留下来的危机重重的局面，我们在过去五年里所取得的成绩也就显得尤其显著，这是没有人可以否认的。

译文：No one will deny that what we have been able to do in the past five years is especially striking in view of the crisis which we inherited from the previous government.

例 3　原文：十年时间，有一两个地方，借百把亿美元，只要讲效益，有什么危险？两百亿也没有什么了不起。（叙事→表态）

译文：What danger is there if one or two places borrow $10 billion over a period of 10 years and make effective use of the money? There will be no trouble even if it is $20 billion.（表态→叙事）

在原因—结果逻辑方面，汉语往往遵循从原因到结果的逻辑顺序，英语则有时将结果置前。

例 1　原文：地球曲率的限度使微波发射的视线路径为三十英里；为了良好的接收效果，需建立间隔为三十英里左右的系列转播塔。

译文：Good reception requires a series of relay towers spaced every 30 miles since the curvature of the earth limits a microwave's line-of-sight path to about 30 miles.

例 2　原文：1988 年，在共和党全国代表大会上，似乎名不见经传的奎尔被布什挑中，成了其竞选伙伴。从那以后，奎尔一直是人们取笑和批评的对象。（因 → 果）

译文：Quayle has been the brunt of jokes and criticism ever since Bush chose him, seemingly from out of nowhere, as his running mate at the 1988 convention.（果 → 因）

在条件—结果逻辑方面，汉语一般是从条件到结果，英语则不尽然。

例 1　原文：如蒙早日寄来样品或产品手册，将不胜感激。

译文：It would be appreciated if samples and brochures could soon be forwarded.

例 2　原文：如果我早点从家出发，就不会误了飞机。

译文：I wouldn't have missed the plane if I had left home earlier.

2. 汉译英中衔接成分的添加——以话语标记语为例

整体而言，英语中的逻辑关系是由衔接词标识的，是显化的；汉语中的逻辑关系则是隐含的，往往不用衔接词标识。因此，汉译英中往往需要添加衔接成分。

例 1　原文：我们坚定不移地加强房地产市场调控，确保调控政策落到实处、见到实效。投机、投资性需求得到明显抑制，多数城市房价环比下降，调控效果正在显现。

译文：We steadfastly tightened regulation of the real estate market and ensured that control policies were fully carried out and achieved real progress. Consequently, speculative or investment-driven housing demand has been significantly curbed, housing prices in most Chinese cities have fallen month on month, and the results of our control measures are beginning to show.

本句中添加了 Consequently，将前后两部分连接了起来。

例 2　原文：年龄看上去有二十五六，不过新派女人的年龄好比旧式女人合婚帖上的年庚，需要考订学家所谓外证据来断定真确性，本身是看不出来的。

译文：She could be 25 or 26, but then the age of modern women is like the birthdates traditional women used to list on their marriage cards, whose authentication required what the experts call external evidence, since they meant nothing in and by themselves.

本句中添加了 then、whose、since 来连接句子，使句子成为一个整体，逻辑清楚，句意明确。显然，这类词语是不可或缺的，否则将会造成语法错误，句意模糊。本句翻译符合英语语言习惯，能够被英语读者所接受和理解。

下面，我们以一种重要的衔接成分——话语标记语（discourse marker）为例说明话语标记语如何参与汉译英中的英语译文重构。话语标记语是一种普遍的语言现象，英语和汉语中都有话语标记语。但英语和汉语中话语标记语的使用存在差异，英语中的明示使用更多，而汉语中的隐含使用更多。下面，我们将分析王佐良、巴恩斯《雷雨》英译本中英语话语标记语的运用。

在话语标记语中，well 和 you know 是出现频率较高的两个话语标记语。我们将重点分析 well 和 you know 这两个重要话语标记语在王佐良、巴恩斯《雷雨》英译本中的运用。

（1）话语标记语 well 的运用

在英语中，well 是出现频率最高的话语标记语，且功能多样、复杂。根据 Jucker (1993)，话语标记语 well 主要有 4 种语用功能：1）面子威胁缓和标记语，主要用来缓和后面一个可能威胁面子的话语；2）话语延缓标记语，标示讲话人因某种原因迟疑或不知如何作答；3）信息短缺标记语，标示当前或前一话语不连贯或内容上有问题；4）会话框标记语，标示话题的转换，开启话轮，自我修正，引入直接引语等。下面，我们将具体分析话语标记语 well 的这四种功能在王佐良、巴恩斯《雷雨》英译本译文重构中的运用。

1）面子威胁缓和标记语

Brown & Levinson（1978）认为，在言语交际中，很多言语行为都可能威胁面子。例如，讲话人要说出听话人不愿听的话，讲话人与听话人意见不一致，听话人的请求遭到了拒绝。当讲话者意识到其话语可能威胁到听话者面子时，往往就会选择一定的手段缓和其威胁的程度。话语标记语 well 便是其中的一种语言手段，可以起到缓和面子威胁的作用。例如：

原文：蘩：鲁奶奶，我也知道四凤是个明白的孩子，不过有了这种不幸的情形，我的意思，是非常容易叫人发生误会的。

鲁：（叹气）今天我到这儿来是万没想到的事，回头我就预备把她带走，现在就请您准了她的长假。（曹禺，2001：188）

译文：FAN：Yes, Mrs Lu, I agree that Sifeng's sensible girl; But now that this unfortunate situation has arisen, ***well***, I'm afraid I'd rather lends itself to misunderstanding.

MA (with a sigh): I never expected to find myself here today. I'm thinking of taking her with me when I go back, so if you'd be kind enough to let her leave you at once.（王佐良、巴恩斯，2001：189，斜体和加重为笔者所加，下同）

周蘩漪的儿子周冲喜欢上了鲁妈的女儿四凤，要帮助她交学费，叫她上学，还要娶四凤。这让周蘩漪惊讶不已，自己的儿子怎喜欢上了一个仆人，所以叫来了鲁妈谈这件事。周蘩漪本想直说四凤不懂事，但怕鲁妈不好接受，所以使用了“不过”“我的意思”等汉语话语标记语使自己的话语更容易被鲁侍萍接受。王佐良、巴恩斯在翻译周蘩漪的话时恰当地使用了英语话语标记语 well 的缓和面子威胁的功能，标示后面周蘩漪要说出威胁面子的不好的事情。马萧（2003：37）指出，当听话人读者在众多的语境假设中面临选择困难时，说话人作者就必须使用标记语对听话人读者的语境假设加以限制和制约，最终消除听话人读者在话语诠释过程中可能出现的误解，并将话语理解引向说话人或作者意欲诠释的方向。王佐良、巴恩斯的英译文中话语标记语 well 的运用对后面话语的理解起到了很好的引导和制约作用，表达出了英语中的程序性意义和语用功能，符合英语的表达方式，从而达到了与原文的异曲同工之妙。

2）话语延缓标记语

当讲话人因某种原因迟疑时，well 便可用作一个缓延标记语，可以避免过长的停顿，并提示对方讲话人要提供的信息还未想好。例如：

原文：蘩：这不是原谅不原谅的问题，我已经安安静静地等死，一个人偏把我救活了又不理我，撇得我枯死，慢慢地渴死。让你说，我该怎么办？

萍：那，那我也不知道，你来说吧！（曹禺，2001：152）

译文：FAN: It’s not a question of forgiving anything. I’d resigned myself to my fate, when along came someone who must need revive me — and then tire of me and cast me aside, and leave me to wither away and slowly die of thirst. Now you can tell me what I should do.

PING: Er, ***well***—I’ve no idea. What do you think?（王佐良、巴恩斯，2001：153）

周萍和周蘩漪间产生了不该有的感情，现在周萍明白过来了，要出走，离开这个家，少见面，说自己爱上她是年轻时一时的糊涂，请周蘩漪原谅。周蘩漪不接受周萍的请求，问周萍该怎么办，周萍不知该怎么办。周萍迟疑的语言表现就是使用了汉语话语标记语“那”。王佐良、巴恩斯的英译文恰当地运用了英语话语标记语 well，使用了其延缓功能，标示了说话者的迟疑。这样，王佐良、巴恩斯的英译文就能很好地表达出原文中的程序性意义和语用功能，符合英语的表达方式，取得了与原文对应的效果。

3）信息短缺标记语

在问—答的会话句式中，当回答者故意缺省一定的信息，不愿意清楚地对某一情况进行陈述，或不能直接向对方提供答案时，well 便可能出现，表明说话人还有额外的信息提供或需要解释。例如：

原文：蘩：四凤给老爷检的衣裳，四凤不会拿么？

贵：我也是这么说啊，您不是不舒服么？可是老爷吩咐，要太太自己拿。（曹禺，2001：160）

译文：FAN: Sifeng looks after his clothes. Can’t she get it for him?

LU: ***Well***, that’s what I said to the master, seeing that you’re no feeling very well, but he insists that you should get it, madam.（王佐良、巴恩斯，2001：161）

鲁贵没有直接回答周蘩漪的问题，而是回答说他也是这样说的。王佐良、巴恩斯的英译文中，在话语开头增添了话语标记语 well，标示后面鲁贵不能直接提供周蘩漪希望获得的信息，是一种信息短缺标记。这暗示鲁贵的回答是不完全的，留有余地，让周蘩漪猜测，以补全余下的信息空缺。王佐良、巴恩斯的英译文中，巧妙地增添了话语标记语 well，对话语的理解起到了很好的引导和制约作用。如果话语表层不运用话语标记语 well，只翻译命题内容，英译文的话语就显得突兀，致使程序性意义表达不足，造成语用功能和人际功能的损失。

4）会话框标记语

① 话轮开启标记语

在言语交际中，人们往往用一些话语起始成分来开始自己的话题。话语标记语 well 便是这种起始成分之一，例如：

原文：

鲁贵下。

蘩：（向鲁妈）我先把家里的情形说一说。我家里的女人很少的。（曹禺，2001：184）

译文：

（LU Gui goes out.）

FAN(to Lu Ma): ***Well***, I’d better tell you something about the family first. You see, there are hardly any women in the house. (王佐良、巴恩斯，2001：185)

周蘩漪和鲁贵说完话后，转过来和鲁妈说话。王佐良、巴恩斯的英译文中增添了话语标记语 well，起到开启话轮的功能。在王佐良、巴恩斯的英译文中，话语标记语 well 的增添，补足了程序性意义，符合英语的表达方式。这显示出了译者王佐良、巴恩斯对汉译英中程序性意义和语用功能的重视及高超的翻译水平。

② 话题转换标记语

会话中，转换话题时也往往会使用话语标记语 well，例如：

原文：萍：你，你，你简直——好，好，（强笑）我都承认。你预备怎么样？你要跟我说什么？（曹禺，2001：150）

译文：PING: You’re-you’re-you’re just-oh, all right, all right—(he smiles wryly) I’ll take your word for it. ***Well,*** what are you going to do? What is it you want with me?（王佐良、巴恩斯，2001：151）

周蘩漪说周萍是其父亲的私生子，周萍不承认。周蘩漪指着桌上的照片说周萍就是那年轻姑娘生的小孩。周萍无法再辩解，只好说“我都承认”。王佐良、巴恩斯的英译文中巧妙地增添了话语标记语 well，标示后面的话题要发生转换，周萍已不愿再讨论此话题，起到了话题转换的功能，很好地引导话语过渡到了后面两个问题。如果英译文中不运用话语标记语 well，此处话语的前后衔接就显得突兀，致使程序性意义和语用功能表达不足，从而影响译文的可接受性。

（2）话语标记语 you know 的运用

Schffrin (2007) 认为，话语标记语 you know 的基本功能是元知识标记，标志着信息转变为元知识，用于取得听话人的注意，促使听话人就说话人提供的信息建立互动中的注意焦点，并且提示听话人为接受说话人的话语而调整自己的取向。话语标记语 you know 传递是有关语言本身的信息或所表示的言语行为，它可以提醒交际对方已知或应该知道的某种信息，以增加交际双方的认知共性，推进交际互动。例如：

原文：贵：　大海，到底你是矿上打粗的，连一点大公馆的规矩也不懂。

　　　四：　人家不是周家的底下人。（曹禺，2001：32）

译文：LU:　That's just like you, Dahai, a ham-fisted miner without the least idea how to behave in a big house.

　　　FENG: He's not a servant here, ***you know***. (王佐良、巴恩斯，2001：33)

原文中，四凤此处用“人家”，而不是用“哥哥”或“他”指称鲁大海的主要目的不是说她相信父亲鲁贵知道哥哥大海不是周家的底下人这个事实，而是标示相信父亲知道哥哥不是周家仆人的隐含意义。王佐良、巴恩斯的译文中巧妙地增添了话语标记语 you know，很好地传达了此语用功能。假设只译为“He's not a servant here.”，便只翻译了语义内容，无法传达此语用功能，造成翻译中的语用失误。再如：

原文：蘩：　我希望你明白方才的情形。这不是一天的事情。

　　　萍：（躲避地）父亲一向是那样，他说一句就是一句的。（曹禺，2001：146）

译文：FAN: I hope you fully realize what that scene this morning was all about. It's not just an isolated incident, ***you know***.

　　　PING (evasively): Oh, well, Father's always been like that. What he says goes. (王佐良、巴恩斯，2001：147)

周蘩漪说“这不是一天的事情。”，并不是仅仅为了指出这个事实。正如前一句“我希望你明白方才的情形”，周蘩漪说“这不是一天的事情。”的主要目的是争取周萍的理解，这才是这句话真正的语用功能。王佐良、巴恩斯的译文中巧妙地增添了话语标记语 you know，在英译文中浮现出了此语用功能。如果只译为“It's not just an isolated incident.”，就只翻译了其命题内容，无法实现周蘩漪意欲获得周萍同意的语用功能，造成译文中的语用损失，从而影响翻译效果。

通过以上王佐良、巴恩斯《雷雨》英译本中两个话语标记语 well 和 you know 的运用分析，我们可以看出汉英翻译中话语标记语对正确传达出原文的程序性意义和避免语用功能损失有重要作用。特别是在口语体的汉英翻译中，我们认为，话语标记语语用功能的合理使用是翻译能力的重要组成部分，应引起足够重视。

3. 汉英翻译中的重复问题

重复在汉语中是一种重要的语篇衔接手段，除此之外汉语中还有着丰富的叠词，这与汉语的语音文字特点和思维习惯有着密切关系。而在英语中，语篇衔接手段以替代为主，重复多用于修辞和强调。汉语除去显性重复外，还包含着大量的隐性重复，若不充分考虑深层意义，英译时很容易产生冗余，降低译文的可读性。

语言表述的普遍原则之一是经济原则——用尽量少的形式表达尽量多的语义内容，力求简洁精练。但由于英语属于形合的语言，句中的词语或分句之间用语言形式手段连接起来，表达语法意义和逻辑关系，句子组合主要通过外显形态标记来表现，而汉语属于意合的语言，词语和分句之间不用语言形式手段连接，句中的语法意义和逻辑关系通过词语或分句的含义表达，在语言组织层面两者有着相当大的差异。重复在汉语中是一种常见的现象，小到词句，大到语篇，重复发挥着不同的作用，而英语总体上避免重复。虽然英语语篇中有时也会使用重复，但多数是为了在修辞上起到强调的作用。在汉语中合理的重复如果都按重复的形式译入英语中，译文就会冗赘拖沓，可读性差。对于重复的含义，归结起来为同一个语言成分的多次出现或相同语言成分的重现。重复既包括同一词的多次出现，也包括相同或相似意义成分的多次出现，前者为显性重复，后者为隐性重复，也有学者将前者称为词复，后者成为意复。

（1）汉英重复对比

1）英语中的重复

连淑能指出，通常除非有意强调或出于修辞的需要，英语总的倾向是尽量避免重复。讲英语的人对于随意重复相同的音节、词语或句式往往感到厌烦。他将英语中不合理的重复分为了四种：

音节重复：

Close examination of the results of the investigation led to a reorganization of the department.

应改为：Close study of the results of the inquiry led to a reorganization of the department.

词语重复：

We listened to an account of the customs of the inhabitants of the village.

应改为：We listened to an account of the villagers' customs.

句式重复：

Now is the time for everyone to come out to vote, for everything depends upon this election. All are against corruption, and so they should vote the Reform thicket. This is not a foolish thing, for the voters can elect anyone they want. But the people must turn out heavily, for if they do there is little doubt that they will elect the men they want.

改 为：Everybody should turn out to vote in this election, for the triumph of the Reform party means the end of corruption in office. If the voters will only come to the polls in large enough number, they can surely elect the men they wish to see in power.

意义重复：

He asked the divisions to give their mutual cooperation to the project.

改为：He asked the divisions to cooperate on the project.

从中可以看出，英语中小到词根、大到语篇都尽量避免重复，其丰富的近义词和灵活的句法成为避免重复的重要手段。

2) 汉语的重复

王力指出，汉语的显性重复可有如下分类：

① 主语与表语重复

不懂就是不懂，不要装懂。

We must not pretend to know when we do not know.

② 主语与宾语重复

宾语就是主语加“的”字，表示互不相干，类似英语的 do your own part。

他说他的，我干我的。

Let him say what he likes; I'll just get on with my work.

③ 主语与谓语重复

主语就是谓语加“的”字。这种格式连用两个（以上）相同的结构，有列举的性质。

火车上看书的看书，聊天的聊天。

On the train some were reading and some chatting.

④ 主语与宾语的修饰语重复，一般表示评估。

穷也有穷的好处。

Poverty has its advantage.

⑤ 重复谓语

a. 含“虽”“虽然”的意思，重复的谓语之间插入“是”“却”等字。

这东西旧是旧，可还能用。

Yes, it's old, but it can still be used.

b. 含“即使”“虽然”的意思，重复的谓语之间插入“也”“都”等字。

这个我连想都没想过。

I haven't even thought of it.

c. 含“容忍”“无所谓”的意思，重复的谓语间插入“就”字。

丢了就丢了吧，以后小心点。

If it's lost, it's lost. Just be more careful from now on.

⑥ 重复带宾语的及物动词

及物动词与补语之间不能被宾语隔开而必须重复这个及物动词。

他读书读得很多。

He has read a lot.

⑦ 重复“也好”“也罢”之类，置于并列的谓语形式之后，表示假设或选择。

刮风也罢，下雨也罢，他都坚持跑步。

He keeps up running whether it’s windy or rainy.

⑧ 重复“各”或“自己”，英语则往往使用代词以回避重复。

他自己打自己。

He beat himself.

当然，除此之外，汉语还有其他重复的情况。

汉语的隐性重复

英语中的意义重复与汉语一致，但英语中此类重复是不合理的，而在汉语中却可以接受，“相互合作”“再次重复”“新的发明”“过去的历史”……这样的例子不胜枚举。汉语的重复可以分为冗余的修饰语、冗余的成对词、一事两说和重复指称。根据汉语特点，汉语意义重复的类型如下：

① 重复的修饰语

他所担任的工作 his work

② 不言自明的修饰成分

广泛团结社会各界 unit people from all walks of life

③ 重复的成对词，尤其见于四字成语和谚语。

另外还有 in addition　　发号施令 issue orders

物以类聚，人以群分。Birds of a feather flock together.

④ 一事两说

我们必须准时，不能迟到。We must be on time.

⑤ 两个意义相同或相近的词根构成的合成词

孤独 solitude　　古老 antiquity

（2）汉英重复差异产生的原因

中国人主张“天人合一”“阴阳调和”，体现在文化上就是求和谐、求平衡，反映在语言上就是重意合，词语重平衡和对仗，多用对仗结构，重复较多，汉语讲究均衡美的特点往往造成用词用句的重复倾向（连淑能，188）。与此相反，西方哲学则主张“人物分立”，重形式论证，注重语言逻辑和句子的完整，除非有意强调或出于修辞的需要，总是尽量避免重复。

在语音上，周流溪指出，英语音位之间的配合制约较少，汉语则较多，即在英语中音位的配合很自由，从而可以构成的音节形式很多。而在汉语中，音位的配合则有诸多限制，从而可以构成的音节形式少。对于汉语而言，连声调在内，一共只有 1 000 多个音节；不算声调，只有 400 多个音节，这构成了汉语重复的语音基础。

申小龙指出，汉语擅于“观物取象”，即取万物之象，加工成为象征意义的符号，来反映、认识客观事物的规律，比如：龟裂、蜗居、球菌、食物链等等；而西方语言崇尚理性、知性，表达倾向于抽象，其“喻”的使用频率远远低于汉语。在引语使用上，汉语文章善于引经据典、旁征博引。有些名人名篇虽被频繁引用，仍然保持丰富的表现力，而英语中引语过多，则被称为“陈词滥调”（cliché）。对待习语的态度，中西方也表现出很大的不同，汉语文章讲究用四字成语，成语的运用使文章流畅、表达力强，增加文章文采；而西方人不主张多用所谓“陈词滥调”。

英语衔接手段比汉语更为复杂多样，同义词或近义词、上义词、统称词等等都可以避免重复，而汉语语篇衔接以重复为主，正如胡壮麟所言，词汇衔接中最直接的方式是具有同样语义、同一形式的词汇在同一语篇中反复出现。汉语意合的本质决定了汉语主要通过重复同一词达到语篇的衔接。

潘文国在《汉英语对比纲要》一书中提出，汉语重重复而英语重替代反映了形合和意合的辩证法，即纯粹用意合或纯粹用形合的语言都是少见的，各种语言都使用意合手段，各种语言也都使用形合手段，只是使用的范围、程度各不相同。拿英语和汉语比较来看，在句子及句子以下层面，英语比较稳定而多样的形式（包括形态），可以控制句子内部各语言要素间的关系，因此以形合为主；到了句以上，英语似乎没有必要再用如此强的形式来限制自己了，为了体现变化，因而采用了意合手段，同义词、上义词、统称词、代词等基本上都是词汇手段，把它们联系起来的不是形式，而是意义。汉语的情况正好相反，在句子（或相当于句子）的较短的语言片段内，主要靠的是意合，用“意脉”贯穿全句；而到了较大的语言片段里，为了保持“神”不散，就要用适当的“形合”手段来增加凝聚力，而重复同一个词是最好的办法，可以使读者、听者的意念中心不致走散。汉语不喜欢使用同义替代的手段，因为会使精神分散；也不喜欢使用代词，因为容易变得所指不明。结果由于强调重复，反而变成了某种意义上的“形合”。

（3）汉英翻译中重复的处理

1）显性重复的英译

替代

使用代词（主要是人称代词、物主代词、指示代词以及用于非限定性定语从句的关系代词等）来回避重复，这是英语中最普通、最常见，也是最有效的回避重复的方法之一。例如：

例 1　原文：共同富裕的构想是这样提出的：一部分地区有条件先发展起来，一部分地区发展慢点，先发展起来的地区带动后发展的地区，最终达到共同富裕。

译文：Our plan is as follows: where conditions permit, some areas may develop faster than others; those that develop faster can help promote the progress of those that lag behind, until all become prosperous.

例 2　原文：中印两国之间的问题并不是很大，既不存在中国对印度的威胁，也不存在印度对中国的威胁，无非就是一个边界问题。

译文：The problem between China and India is not a serious one. Neither country poses a threat to the other. The problem we have is simply about the border.

用同义词、上义词或者统称词来变换，例如：

例 3　原文：他去抓那小猫，那小猫却上了树。

译文：He went to catch the kitty but that little animal went in a tree.

例 4　原文：此次会议总结了过去时期的经验，决定了各项方针。这种总结经验和决定方针的工作，是我们大家一起来做的，……

译文：The present session has summed up our experience in the past period and laid down various guiding principles. We have done this work jointly...

换用近义词，例如：

例 5　原文：我代表国务院，向全国各族人民，向各民主党派、各人民团体和各界人士，表示诚挚的感谢！向香港特别行政区同胞、澳门特别行政区同胞、台湾同胞和海外侨胞，表示诚挚的感谢！向关心和支持中国现代化建设的各国政府、国际组织和各国朋友，表示诚挚的感谢！

译文：On behalf of the State Council, I wish to sincerely thank the Chinese people of all ethnic groups, the democratic parties, people's organizations, and people from all sectors of society. I wish to express my sincere gratitude to our compatriots in the Hong Kong and Macao special administrative regions and in Taiwan, as well as overseas Chinese. I also wish to express my sincere appreciation to governments of other countries, international organizations, and foreign friends around the world who show understanding for and support China in its pursuit of modernization.

使用替代的特殊形式，即使用 in the same way、the other way around、likewise、similarly、vice versa、"so do + 主语"以及关系从句等。例如：

例 6　原文：成绩有两重性，错误也有两重性。

译文：Achievements have a dual character, and so have mistakes.

例 7　原文：一个人的工作，究竟是三分成绩七分错误，还是七分成绩三分错误，必须有个根本的估价。

译文：We must have a fundamental evaluation of a person's work and establish whether his achievements amount to 30 percent and his mistakes 70 percent, or vice versa.

例 8　原文：所以，不仅地方对中央有要求，中央对地方也有要求。

译文：Therefore, not only do the local authorities have demands on the central governments, but the same is true the other way around.

使用合并，即将语句中相同的词提取出来，使文字变得简洁紧凑。如果汉语句子中两次或多次出现的词或短语与其在不同位置出现的下文都可以搭配，就可以将其提取出来一起表达。例如：

例 9　原文：以开放促改革、促发展、促创新。

译文：We will spur reform, development and innovation through opening up.

例 10　原文：

我们要继续坚定不移地坚持以经济建设为中心。

我们要继续坚定不移地推进改革开放。

我们要继续坚定不移地保持社会稳定。

我们要继续坚定不移地贯彻执行独立自主的和平外交政策。

译文：We will unswervingly focus on economic development, press ahead with the reform and opening-up, maintain social stability and pursue the independent foreign policy of peace.

若全部译出，反而削弱了语气，且句子累赘。

在不影响明确、完整地传达原义的前提下，可以根据英语表达习惯，将汉语中重复出现的词语或结构删去，来避免重复，使译文简明扼要。例如：

例 11　原文：解决得好，对经济的发展就很有利，解决不好，就会糟。

译文：If we handle it properly, it will greatly help promote the economic development; if we don't, things will go badly.

例 12　原文：是迅速进步，不是慢慢地进步。

译文：We need rapid progress, not slow.

2）隐性重复的英译

汉语隐性重复的现象大体上可以用合并和省略的方法避免重复，使译文更为简练。

汉语原文中用几个同义词来表达同一意思，英译时将这几个词合并。例如：

例 1　原文：提起此人，人人皆晓，处处闻名。

译文：The name of this person is a household word all over the country.

例 2　原文：经济运行中又出现不少新情况、新问题。

译文：In addition, China's economy is encountering new problems.

省略原文中不言而喻的词，例如：

例 3　原文：胜利完成四川汶川特大地震灾后恢复重建任务，积极推进青海玉树、甘肃舟曲、云南盈江抗灾救灾和恢复重建工作。

译文：We completed reconstruction in Wenchuan, Sichuan, which was hit by a massive earthquake in 2008, and made major progress in disaster relief and reconstruction in Yushu, Qinghai; Zhouqu, Gansu; and Yingjiang, Yunnan.

例 4　原文：他强调国务院的各个部门在反腐败斗争中负有重要的责任，并说它们处在非常重要的位置上。

原译：He stressed that all State Council departments have an important responsibility in the struggle against corruption and said they are in a very important position.

改译：He stressed that all State Council departments have an important responsibility in the struggle against corruption.

省略原文中的范畴词。

汉语中有大量意义空泛但语法上不可或缺的词，如“任务”“现象”“情况”“过程”“工作”“事业”“因素”“态度”“局面”“状况”等。这些词表明事物的范畴或属性，大多没有实质内容。这类词语若照搬到英语中势必冗余，因此译者应“忍痛割爱”，予以删除。例如：

例 1　原文：听了她家的困难情况后，大家都伸出了援助之手。

译文：After hearing her family difficulties, they offered to help.

例 2　原文：这个国家一直有严重的失业现象。

译文：There has been serious unemployment in this country.

例 3　原文：那时他们最渴望的就是结束这摇摆不定的局势。

译文：What they wanted was an end of uncertainties.

例 4　原文：他讲话时态度坚定。

译文：He spoke with firmness.

4. 汉译英语篇的四大类问题

段连城先生在《中国翻译》1990 年第 5 期上的文章《呼吁：请译界同仁都来关心对外宣传》阐释了汉译英语篇的四大类问题。这四大类问题在汉译中较为突出，也较难处理，对这些汉英语篇的重大差异应予以充分重视。现摘录如下。

（1）某市的画册有这样一段文字：

市内外有名胜古迹 300 多处，市中心有赵武灵王操演兵马和观赏歌舞的武灵丛台，市郊有国家重点文物保护单位——赵主城遗址，城北有明代所建“蓬莱仙境”般的黄粱梦吕仙祠，市西南有可与龙门、敦煌媲美始凿于北齐的响堂山石窟。[这里] 又是典故之城——黄粱美梦、毛遂自荐、负荆请罪、完璧归赵等众多成语典故，脍炙人口，给人启迪。

译文如下：

There are over 300 scenic spots and historical sites inside and outside the city. In the civic center stands the Wuling Congtai Terrace, where the King Wuling drilled warriors and enjoyed signing and dancing performances; in the outskirts remains the ruined City of the State of Zhao, the monument specially protected by the state, in the north lies the fairyland-like Golden Millet Dream Temple built in the Song Dynasty; in the southwest lies the Xiang Tang Caves Temple built in the Bei Qi period, which is thought to be as famous as Longmen and Dunhuang. Being a town of allusions, XXXX certainly has numerous greatly inspired allusions, such as — "Golden Millet Dream (pipe dream)," "Mao Sui Recommending Himself (volunteering one's services)," "Bearing the Rod for Punishment," "Returning the Jade Intact to Zhao," etc., which are widely loved and quoted by people.

这样一段充满了陌生的中国地名、人名、朝代名和典故的文字，外国读者只能望洋兴叹。譬如，"负荆请罪"译成"扛一根处罚的棍棒"，处罚谁？为什么？

（2）某地区的画册有一篇书记写的序言，其中说：

自十一届三中全会以来，我地区广大干部群众坚持四项基本原则，坚持改革开放，把工作重点转移到社会主义现代化建设上来，团结奋斗，在物质文明和精神文明建设上都取得了巨大成就。

译文如下：

Since the Third Plenary Session of the Eleventh Central Committee, the board masses of cadres and people in our prefecture, adhering to the Four Cardinal Principles and persisting in reform and opening, have shifted the emphasis of work to socialist modernization construction, united in struggle and achieved great successes in building both material and spiritual civilization.

作为试验，我曾把译文交给一位美国老专家，请她鉴定一下一般外国读者能读懂多少。她标出了不懂或难懂之处，其中包括"十一届三中全会""四项基本原则""广大干部群众""工作重点转移""精神文明建设"等。这类我们人人都能脱口而出的政治语言，对外国人却很陌生。

（3）北京某大报有这样一条报道：

市委、市政府决心变压力为动力，借各方面对本市服务工作关心、支持和期待的东风，把服务工作大大提高一步。为此，明确提出要继续扩大企业自主权，把应当放给企业的生产经营和业务管理权，全部放给企业，该放到那一级就放到那一级，任何部门不许截留；要继续坚持和不断完善企业内部的经营责任制，打破企业吃国家"大锅饭"和职工吃企业"大锅饭"的状况；要实行鼓励政策，扶持群众生活必需的小商品生产和便民服务项目的经营。

译文如下：

The Municipal Party Committee and Government have decided to turn the pressure into motive force and ride on the east wind of concern, support and expectations from all quarters and bring about a marked improvement in the standard of service. For this purpose it is explicitly provided that continued efforts will be made to expand the decision-making powers of the enterprises—to vest in them all powers for production management and business administration that should be given to the enterprises and to delegate these powers to whatever level necessary and not allow any department to withhold them.

Continued efforts will also be made to improve and perfect the inner-enterprise management responsibility system so as to end the situation in which enterprises "eat from the common rice bowl" of the state while workers and staff members "eat from the common rice bowl" of their enterprises. A policy will be introduced to encourage the production of miscellaneous daily necessities and services for people's convenience.

这里充满中国"行话"（指每个行业的常用术语）的译文，在我们的中央和地方的对外宣传材料上并不罕见。作为试验，我也曾请那位美国友人鉴定这段译文的清晰度。她打了一大堆问号，认为："变压力为动力""借……的东风"等中国的习惯用语"很怪"；扩大企业自主权"任何部门不得截留"，以及"企业吃国家的大锅饭""职工吃企业的大锅饭""便民服务项目"等等中国商业通用的"行话"，一般外国读者会感到模模糊糊，或根本不懂。

（4）某市举办国际龙舟会，彩色印刷了宣传品，原文是：

中华大地，江河纵横；华夏文化，源远流长——（然后才讲到本地，再讲到龙舟节）轻快的龙舟如银河流星，瑰丽的彩船似海市蜃楼，两岸那金碧辉煌的彩楼连成一片水晶宫，是仙境？是梦境？仰视彩鸽割飞，低眸漂灯留霓，焰火怒放，火树银花，灯舞回旋，千姿百态，气垫船腾起一江春潮，射击手点破满天彩球，跳伞健儿绽空中花蕾，抢鸭勇士谱水上凯歌——啊，×× 城是不夜城，龙舟会是群英会！

译文如下：

The divine land of China has its rivers flowing across; the brilliant culture of China has its roots tracing back long—

The light-some dragon boats appear on the river as though the stars twinkle in the milkway. The richly decorated pleasure boats look like a scene of mirage. The splendid awnings in green and gold chain into a palace of crystal. Is this a fairyland or a mere dream? Looking above, you can see the beautiful doves flying about. Looking below, you can see the sailing lamps glittering. Cracking are the fireworks, which present you a picture of fiery trees and sliver flowers. Circling are the lantern-dancers, who present you a variation of exquisite manner. Over there the motor-boats are plowing the water, thus a tide stirs up. Over there, the marksmen are shooting to their targets; thus colorful beads whirl around. Besides, the birds' chirping, the potted landscape's charm, the exhibition of arts and painting, all claim a strong appeal to you. Therefore, we should say: XXXX is a city of no light; its Dragon-Boat Festival a gathering of heroes.

Come on, dear friends! Come on, honorable guests!—

译者可算煞费苦心。我特意请一位美国新闻工作者看看并坦率写出她的评语。她说：full of hyperbole（充满了极度夸张），不仅不知所云，而且令人发笑。

5. 文学翻译中语篇叙事模式的重构

由于中英叙事模式的差异，在英译中国当代小说的过程中，我们需要进行翻译中的叙事重构，以便保持英文叙事的连贯性（包括结构连贯性、素材连贯性和人物性格的连贯性）和忠实性。下面我们以余华小说的英译为例来进行阐释。

余华自1983年开始创作，至今已完成5部长篇小说（《在细雨中呼喊》《活着》《许三观卖血记》《兄弟》《第七天》）、6部中短篇小说集（《世事如烟》《黄昏里的男孩》《鲜血梅花》《战栗》《现实一种》《我胆小如鼠》）、3部随笔集（《温暖和百感交集的旅程》《音乐影响了我的写作》《没有一条道路是重复的》）和1部散文集（《十个词汇里的中国》）。余华前期的小说充满了先锋色彩，在主题上倾向于关注人性中残酷冷漠的一面，习惯于在客观冷静的叙述中呈现给读者一幅幅血淋淋的图面，让人在惊悚之余感慨并领受世界与生活的真实本相。在表达方式上他看重的是零度的呈现，沉溺于叙事技巧的操练和炫耀。而到了后期，即20世纪90年代以来，余华的小说在主题方面更加关注人类苦难的生存状态，他开始用讲述的方式把一个个普通人物的普通而心酸的故事推到我们面前；他一改先锋实验小说的故作深沉和自以为是，而展示出一派成熟后的朴素和写实，其叙述的调子也由冷漠惨烈的呈现转向了温情的关照和呵护，实现了从"先锋"到"大众"的转型（曲娜，2006）。

余华有7部作品被翻译成英文并出版，在此我们仅分析其中3部中的例子(《兄弟》、《在细雨中呼喊》及《许三观卖血记》)。

余华英译作品

序号	英文版书名	中文版书名	译者	出版年份
1	*The Past and the Punishments*	《往事与刑罚》	Andrew F. Jones	1996
2	*To Live*	《活着》	Michael Berry	2003
3	*Chronicle of a Blood Merchant*	《许三观卖血记》	Andrew F. Jones	2004
4	*Cries in the Drizzle*	《在细雨中呼喊》	Allan H. Barr	2007
5	*Brothers*	《兄弟》	Eileen Cheng-yin Chow, Carlos Rojas	2009
6	*China in Ten Words*	《十个词汇里的中国》	Allan H. Barr	2011
7	*Boy in the Twilight*	《黄昏里的男孩》	Allan H. Barr	2014

《兄弟》分为上、下两部，是关于江南小镇两兄弟李光头和宋钢的故事。上部集中讲述这个重新组合成的家庭如何在"文化大革命"劫难中崩溃；下部讲述的是改革开放之

后，李光头如何通过收破烂发家，成为刘镇首富，而宋钢却艰难地生活着，最终卧轨自杀。两个人的命运和小说中描述的两个时代一样，经历了天翻地覆的变化。2008 年，余华凭借这部小说获得由法国著名周刊《国际信使》设立的“首届《国际信使》外国小说奖”；2010 年《兄弟》入选瑞士《时报》评选的“2000 年至 2010 年全球最为重要的 15 本书。译者 Eileen Cheng-yin Chow 和 Carlos Rojas 是一对夫妻，Carlos Rojas 现为美国杜克大学中国文化研究、女性研究与影像艺术助理教授；夫人 Eileen Cheng-yin Chow 为我国台湾世新大学舍我纪念馆馆长、杜克大学中国与日本文化研究客座副教授，两人合作翻译了该部小说。

《许三观卖血记》讲述的是一个出身于农村的丝厂送茧工许三观三十几年的生活经历。回乡探亲的许三观偶然得知乡亲们“卖血”的习俗后随同前往医院，并以挣得的三十五元钱在城里娶了“油条西施”许玉兰；在以后的几十年中，每有家庭变故，许三观都会卖血来挽救危机。许三观为家人卖了 11 次血，直到最后想为自己吃一次炒猪肝、喝二两黄酒卖血时，血头却因为嫌弃他太老而拒绝收他的血。该部小说与《活着》同时入选中国百位批评家和文学家编辑评选的“九十年代最具影响的十部作品”。译者 Andrew F. Jones 也是《往事与刑罚》的译者，在加州伯克利大学东亚系担任副教授，因为“余华的文字同他个人翻译的风格很契合”（陈雅莉，2003），而选择余华的作品。

《在细雨中呼喊》是一本关于记忆的书，是余华发表于 1991 年的第一部长篇小说，描述了一位江南少年的成长经历和心灵历程。小说中“没有一个完整的故事和一条贯穿的情节线，况且时空的转换又常常中断线性的阅读”（潘凯雄，1992），这使得这部小说颇具特色，也为翻译增添了难度。译者 Allan H. Barr，英国籍，现任美国加州波摩纳学院亚洲语言文学系教授，是翻译余华作品最多的译者。2014 年最新出版的《黄昏里的男孩》，收录了余华的十二篇作品，译作中加了一篇小说《我胆小如鼠》。

（1）余华小说英译过程中的语篇叙事模式的调整

众所周知，美国译者葛浩文在翻译中常常更改或调整中国小说的故事情节。例如，从叙事学视角看，葛浩文英译莫言小说《丰乳肥臀》的翻译策略是：有意识地调整原作的叙事结构，删去部分非叙述性的评论性话语，并增补一些解释性话语使叙事更具可接受性（尹婷，2014）。

但是余华并不推崇对原作的大幅度改动。在 2010 年的汉学家文学翻译国际研讨会上，余华曾就作品翻译发表了他的观点。他不同意译者和编辑对他的翻译作任何删减，“我记得当时我的两个译者翻译完以后 A4 纸打印出来以后 800 多页，他根本没看那个书就先让我的翻译给我打一个电话，说有没有可能作一个删减。我当时很不理解，我从来没有听说过这样的事情。后来我让我的翻译转告我的编辑，我说你告诉他，我不同意作任何删减，如果他坚持删减以后我就坚持不出版”（余华，2010），“至于葛浩文翻译的情况，我们首先要承认葛浩文对中国文学翻译到英文世界做了很大的贡献，但是他也有不太好的风格，就是他喜欢‘动外科手术’，他的这个风格不仅仅针对《狼图腾》，其他的很多书他都这么做。当然作为一个作家来说，因为中文的语言翻译成欧美语言的时候差距非常大，包括日语差距也很大，里面肯定有一些‘水土不服’的地方，作这样一些改动，我对我的翻译都说是可以作一些改动的，在字句上不一定完全忠于原著，因为确实有文化差异的问题。所以我觉得文学翻译作品中做一些内科式的‘治疗’是应该的，‘打打针’‘吃吃药’，但是我不赞成‘动外科手术’，‘截掉一条大腿’，‘切掉一个肺’，所以最好不要‘做外科手术’”（余华，2010）。

余华的小说在英译过程中真的像他说的没有删减，没有改动吗？对比余华小说的中英文版本可以发现，事实上，由于中英小说的叙事差异、读者阅读习惯的不同以及编辑的要求等，余华小说英译文中有多处与原文不同的地方。本文主要分析余华小说英译中故事情节的改变，包括三方面：1）添加故事情节；2）删减故事情节；3）调整叙事方式。

1）添加故事情节

在《许三观卖血记》中，有一段是讲述许三观不小心把木桶掉进了井里，一乐提出让许三观用绳子系住他，把他放到井里去把桶捞起来。原文中，对捞木桶的这个过程一带而过。

例 1　原文：

一乐说：“爹，这井太高了，我不敢往下跳；爹，这井太高了，我下去以后爬不上来。爹，你找一根麻绳绑在我的腰上，把我一点一点放下去，我扎一个猛子，能扎一分钟二十三秒，我去把木桶抓住，你再把我提上来。”

许三观一听，心想一乐这崽子的主意还真不错，就跑回家去找了一根崭新的麻绳，他不敢用旧麻绳，万一一乐也像木桶那样被井水吃了进去，那可真是完蛋了。

许三观将一根麻绳的两头从一乐两条大腿那里绕过来，又系在了一乐腰里的裤带上，然后把一乐往井里一点一点放下去……这时三乐又摇摇摆摆地过来了，许三观看到三乐走过来，就说：

“三乐，你走开，你会掉到井里去的。”（余华，《许三观卖血记》，1995: 19-20）

译文：

Yile said, “Dad, the well’s too deep. I’m scared to jump. Dad, the well’s too deep, I’m scared I wouldn’t be able to get back out. Dad, get some rope to tie to my waist. Let me down little by little, and then I’ll dive in. I can dive for one minute and twenty-three seconds. I’ll find the bucket, and then you can pull me up.”

Xu Sanguan, slowly coming to the realization that Yile’s plan might actually work, ran home to grab a length of brand-new rope. He was afraid that if he fastened him with a piece of old rope, Yile might disappear down the well just like the bucket. That would really be the end.

Xu Sanguan wound the two ends of the rope around Yile’s thighs and then fastened the rope to his own belt. Just as he began to let Yile slide slowly down into the well, Sanle came wobbling over toward them. As soon as he approached, Xu Sanguan warned him, “Sanle, go away! You might fall down the well."

Sanle stood quietly to one side as the rope, and Yile with it, slid deeper and deeper into the well. Soon the rope went taut and tugged sharply at Xu Sanguan's belt.

Xu Sanguan began to slowly and softly count the seconds to himself as Sanle, mouth agape, looked on. "Ten seconds... twenty seconds... thirty seconds... forty seconds..." Xu Sanguan paused to take a deep breath and continued, "Fifty seconds... sixty seconds... one minute and ten seconds..."

There was a sudden sharp tug on his belt that dragged Xu Sanguan a step closer to the mouth of the well. He braced his feet against the stone steps and began to pull with all his might on the rope. Sanle took up the count where his father had left off, sounding out the seconds as Xu Sanguan panted with the effort of pulling the rope up from the depths: "One minute and eleven seconds... one minute and fifteen seconds... one minute and twenty seconds..." Xu Sanguan heard what sounded like the distant echo of a heavy stone falling into the water, and then a gasp and a splutter as Yile emerged above the surface of the water.

Dripping wet, he clambered the last few steps out of the well and shouted through pale blue lips, "Dad, I found the bucket! Dad, I almost couldn't hold my breath long enough! Dad, the bucket was caught under a ledge! Dad, how long was I down in the well?"

Sanle ran eagerly forward to announce the total but was quickly and dismissively waved away by Xu Sanguan, who was stroking the water from Yile's forehead with his other hand.

"Sanle, didn't I already tell you to get out of here?" (Yu Hua, 2004: 49-50)

通过原文与译文的对比，我们发现，译文中加入了一段详细的描写（译文中的斜体部分）：因为一乐说他可以在水中憋气一分二十三秒，所以他进入井下后，许三观一直在仔细地为他计时；还添加了一段三乐在许三观停止计时后继续为一乐计时的描述，将整个过程叙述得有头有尾、生动形象。

2）删减故事情节

例 2　原文：

李光头和宋钢拉着李兰的衣服，跟随着她的步伐又去了照相馆。**李兰在整理宋凡平的遗物时，发现了那张蓝色的发票，她将发票拿在手里看了很长时间，才想起来曾经照过一张全家福的照片，那是她去上海治病前照的。宋凡平一直没有将照片取回来，她心想肯定是她一到上海，宋凡平就出事了。**

照相馆的人拿着发票找了很久，才找到他们的全家福。李兰接过照片的那一刻，她的手颤抖不已，她将照片和黑纱白布一起捧在了胸前，走出了照相馆，继续昂首挺胸地走在大街上。（余华，《兄弟》，2005: 152）

译文：

Grasping on to Li Lan's shirt, Baldy Li and Song Gang followed her into the photography studio. As she received the photograph her hands would not stop trembling; she hugged the photograph close to her chest, along with the black sash and white cloth, and continued her proud journey down the main street.（Yu Hua, 2009: 156）

通过原文与译文的对比，我们发现译文中删减了李兰如何发现照相的发票、拿到发票时的心情，以及照相馆工作人员如何找到照片这些叙述（原文中的黑体部分）。

3）调整叙事方式

《在细雨中呼喊》是余华创作的第一部长篇小说，先锋色彩非常明显。首先是它的叙述视角，小说中的"我"实际是作者在叙述与叙述对象之间设置的第三者，借此来实现间接叙事（杨其林，2011: 110）。对此，余华在《虚伪的作品》中谈道："在叙述和叙述对象之间存在的第三者（阴沉的天空），可以有效地回避表层现实的局限，也就是说可以从单调的此刻进入广阔复杂的现在层面"，"通俗的说法便是将别人的事告诉别人"，是"无我"的叙述方式（余华，2004）。在这部小说中，"我"又被赋予了双重身份——成年的"我"和童年的"我"。小说是站在成年的"我"的位置去回顾童年的"我"的感觉和经历，因此，小说中经常出现现在与过去的重逢（杨其林，2011: 110）。因此，小说的时空顺序经常交叉，在回忆过去时，时常插入现在的感受。但在英文叙事中，这种叙事的方式不一定被接受，因此译者在英译过程中需对叙事方式进行适当的调整。

例 3　原文：

在我记忆里，哥哥进入高中以后，身上出现了显著的变化。**现在想来，我倒是十分怀念十四岁时的哥哥。那时的哥哥虽然霸道，身上的骄傲却令人难忘。我的兄弟坐在田埂上，指挥着苏家兄弟为他割草，这情景在很长一段时间里一直代表着哥哥的形象。**

我哥哥升入高中没多久，开始结交城里同学。与此同时，他对村中孩子的态度变得越来越冷漠。……（余华，《在细雨中呼喊》, 2008: 13-14）

译文：

When my big brother went to high school his behavior changed quite markedly. *(I found I now recall rather fondly my brother at the age of fourteen. Though he was a real dictator, there was something unforgettable about his arrogance. Sitting on the bank, directing the Su brothers' grass-trimming activities — for a long time this was the image of him that was foremost in my mind.)* Once he began to mix with the children from town, he became increasingly standoffish toward the village boys...（Yu Hua, 2007: 16）

本来原文正在叙述哥哥的事情，但现在突然加上了"我"现在的看法或回忆（原文中的黑体部分）。通过原文与译文的对比，我们发现美国译者白亚仁（Allan H. Barr）对中文中插叙的翻译方法是将观察部分用括号与叙事部分分开。

例 4　原文：

在暑假即将来到的一个中午，我很早就来到学校。**那时教室里几个女同学的高声说笑，使我缺乏足够的胆量走进去。直到现在，当一个屋里全是女性或者陌生人时，让我独自进去依然是一件可怕的事。那么多目光同时注视着我，我将惊慌失措。**当时我是打算立刻走开的。可我听到了曹丽的声音，她的笑声紧紧攥住了我。……（余华，2008: 90）

译文：

Shortly before the start of the summer vocation, I came back to school early after lunch, but was deterred from entering by the sound of girls talking and laughing loudly inside. *(Even now, if it is all women or all strangers in a room, I find it an intimidating experience to go in on my own. with so many eyes resting on me all at once, I am nervous and flustered.)* I meant to walk away immediately, but I heard Cao Li's voice and her laughter kept me rooted to the spot...（Yu Hua, 2007: 100）

这一段的叙事特点与上个例子中是类似的，在回忆过去的过程中，忽然加入了“我”现在的感受（原文中的黑体部分）译者采用了同样的处理方式，即在英译文中将现在的感受和解释放到了括号中。

（2）余华小说在英译过程中语篇叙事模式调整的原因分析

英语中的叙事是有一定范式的，而且这种范式具有约束性，需要得到遵守。

根据哲学家 Walter Fisher（1984，1985，1987）的叙事范式（narrative paradigm）理论，英文中的叙事需遵循连贯性原则。该原则包括三个方面：一是结构连贯性，即叙事需具有内部的一致性，不能有严重的逻辑缺陷。二是素材连贯性，即一种叙事如何与我们所熟悉的同一问题的其他叙事相关联的问题。更具体地说，哪些“事实”可能被轻描淡写或完全忽略？三是人物性格的连贯性，叙事所牵涉的角色的前后一致性。如果一个人物的价值倾向在情节前后有明显的矛盾冲突，读者就会判断所描述的这个人物不可靠，因此叙事也不可靠。

中国当代文学虽然已取得了很大成就，但仍存在诸多问题。相对于中国现代文学而言，中国当代文学还不够成熟。德国汉学家顾彬（2009：94）把两者间的差异作了如下的比喻：

我把中国现代文学跟五粮液比较起来，把中国当代文学跟二锅头比较起来。要看中国现代文学的话，得需要很长时间来看懂，比较复杂，特别是钱钟书、鲁迅、周作人这一批人，要看懂了的话，需要很长时间，慢慢看。

对于中国当代小说，顾彬（2009：89）指出了三大问题：一个是语言的问题，一个是形式的问题，一个是意识的问题。例如，莫言写的那个《生死疲劳》很多地方对不上（顾彬，2009：89）。在一定程度上可以说，中国当代文学在西方看来在叙事范式上还存在一定的不足。同时，又由于英语文学相对来说具有较为固定的叙事范式，因此在客观上，英译中国当代文学的过程中叙事的调适就是必然的。

葛浩文对中国当代文学的英译可以说是大刀阔斧的“外科手术式”的翻译。例如，在翻译《狼图腾》时，葛浩文作了大量的删减，将原文的54万多字删减到50万字，删去了近5万字的内容。与葛浩文的翻译不同，我们看到余华作品英译者或英译本编辑对原作故事情节的添加或删减，采取的是“内科治疗式”的翻译方法，主要目的是使其适应英文的叙事范式。这种翻译过程中的叙事重构，我们称之为叙事调适。下面，我们借助Fisher的叙事范式理论和译者本人的解释分别探析余华的三部小说《许三观卖血记》、《兄弟》和《在细雨中呼喊》在英译过程中进行叙事调适的原因。

对于《许三观卖血记》英译本中故事情节的添加，我们通过电子邮件向本书的美国译者Andrew F. Jones寻求解释。琼斯的解释是：添加这一段事实上是编辑提出来的，因为原文的叙述不够清晰，没有清楚地表述事情的发展过程和结果，编辑希望余华能再补充一下；余华表示译者可以加上一段他认为合适而且完整的叙述，译者将添加的段落回译成中文给余华，也得到了他的认可。（译者琼斯回复的电子邮件原文如下：I do remember that the additions I made to the scene with Yile down in the well were prompted by the US editor, who felt that the scene was unclear and insufficiently developed and requested further delineation from Yu Hua. I asked Yu Hua what to do, and he told me to go ahead and make a few minor additions as I saw fit. I remember translating the changes back into Chinese for his approval, and that he liked them.）由此可见，美国译者Andrew F. Jones英译《许三观卖血记》中扩充的一段描写是为了弥补英文叙事中素材的连贯性。

对于《兄弟》英译本中故事情节的减略，我们向本书的美国译者Eileen Cheng-yin Chow和Carlos Rojas发邮件，请教删减的原因，但是译者一直没有给我们回复。我们认为，在英译文中对这一段进行删减的原因应是：中间这一段属于插叙，读者一定记得他们照过全家福，他们唯一照过的全家福，李兰应该也不会忘记。前面一直在讲述李兰如何骄傲地去买白布和黑纱，这里又讲述她如何骄傲地取照片。插叙的这一段事实上阻断了正常的故事进展，读者此刻更关注的是李兰的举动和心情，所以删掉这几句话会使英译文的叙事更加通畅，更符合英语小说的叙事方式。因此，美国译者Eileen Cheng-yin Chow和Carlos Rojas减略《兄弟》原作中的插叙的那部分是为了保持英文叙事中的结构上的连贯性。

对于《在细雨中呼喊》英译本中为何将观察部分用括号与叙述部分分开，我们也通过电子邮件请教了本书的译者白亚仁（Allan H. Barr）教授。白亚仁指出：原文一直在叙述我记忆中的哥哥进入高中的变化，现却突然加上了一段“我”的观察，显得非常突兀与不协调，打破了原本的叙事顺序，进而使得整体叙事显得破碎。因此，在译文中，译者将现在“我”的观察部分放到了括号里边，以保持原有的叙事流不被打破。（译者白亚仁回复的电子邮件的原文如下：I added the parentheses in these examples because I felt that their addition enhanced the smooth flow of the text. In English, without the parentheses, the sudden switch to an observation made from the present vantage point seems a little jarring, a little too abrupt; there is a danger that the narrative will seem too fragmented, too jerky. I do not know how other readers react to the parentheses—nobody has ever told me, and I have never asked! But I was a reader before I became a translator, and my translation reflects my outlook and experience as a reader. I would expect other readers to share my feeling on this.）由此可见，白亚仁将《在细雨中呼喊》原作中叙事中的观察部分用括号与叙述部分分开也是为了保持英文叙事中结构的连贯性。

练习题：

一、请将以下语篇翻译为英语。

语篇翻译练习 1

守住书香——电商来袭下的中国实体书店

北京师范大学附近的野草书店要关门了，民营连锁书店“纸老虎”宣布最多三个月也要关门,连国内最大的广告书店“龙之媒”也宣布要在年底关闭现存的三家店……

在中国，随着一家又一家的书店相继没落，被认为是城市文化地标、代表着城市文化内涵的实体书店还能走多远，应该如何生存，再次成为人们关注的焦点。很多人哀叹，面对当当、京东、卓越等网络书城的低价竞争，中国实体书店将集体经历寒冬，有人甚至认为实体书店已经没有存在的必要。

尽管实体书店愈来愈举步维艰，但人们依旧相信，实体书店是网络书店或其他形式所取代不了的。“一个城市有图书馆、书店、报亭，这个城市才是完整的。虽然实体书店正在经历电子阅读和网络书店的挑战，但挑战并不表明他们会消失。”北京大学信息管理系主任王余光教授说。

同样是实体书店的万圣书院就是迎接挑战的成功者。万圣书院之所以能够在电子时代屹立不倒，与其选址科学、定位准确以及根据市场调整营销策略有很大关系。万圣书院周边有北京大学、清华大学等中国知名高校和中关村高科技园区，来此购书的以大学生、大学教职人员、IT 和金融界的高端人才居多。万圣书院还采取线上线下同时卖书，这已经成为越来越多的实体书店采用的销售方式。除此之外，还有一些实体店采取了书店和咖啡共存，或者文化沙龙的模式。“字里行间”书店就是利用这种方式发展极快的一家书店。

但是，大部分实体书店没有这样的“运气”和“先知”。电子图书阅读和下载的便利还有网上书店的大幅折扣，受到越来越多年轻人的推崇。大量实体书店的倒闭，折射出目前我国民营书店的整体困境。

如今，从官方到民间，中国保护实体书店的呼声越来越高。业内人士建议，中国政府应该建立一个适用于实体书店发展的中、长期规划。通过财政补贴及政府资助，在短时期内解决实体书店的运营问题，长期内则应出台税收优惠和规范定价制度，提高盈利水平，促进公平竞争。

实体书店要生存发展，国家的政策扶持固然重要，但最重要的还是立足市场，寻求自己的特色经营之道。文化产业作为国民经济的重要组成部分，终将随着国家经济结构的调整逐步发展完善，而保护作为城市文化地标代表的书店，也是文化及其产业健康发展的一个标志。

语篇翻译练习 2

初到中国旅游可到哪些地方

一、第一次到中国旅游，应当先去哪些地方？

答：这首先要看您能安排多少时间。一般地说，第一次到中国应当先到北京、上海、西安等地。

北京是中国的政治、文化中心。在这里您可以游览万里长城中的一段——八达岭，明、清两代皇室居住的地方——故宫。清朝御花园——颐和园和北海，还可品尝到正宗的北京烤鸭、涮羊肉。

上海是中国最大的城市，在这里选购物品最合适，上海品种繁多的小吃、糕点和手工艺品、纺织品，会使您感到满意。离上海仅有几小时路程的苏州和杭州，是中国园林艺术的代表，被人称为“天堂”。

西安是古丝绸之路的起点，也是中国历史上建都最多的城市之一。新发掘的秦兵马俑被称为“世界第八大奇迹”；大雁塔、鼓楼是唐代留下来的建筑，您可以到杨贵妃洗澡的华清池去洗温泉澡，作为炎黄子孙还可以去拜谒离西安不远的黄帝陵。在西安还可以欣赏到仿唐音乐和歌舞，尝品唐菜。

二、什么时侯到中国旅游最佳？冬季去什么地方好？

答：中国幅员广大，各地景色、气候差异很大，可以说一年四季都可以旅游。如到上述所说的北京、上海、西安最好是在春、秋两季。

冬季您若怕冷的话可以到没有酷暑和严冬的“春城”——昆明，那里有引人入胜的石林和滇池，还可到西双版纳去欣赏亚热带风光。也可以去桂林，沿着漓江顺水而下到阳朔，“桂林山水甲天下，阳朔山水甲桂林”，这个旅游项目不会使你失望。没有见过冰雪的港澳同胞，不妨在一、二月份去哈尔滨，那里是冰雪的世界，可以观雪景、看冰灯、滑雪、滑冰。

三、在中国有什么东西最值得买？在什么地方买最合适？

答：中国的手工艺品、丝绸、瓷器、地毯、棉纺织品在世界上享有盛名，而且比在世界其他地方购买价格更合理，挑选余地更大。中国各地都有自己独特的产品可买，比如说北京的景泰蓝、地毯；上海的中国服装、棉纺织品；杭州的丝绸；苏州的古玩；到西安您可以买兵马俑、唐三彩。如果您嫌麻烦，也可以在北京、上海的友谊商店里将东西一次买齐，大城市的友谊商店一般货源都比较充足，而且一般可以代您托运。爱好艺术的游客还可以在中国购买字画和古玩。但记住一定要有发票和正式鉴定标记（即红漆标记），才不致在海关遇到麻烦。

语篇翻译练习 3

中资银行上半年业绩再创新高

中资银行再度交出了亮丽业绩，不过它们仍无法消除以下担忧：不良贷款问题和经济放缓，有可能让它们的好运气转化为厄运。

当西方银行因难以安度全球金融危机而大举裁员时，中资银行却表示，它们将继续在国内大举扩张，同时在国际上慢慢扩大影响。

在过去一年的大部分时间里，话题一直集中在一种背离现象上：中资银行屡屡实现创纪录的业绩，可市场却坚定地认为，它们以往过度放贷的“账单”只是还没到期。

中国四大银行本周陆续发布了业绩。中国农业银行 (ABC) 上半年净利润增长 45%。中国银行 (BoC) 增幅最小，为 28%。全球市值最大的银行中国工商银行 (ICBC) 增长 29%。中国第二大银行中国建设银行 (CCB) 增幅为 31%。银行股本周表现平平，自年初以来则跌幅深重，投资者似乎把注意力放在了银行成功基础的“裂缝”上面。

自 2008 年末以来，中国信贷激增，而投资者仍对此深感担忧。当时，中国政府推出了一项以信贷推动的经济刺激方案，并以银行作为排头兵。近几个月来，这种做法的风险已开始显现，官员们试图就发放给地方政府的贷款作出解释——据国家审计局统计，总额约为 10.7 万亿元人民币（合 1.65 万亿美元）——并估计可能出现违约的数额。

各银行在中期业绩中，披露了迄今最全面的潜在不良贷款情况。中行表示，共向地方政府融资平台提供了 5 320 亿元人民币贷款，比 2010 年末的数字增长 40%。这是把一大批企业贷款重新归类为政府贷款后的数据。

同时，各银行竭力保证这些贷款是健康的，并且自己已做好了应付违约的准备。建行表示，该行发放给地方政府的贷款 84% 都有现金流拨备，超过了监管要求。建行董事长郭树清表示，建行不需要进行股权融资。

中行行长李礼辉表示，中行不良贷款拨备覆盖率为 217%，亦远高于监管规定。

然而，巴克莱资本（Barclays Capital）中国银行业研究主管颜湄之（May Yan）表示：“这是一个对银行在尽职调查和披露方面的可靠性的信任问题。（地方政府贷款的）影响或许不大，但银行估算现金流的方式令人怀疑。”

二、分析并总结你自己汉译英实践中的语篇翻译对策。

第五章 汉英翻译常见错误例析

第一节 注意英语使用的准确性

1. 译文表述不确切，如：

例 1　原文：按人口计算，中国是世界上最大的国家；按领土面积计算，是第三大国家，仅次于俄罗斯和加拿大。

不合格的译文：According to population figure, China is the largest country in the world; and according to area, it is the third largest, only next to Russia and Canada.

此译文有以下问题：（1）汉语“按人口计算”和“按领土面积计算”用英语 according to 的结构来翻译，是不确切的。我们中国人往往一见到“按”字，就首先想到翻译成 according to 或者 in accordance with，这是不妥的，因为“按”字并不能和 according to 或 in accordance with 对等。其实，在这里可以用 in terms of 这样一个短语，表示“就……来说”“按……来说”，是地道的英语。（2）population figure 里的 figure 可以不要，说 population 就可以了；in the whole world 里的 whole 可以不要，说 in the world 就可以了；it is the third largest 里的 largest 也可以不要，而承接着前面的结构下来，说 it is the third 就可以了。但“领土面积”只翻成 area，是不够的，应当翻译成 territorial area。修改后的译文如下：

In terms of population, China is the largest country in the world; and in terms of territorial area, it is the third, ranking only after Russia and Canada.

（本例引自 李学平《通过翻译学英语——150 实例使你迅速提高汉译英能力》）

2. 褒贬义使用不准确，如：

例 2　原文：中国政府和人民愿与国际社会一道，共同应对风险挑战，共同分享发展机遇，为人类和平与发展的<u>崇高</u>事业做出新贡献！

译文：The Chinese government and people are willing to work with the international community to respond to risks and challenges, share in development opportunities, and make new contributions to humanity's lofty causes of peace and development.

lofty 一词的选用有失妥当。因 lofty 一词有“高傲、傲慢”之意，含有贬义，因而不适用于此语境。此处改为 noble 会更加得体。

3. 语体使用不准确，如：

例 3　原文：……在推动解决热点问题和全球性问题上发挥建设性作用，履行应尽的国际责任和义务。

译文：...playing a constructive role in helping resolve hot issues and global problems; and fulfilling our international responsibilities and duties.

hot issues 作为“热点问题”的英译，存在语域（register）使用不当的问题。本句话取自 2011 年的《政府工作报告》。“hot issues”不适合用在像《政府工作报告》这样的庄重的政治文体中。根据语域特点，contentious issues 在此更合适。

4. 词义含糊，如：

例 4　原文：综合判断国际国内形势，我国发展仍处于可以大有作为的重要战略机遇期。

译文：Looking at the overall international and domestic situations, we have concluded that China's development is still in an important period of strategic opportunities.

strategic opportunities 一词表达不准确，词义含糊。

例 5　原文：去年对外贸易总额达到 2.97 万亿美元，开放型经济水平快速提升。

译文：Last year, total foreign trade volume reached US$ 2.97 trillion and the openness of the economy increased rapidly.

openness 一词在此表达不准确，词义含糊。

5. 派生词使用不准确，如：

informationization（信息化）、multipolarization（多极化）、marketization（市场化）、internationalization（国际化）等。在外国读者看来，此类词语读起来不自然。一位美国读者指出，“Some of the words are examples of business jargon. They are ugly and really rather meaningless. For example, “informationization,” “marketization” and “internationalization.” It looks as if the translator is trying to show off. It would be better to use ordinary words to express these ideas.”。

例 6　原文：从国际看，世界多极化、经济全球化深入发展，和平、发展、合作仍是时代潮流。

译文：From an international perspective, world multipolarization and economic globalization are deepening, and peace, development and cooperation remain the current of the times.

例 7　原文：从国内看，我国发展的有利条件和长期向好的趋势没有改变，工业化、信息化、城镇化、市场化、国际化深入发展，……

译文：From a domestic perspective, factors favoring China's development and the positive long-term development trend have not changed. Industrialization, informationization, urbanization, marketization and internationalization are all intensifying;

实际上，这类词都可用普通词代替，可用 extensive use of information tools 代替 informationization。

第二节 汉译英中的冗余词

在中国翻译协会第六次会员代表大会上，原外交部翻译室主任施燕华女士回忆了中国翻译逐步与国际接轨的经历。起初我国的翻译完全按照中国的国内政治思路来，比如“最最最强烈抗议”，英文中本没有相应的说法，外交部的翻译室就给创造出了完全中国特色的译法：“strongest strongest strongest protest against…”。随着中国与国际慢慢接轨，外交部的翻译开始强调以别人听得懂的方式来翻译，而且翻译可以根据语境灵活翻译。随着时代的发展，中国外文局原副局长黄友义（2004）提出了外宣翻译的三贴近原则：贴近中国发展的实际，贴近国外受众对中国信息的需求，贴近国外受众的思维习惯。对于从事外宣工作的翻译人员来说，黄友义特别强调了第三点，即最应该注意时刻不忘要按照国外受众的思维习惯去把握翻译。最好的外宣翻译不是按中文逐字逐句地机械地把中文转换为外文，而是根据国外受众的思维习惯，对中文原文进行适当的加工，有时要删减，有时要增加。

翻译中的迁移性冗余指的是，并不按照译文语言的内在组合规律，而是将原文中的语言组合形式直接迁移到译文中，从而造成译文的冗余性表达，并影响译文的交流效果的现象。例如，在中文中我们可以说“我们必须厉行节约，减少不必要的开支”。实际上，这句话中的前后两个小句讲的是一回事，即中文中的“一事两说”现象。在英文译文中，一般应只保留一个小句。如果直译为“We must practice economy and reduce unnecessary expenditures.”，就会造成英文译文中的迁移性冗余，影响译文的表达效果。所有英语文体权威专家都认为，英语文体贵在简洁。Strunk（1979:23）在其名著《文体的要素》中指出，有力的文章是简洁的。一句话不应包含多余的词，一段话不应包含多余的句，正如一幅画不应包含多余的线条，一台机器不应包含多余的零件。

这也就是说，我们应该把一句话中不起任何作用的词删掉。对于中译英中的迁移性冗余问题，在外文出版社和中央编译局做过八年译文修改工作的翻译专家平卡姆（2000：2）曾一针见血地指出，词语冗余（unnecessary words）是中式英语的标志。也就是说，词语冗余是汉译英的一大棘手问题。根据平卡姆（2000），汉译英中的迁移性冗余主要有五大类：1）冗余的名词和动词（unnecessary nouns and verbs）；2）冗余的修饰语（unnecessary modifiers）；3）冗余的成对词（redundant twins）；4）一事两说（saying the same thing twice）；5）重复指称（repeated references to the same thing）。

1. 冗余的名词

第一类冗余的名词为意义已包含于其他成分的名词。例如：

1）中文原文：经济增速陡然下滑。

英文译文：The pace of our economic growth suddenly slowed down.

根据 *Longman Dictionary of Contemporary English*（2003 版）（以下简称 LDCE），slow down 的意思是 to become slower or to make something slower，该词本身已含有"速度"之义。例如，我们可以说"Growth in sales has slowed down."。因此，该句中的 pace 一词是由于中文迁移带来的冗余的名词，可删除，仅保留 slowed down 即可。

第二类冗余的名词为范畴名词。例如：

2）中文原文：进一步提高服务业发展水平和在国民经济中的比重。

英文译文：We will further raise the development level of the service sector and its proportion of the national economy.

3）中文原文：做好人口和计划生育工作。

英文译文：We will do a good job in population and family planning work.

以上两句中的"水平""工作"是中文中的范畴名词。平卡姆（2000：5）指出，这一类词要特别注意，因其是中式英语中最常见的冗余词。中文中的范畴名词较多，再如：问题、领域、情况、做法、事业、局面等。这些范畴名词实际上无实质内容，因此在英译时一般可省略。例如，"经济领域的改革"可译为 reforms in the economy 或 economic reforms，而不是 reforms in the sphere of the economy。因此，以上两句译文中的 level 和 work 可省略不译。

2. 冗余的动词

汉化英语中大多数的冗余动词出现在短语或词组中。例如：

A: It is impossible for us to accomplish the transformation of the whole society overnight.

B: It is impossible for us to transform the whole society overnight.

在此句中，accomplish 一词并无实质意义，因此可去除。

在动词方面，特别要注意的两个词是 make 和 have，这两个词组成的词组实际上就是单个动词的意思：

to make an investigation of =to investigate

to make a proposal that =to propose that

to make an analysis of =to analyze

to have trust in =to trust

to have adequate knowledge of=to know enough about

to have respect for=to respect

当然，还有其他的词，例如：

to provide assistance to=to assist

to carry out the struggle against=to struggle against

to conduct reform of =to reform

还要注意一些引介性动词短语（introductory verb phrases）的使用。例如：

The principal task at present is to do a good job in disseminating and applying the results of scientific and technological research.

此句话中的引介性动词 do a good job 并无实际意义。从逻辑上讲，要做的任务不是 do a good job，而是 disseminate and apply。因此，这句话可修改为：

The principal task at present is to disseminate and applying the results of scientific and technological research.

All enterprises must pay attention to promoting excellent workers.

此句话的要义是企业必须提拔优秀员工，而不是仅仅要去注意这件事。如果他们提拔了优秀员工，他们肯定就会注意提拔这件事了。因此此句中的 pay attention to 使用不合适。这句话可修改为：

All enterprises must see to it that excellent workers are promoted.

3. 冗余的修饰语

程镇球（1980：232）指出，从事汉译英笔头工作的同志常会碰到一个棘手的问题，那就是如何在译文里处理好原文中的修饰词。这里讲的修饰词指的是修饰名词的形容词或词组和修饰动词、形容词的副词或词组。在中文政治文献中，为了加强语气，通常使用修饰语较多，特别是副词性修饰语。当然，英语中也有滥用修饰语的现象。但相对来说，英文中的修饰语要少得多。在中文政治文献的英译中，这是译文中迁移性冗余的重要方面之一。我们先看一下形容词的问题。例如：

1）中文原文：有力地彰显了社会主义制度的无比优越

英文译文：powerfully demonstrates the incomparable superiority of the socialist system

根据 LDCE，superiority 的意思是“ the quality of being better, more skillful, more powerful etc than other people or thing”，该词本身已包含比较义，所以不能再加上 incomparable 来修饰。

我们再看一下副词的问题，副词的情况要比形容词的情况严重得多。

2）中文原文：严厉打击偷骗税行为，

英文译文：strictly crack down on tax fraud,

根据 LDCE，crack down 的意思是“to become more strict in dealing with a problem and punishing the people involved”，该词本身已含有 strictly 之义。正如“坚决禁止”不能译为 firmly banned，而只须译为 banned 即可。因此，本句译文中的 strictly 是迁移性冗余，应删掉。

在英文中，relatively、quite、rather 等属于限定词（qualifiers）范畴。限定词并不是用来强化语气的词，而是用来弱化语气的词，往往表现了作者的迟疑不决。平卡姆（2000：43）举了这样一个例子：

原译文：We have dozens of thousands of students studying abroad, and it is quite important to create suitable conditions for their work after they come back.

修改后译文：We have tens of thousands of students studying abroad, and it is important to create suitable conditions for their work after they return.

平卡姆将原译文中的限定词 quite 拿掉了。平卡姆（2000：43）认为，没有必要犹豫不决，不直接说出这是重要的。实际上，这正是讲话者的本意。因此，我们认为，public administration and services are relatively weak 应修改为 public administration and services are weak，省去 relatively 不译。

basically 一词也是限定词，在此处可省去不译。平卡姆（2000：44-45）举了一个类似的例子：

原译文：...under the most difficult circumstances, Zhou Enlai resolutely and carefully set to work, basically guaranteeing the peaceful resolution of the Xi’an incident.

修改后译文：...under the most difficult circumstances, Zhou Enlai resolutely and carefully set to work, guaranteeing (or ensuring, or bringing about) the peaceful resolution of the Xi’an incident.

4. 冗余的成对词

冗余的成对词指的是，中文中经常出现两个意义非常相近的词并列使用的现象。实际上，这就是一种重复。在中文里，这种重复可以接受，但在英文中往往不可接受。平卡姆（2000：63）举了译文中出现的例子：help and assistance、stir up and incite、prudent and cautious、firmly and resolutely 等。

中文原文：我们要全面正确履行政府职能。

英文译文：We will fully and properly perform government functions.

根据 LDCE，properly 的第一个义项的意思是“correctly, or in a way that is considered right(=right)”，第二个义项的意思是 completely or fully(=thoroughly)。所以，properly 已含有 fully 之义，只用一个 properly 足矣。

A: Although the road before us is rough and bumpy, we believe that the favorable situation will continue.

B: Although the road before us is rough, we believe that the favorable situation will continue.

A: The present boom of foreign investment in China has prompted the country to consider and eventually work out ways to use such investment more efficiently.

B: The present boom of foreign investment in China has prompted the country to work out ways to use such investment more efficiently.

A: Even if problems do emerge, they can be easily corrected or solved.

B: Even if problems do emerge, they can be easily solved.

5. 一事两说

一事两说指的是同一思想的两次无谓的重复。在中文里，这是可以接受的，但在英文里是不可接受的。根据平卡姆（2000），一事两说主要有三种情形：

1）简单重述

We must practice economy and reduce unnecessary expenditures.

2）显而易见的陈述

China's socialist system of law has now been basically established, so that the situation in which there were no law has changed.

3）镜像陈述

即先正说，再反说，前后讲的实际是一回事。

We must pay close attention to the formulation of annual plans and not neglect it.

下面，我们看以下例子。

① 中文原文：整顿和规范市场秩序，努力营造便利、安全、放心的消费环境。

英文译文 : We will overhaul and standardize markets to create a convenient, safe and worry-free environment for consumers.

“安全”和“放心”是同义的。safe 基本上就是 worry-free 的意思，因此只须保留一个即可。

② 中文原文：切实解决人民群众最关心、最直接、最现实的利益问题。

英文译文：We should effectively solve the most practical problems of the greatest and most direct concern to the people.

“最关心”、“最直接”和“最现实”基本上来说指的是一回事，因此英译中保留一个即可。该译文同时保留了 the most practical、the greatest 和 most direct 三个最高级修饰语，语气过重，且有不切实际之嫌。

此外，我们还要注意语篇层面的迁移性冗余。程镇球（1980：245）指出，由于汉英两种语言差别较大，在汉语里有些修饰词可以重复，不显得累赘，有时还起强调的效果，或者读起来更为顺口，可是译成英文就不一样，会显得多余，念起来别扭，产生削弱原意的结果。这里讲的重复主要指的是语篇层面的重复。在中文里，这种语篇层面的重复是可以接受的，但在英文中不被接受。如果全部照译，将会出现语篇层面的迁移性冗余，影响译文的表达效果。下面，我们看2010年《政府工作报告》英文版节能减排部分对汉语语篇层面上重复的修饰词的处理。

中文原文：

打好节能减排攻坚战和持久战。

一要以工业、交通、建筑为重点，大力推进节能，提高能源效率。

二要加强环境保护。

三要积极发展循环经济和节能环保产业。

四要积极应对气候变化。

英文译文：

We will strive to conserve energy and reduce emissions.

First, we will energetically promote energy conservation and raise the efficiency of energy consumption, especially in industry, transportation, and construction.

Second, we will strengthen environmental protection.

Third, we will energetically develop a circular economy and the energy conservation and environmental protection industries.

Fourth, we will actively respond to climate change.

我们看到，中文中的修饰词在译文中全部保留下来了。这并不是一种好的翻译方法。下面，我们看胡锦涛主席2010年4月13日在华盛顿核安全峰会上的讲话《携手应对核安全挑战共同促进和平与发展》中的一段话的译文是如何处理重复的修饰词的。

中文原文：

借此机会，我愿提出五点主张：

切实履行核安全的国家承诺和责任。

切实巩固现有核安全国际法框架。

切实加强核安全国际合作。

切实帮助发展中国家提高核安全能力。

切实处理好安全与和平利用核能的关系。

英文译文：

I wish to propose, in this connection, that we take earnest steps in the following five areas:

First, honor national commitments and responsibilities.

Second, consolidate the existing international legal framework.

Third, strengthen international cooperation.

Fourth, help developing countries enhance nuclear security capacity.

Fifth, handle properly the relationship between nuclear security and peaceful use of nuclear energy.

我们看到，该译文将五个“切实”巧妙地转换为了一个 earnest，从而避免了英文译文中修饰词的罗列现象。程镇球（1980：244）发现，五届人大《政府工作报告》第 20 页，在短短的一页里，有十一次出现“搞好”“抓好”，如果统统照原文字面译出，就显得重复累赘、强调过头，反而削弱了表达效果。英文删去了七个“搞好”“抓好”。这就是说，在语篇层面上，只要译文能够表达原文的意思，一些修饰词应当尽量不译或少译。这是我们应对中译英中的迁移性冗余的总体策略。

第三节 如何避免中式英语

中国的译者不但要做英译汉的工作，而且要求承担汉译英的任务。在汉译英方面，最大的一个问题就是我们往往使用中式英语。

怎样才能避免中式英语呢？换言之，在使用英语的时候，应注意英语的哪些特点呢？我认为可以考虑三个要点：1）替代（substitution）；2）主语（subject）；3）主从（subordination）。抓住了这“三 S 要点”，可以大大减少中式英语。

汉英两种语言有一个重大的差别，那就是“英语不喜欢重复，如果在一句话里或相连的几句话里需要重复某个词语，则用代词来代替，或以其他手段来避免重复。汉语不怕重复，连续使用某个词语是常见的事。汉语也用代词，但不如英语用得多。所以汉译英时要千方百计避免重复，多用代称；英译汉时则要少用代称，多用实词。”关于这个问题，外国语言学家和语法学家都有详细的论述。

例 1　原文：哈佛是最早接受中国留学生的美国大学之一。中国教育界、科学界、文化界一直同哈佛大学保持着学术交流。

译 文：Harvard is among the first American universities to accept Chinese students. The Chinese educational, scientific and cultural communities have all along maintained academic exchanges with this university.

这个例子，原文“哈佛”出现两次，而译文中 Harvard 只出现一次，第二次使用了代称 this university。这样译既避免了重复，又体现了两句之间的联系，译文也显得流畅。而如果译者忽视了英语的这一特点，注意力过分集中在单个句子上，照样重复，译文便成了两个孤立的句子了。

关于主语，这里主要是指译文以什么作主语，也就是考虑主谓怎样搭配的问题。“英汉两种语言的主谓搭配，在大多数情况下是相通的。英语里一个主谓搭配，译成汉语后可以保持原来的搭配。但有时却不行，汉译英时也是一样。一般说来，汉语的主谓关系没有英语那么密切。英语对于主语能否作后面的动作考虑较多。因此，译文以什么作主语，怎样和谓语搭配，是一个经常需要斟酌的问题。”

例 2　原文：鲁镇的酒店的格局，是和别处不同的：都是当街一个曲尺形的大柜台，柜里面预备着热水，可以随时温酒。

译文 1：The layout of Luzhen’s taverns is unique. In each, facing you as you enter, is a bar in the shape of a carpenter’s square where hot water is kept ready for warming rice wine.

译文 2：The wine shops in Luzhen are not like those in other parts of China. They all have a right-angled counter facing the street, where hot water is kept ready for warming wine.

原文以“格局”为主语，译文 1 以 layout 为主语，与原文完全吻合，但一篇故事这样开始，英译显得颇为突然，远不如译文 2 以 wine shops 为主语，因为整篇故事就是围绕着酒店展开的。此外，译文 1 第二句不得不换用 bar 作主语，而英语一般是不喜欢不断更换主语的。译文 2 第二句用 they 作主语，与第一句呼应，译文就显得流畅自然。

英语中大量使用定语从句、分词短语、介词短语等，汉语则没有这么多表达方式。“因此英译句子里主从关系很少，体现出不同的层次。这与汉语有很大的不同。汉语……多用并列动词或并列分句，因此汉语句子里并列关系居多，层次不甚明显”。

例 3　原文：海洋覆盖了地球表面的 71%，是全球生命支持系统的一个基本组成部分，也是资源的宝库，环境的重要调节器。

译文：The ocean, which covers 71 percent of the earth’s surface, is a basic component of the global bio-support system. It is also a treasure house of resources and an important regulator of the environment.

原文的第一个谓语，译文用一个 which 引导的从句来表述。“覆盖了地球表面的 71%”是对客观情况的描述，也可以说是表述了一个已知的事实，它不是句子的重点，后面才是句子的重点。译文把次要的部分用从句处理，这就突出了层次，突出了句子的重点。

抓住以上三个要点，可能避免许多中式英语。中国人介绍中国的情况，写出来的英文有中文的味道也许是不可避免的。但我觉得至少应该做到两点：一是不要让外国读者产生误解，二是不要违反英语的词法句法，也就是不要把汉语的词法句法强加在英语身上。

美国翻译理论家奈达说过这样几句话：

Each language has its own genius—Rather than force the formal structure of one language upon another, the effective translator is quite prepared to make any and all formal changes necessary to reproduce the message in the distinctive structural forms of the receptor language. To preserve the content of the message the form must be changed.

有些译者不喜欢翻译理论，我也一向偏重于实践，对理论没有研究，然而理论自有其存在的价值。我觉得以上奈达的两段话，对我们避免中式英语，提高译文质量，是大有好处的。

（本节内容转自庄绎传．也谈中式英语．《中国翻译》，2000（6））

练习题：

一、请分析以下原译和改译。

1. 中方认为，欧方在该案的立案、调查和裁决过程中存在诸多与 WTO 规则不符之处，违反了欧盟在 WTO 项下应承担的义务。

原译：We think that in the initiation, investigation and determination of this case, the Commission didn't comply with the WTO rules on multiple occasions, thus acting inconsistently with its obligations under the WTO agreements.

改译：We believe that many WTO rules were not followed when the case was filed, investigated and decided, and that the EU has thus not fulfilled its obligations under the WTO.

说明：改译选用了更简洁的表述方法，遵循英译文要简洁的原则。

2. 名流酒运用传统工艺结合现代科学技术，配料讲究，工艺独特，金黄透明，味道纯正，富含人体必需的多种氨基酸和微量元素，保持原汁原色原味，是不加任何色素和添加剂的天然养生酒。

原译：Rich in amino acid and micro-elements necessary for human health, Mingliu Wine is a nourishing wine made from natural ingredients, without any coloring material or additives. Traditional method is employed for production as well as modern technique, with particularly chosen ingredients and unique expertise. The Wine presents a clear golden color and a pure unadulterated taste, preserving the original nutrition and flavor.

改译：Today, Mingliu Wine is brewed using a combination of traditional techniques and modern technology. The carefully selected ingredients go through a unique process, without additives of colourants, to produce a golden, transparent brew with a pure flavor. The wine is rich in essential amino acids and trace elements, and has a high nutritional value.

说明：原文叙述的内容包括工艺技术、配料、产品特点，但各部分内容排列较乱。改译中进行了重新排列，按照逻辑顺序，先讲工艺、配料，再讲产品特点。

3. 目前，石化产业在快速发展中长期积累的矛盾日益凸现。经济发展方式比较粗放，结构性矛盾比较突出，行业经济规模大而不强，资源环境约束加大；去年下半年以来，受国际金融危机影响，石化产业受到严重冲击。迫切需要通过结构调整和产业升级，提高行业整体素质和市场竞争力；迫切需要认真贯彻“自主创新、重点跨越、支撑发展、引领未来”的方针，按照行业发展必须依靠科学技术、科学技术必须面向行业经济发展的要求，加快科技成果转化，为石油和化学工业的结果调整和产业振兴提供强大的技术支撑。

原 译：At present, the fallout of fast growth, like extensive growth, structural imbalance, mounting resources and environmental constraints, begins to set in. Since the second half of this year, the global financial tsunami has taken a heavy toll in petrochemical industry. It is imperative to strengthen the industry and sharpen its competitive edge by restructuring and industrial upgrading. It is also critical to abide by the principle of "Making Breakthrough, Enhancing Growth and Shaping the Future of the Industry by Independent Innovation" and adhere to the guideline that industry development and science and technology must go hand in hand, translate the scientific findings and technological advancement into economic gains in a more efficient manner, and lay a solid technological groundwork to restructure and rejuvenate the petrochemical industry.

改译：At this point, a number of problems have surfaced as a result of many years of fast expansion. These include overly extensive growth, structural imbalance, lack of competitiveness in spite of large scale, and increasing constraints in natural resources and the environment. Since the second half of last year, the Chinese petrochemical industry has been hit hard by the international financial crisis. There is an urgent need for structural adjustment, an upgrading to raise the industry's overall quality and competitiveness. Another urgent need is to encourage "indigenous innovation in key areas to support current and future development." As innovations are commercialized faster, growth will drive technology and technology will serve development. This will all lay a sound basis for restructuring and invigorating the whole industry.

说明：原译第一句头重脚轻，且"fall out of fast growth...begins to set in"是不好搭配，因 fallout 是否定的含义。原译第四句，结构累赘，且 lay a solid technological groundwork to 是错误搭配，因为没有 weak groundwork。

二、分析并总结你自己汉译英实践中的错误及改正对策。

第六章

汉英翻译名家经验谈

第一节 程镇球：汉英翻译问题

汉英翻译问题

程镇球

（一）

汉英翻译有口笔之分，范围包罗万象，有文艺、科技、经贸、外事、新闻宣传、广播电视、旅游等等，存在的问题也不少。总的来讲，可以概括为两个问题：

1）应译未译，或译得有限，主要涉及当代和古代的文、史、哲名著。

2）已译质量不高，有的很差，特别在对外宣传方面（这里作广义解释，包括政治、经贸、文教等各个领域）。

有的人会说，汉英翻译如此，英汉翻译又何尝不如此。这两个问题在英汉翻译中也确实存在，但是不像在汉英翻译中那样突出，这和汉英翻译的特点是分不开的。

汉英翻译有什么特点呢？国内外翻译界人士都认为：在一般情况下，翻译应以译入本国（族）语为主。例如 I. F. Finlay 在所著 *Translating* 一书中指出：

“... it is the general consensus of opinion amongst professional translators in this country that translators should, unless bilingual (bearing in mind all that this implies), translate solely into their mother tongue or,...‘their language of habitual use.’”

也就是说，中国人应以英（外）汉翻译为主。因为除了少数例外，人们对母语的掌握比总要对外语的掌握好些。真正精通两种语言 (bilingual) 的人是不多的。

但是我们需要对外介绍中国各方面的情况，进行国际交流，也就是说，需要进行大量的汉英翻译工作。汉英翻译有相当的难度，产生这样那样的问题，也就在所难免。但我们不应该放松努力，要正视汉英翻译中存在的问题，尽可能提高质量，改进工作。

（二）

改进汉英翻译工作的当务之急，一是尽量消灭大错，二是努力提质量。当然消灭差错也是为了提高质量，但二者并不完全等同。

总的说来，我国译者的英语水平还不高，拼写错误、用词不当，到处可见，有时甚至笑话百出。段连城同志在《中国翻译》1990 年第 5 期的文章中举了大量的例证。在这里我想加一些例子（多半是来自外国报刊杂志上），以说明问题确实相当严重。

Swine Chocolates（浙江绍兴友谊工厂出品）

Air China Infright Magazine, Nov. 1989

Huaying Apartment Complex warmly welcomes the presence of extinguished guests from abroad.

文字上的毛病也不少。例如 1989 年 12 月我们去广东参观一家工厂，该厂产品远销海外许多国家，英文介绍材料上写道：

We are soled to more than fifty countries.

有人发现中国民航的旅行包上曾印着：

We welcome you to fly CAAC.

据说《中国日报》有过这样的新闻标题：

A non-smoker with designs on fags * (fags: BrE. cigarettes; AmE. homosexuals).

对这类差错，我看应该区别两种不同的情况：小地方、小单位人力有限，有时难免出差错，要求可以从宽；大地方、大单位人力物力充裕，对外影响也较大，要求应该从严。翻译事关国家形象，我们呼吁有关部门领导及时组织力量，对重点涉外单位的英语宣传介绍材料进行一次检查，尽力消灭大的差错。

（三）

关于如何提高汉英翻译的质量，这里仅就几个方面同大家探讨。

第一，翻译质量要高，译员的素质就要好，这是不言而喻的。但是培养一个好的汉英笔译人员并不容易。首先，要能吸引有才华的人来干这一行。笔译人员在后台工作，默默无闻，不像口译工作那样可以出头露面，周游列国，有机会见到世界名人，工作本身就有相当的吸引力。成为一名合格的汉英笔译人员需要较长时间的实践和磨炼，但是他们没有得到应有的社会尊重和适当的物质待遇。现在愿意终身从事汉英笔译事业的青年寥寥无几，老一代译者深感后继乏人。其次，缺乏领导的支持。有些领导口头上也说要重视翻译，但实际上并非如此，他们并不懂得翻译的艰苦。一篇中文稿写好了，既没有给翻译讲文章的中心感想和应注意的地方，又没有考虑给翻译以推敲的时间，只要译文能按时完成，质量好坏并不太在乎。这种情况恐怕一时也难以改变。我们对青年翻译当然应该严格要求，要讲求无私奉献，但是思想教育不等于政策。如果领导在思想上对汉英翻译不重视，不采取“倾斜政策”，汉英笔译的前途是不容乐观的。

第二，就译文本身而言，提高汉英翻译质量的一个关键问题是避免所谓的“中式英文”(Chinglish)。翻译是用一种语言文字来表达另一种语言文字所体现的思想内容。思想要通过文字才能表达出来，但文字不完全等于思想。形式与内容既统一又矛盾。翻译的最大课题之一就是摆脱原文字面的束缚。

汉英翻译中，译文受原文字面影响的问题很多。现在举三个方面常见的现象说明一下。

1）搭配（collocation)

受到汉语字面影响而搭配不当的例子经常碰到，例如：

抓紧施肥 grasp manure (pay close attention to or attend to the question of manure)（这个错误译法曾在许多人中传为笑谈）

取得成就 make achievements (have or record achievement)

学习知识 learn knowledge (acquire or attain knowledge)

把中国建设成为 build China into (turn or transform China into)

犯个人主义的错误 make mistakes of individualism (mistakes of succumbing to individualism)

我们有过这样的经验 We had the experience that (It was our experience that)

热烈祝贺亚运会 Warmly congratulate the Asian Games (Hail or Greet the Asian Games)

附带提一下，亚运会有这样一句口号：“争取运动成绩与精神文明双丰收”，译成 For a good harvest both in sports and morals，“丰收”译成 a good harvest。太拘泥于字面了。“精神文明”不好译，译成 morals 也费了一番苦心。但是 morals 另有含义，*Longman Dictionary* 的解释是：standards of behaviour, esp. in matters of sex。这句口号译成 For better (athletic) records and sportsmanship 是否稍好些？

2）拟人法（personification）

拟人法的现象在汉语中常见，而在英语中，多数情况下，是视为修辞上的一种毛病。因此在汉英翻译中要注意这个区别，避免受汉语影响而出问题。例如：

我们的事业从胜利走向新的胜利。

Our cause has won victories one after another.

cause 是没有生命的，而 win victories 的主语一般是人，二者用在一起，就把 cause 拟人化了。英译文虽然在语法上站得住脚，但不符合英语习惯用法，不是地道的英语。译文需要改写，或者加主语，如：

We have won one victory after another for our cause.

或者改用被动语态，如：

A series of victories have been won for our cause.

以下两个例子也属同一性质：

汉字在历史上有过不可磨灭的功绩。

The system of Chinese characters has played an invaluable role in our history.（不是 Chinese characters have made indelible contributions in history.)

宗教不得干预政治。

It is impermissible to interfere with politics in the name of religion.

(不是 Religion must not interfere with politics.)

3）修饰词 (modifier)

汉语里修饰词用得较多，例如：顺利进行，胜利完成，热烈拥护，积极支持，努力做到，认真贯彻，彻底粉碎，深入批判，广泛开展，严肃处理。甚至有些人的文章里还出现"不切实际的幻想""毫无根据的诽谤"等等。

一般说来，英语里的修饰词不像汉语里那么多，不少指导写作的书都告诫不要乱用修饰词。因此，汉语里的修饰词不一定非统统照译不可，而应加以推敲，决定如何处理。英译文里修饰词过多会显得装腔作势，效果适得其反，原来想加以强调的反而削弱了。试看下面的例子：

进一步简化手续，及时地积极地从国外引进，并且认真组织科学技术人员和广大职工做好消化和推广工作。

We should simplify procedures and take prompt action to import urgently needed technology…organize scientists, technicians and workers to assimilate and popularize imported technology.

如果照原文字面在 simplify 前加上 further，在 prompt 后加上 and vigorous，在 organize 前加上 earnestly 或 actively，在 workers 前加上 the mass of，文字会显得重复和累赘，不能很好传达原文的意思。

此外，有的修饰词要不要译，需要根据情况仔细斟酌，因为有时译了反而有损原意，例如"胜利召开"如译为 successfully convened，会使人感到召开前遇到不少困难和阻碍，最后才得以开成，而原文可能根本没有这种含义。

（四）

汉英翻译中一个最棘手的问题涉及词汇和短语，特别是政治性词汇和短语，由于中、外社会背景和文化传统的差异，翻译难以处理恰当。但是政治类词语关系重大，翻译时必须既要扣紧原文，又要使外国读者能够正确理解。我们可以用"资产阶级自由化"为例来加以说明。这个词现在译为 bourgeois liberalization，但是 liberalization 在西方是褒义词，毫无贬义，英语里也很难找到合适的匹配词。根据中央负责同志的讲话精神，译时似乎可以作适当解释。事实上，西方报刊也已经加以解释，如 bourgeois liberalization, meaning Western influence，只是与我们的解释不同而已。"资产阶级自由化"是不是可以译为 bourgeois liberalization 或者 the attempt to restore capitalism in the name of liberalization? 或者把译文中的 restore capitalism 改为 overthrow the government；或者更简单地译为 bourgeois liberalization aimed at capitalist restoration。口译中这样译似乎问题不大，但笔译要见诸文字，要求更为严格，可以考虑用上面的译法作为基础，讨论后加以完善。当然，也不需要每次都译成“资产阶级自由化”，第二次、第三次出现就不必全部重复，单用 bourgeois liberalization 也就够了。

同样，“和平演变”是否可以译为 peaceful evolution, or the attempt to transform socialism into capitalism by peaceful means，或者简化为 peaceful evolution aimed to subvert socialism (or the socialist state)。

这一类政治性词汇和短语还有不少，都需要进一步研究探讨。相应的英译，希望能引起广泛重视。

（五）

最后，简单谈一下翻译理论联系实际的题。翻译理论源于翻译实践，又用来指导翻译实践，这是大家都会同意的。目前存在的情况是：在翻译单位，由于工作需要，往往强调解决实际翻译问题的能力，不太重视理论。而另一方面，教学单位要求学科的系统性、科学性，往往翻译实践不多，谈起翻译理论来却头头是道。这两者之间是不是有些脱节，而且有越来越隔离的倾向呢?

翻译是实用的学科，最终还要看有没有培养出好的翻译人才，译出好的翻译作品。英语里有这样一句谚语：“The proof of the pudding is in the eating.”。对翻译来说恐怕应该是：“The proof of the translation is in the reading (whether it reads well or not).”。

因此，有些西方学者强调翻译理论和实际的联系要更密切些，有的甚至认为翻译中的具体实例要比论点更有意义。

为了使翻译单位与教学单位相互通气，双方应该进行交流，加强来往。外语院系的翻译教师可以去工作单位实习调查，而工作单位有经验的翻译可以去外语院系听课和参加座谈，这种交流可能对教学单位更为重要，因为归根结底教学是为工作单位培养人才的，了解工作单位的需要和问题，对进一步改进翻译教学是有好处的。

1) 对于 bilingual 的解释，有些英汉词典并不确切，如《新英汉词典》（增补本，1985 年版）：① 两种语言的：用两种语言写（印）的；② 使用两种语言的。《英华大词典》(1984 年版)：① 两国语言的；② 能讲两国话的；③ 用两种语言书写（印刷）的。请比较 *Longman Dictionary of Contemporary English* (1987): able to speak two languages equally well; *Webster Ninth New Collegiate Dictionary* (1983): using or able to use two languages esp. with equal fluency。

2) “He[one who writes or speaks in a foreign language] will be ‘caught’ out every time, not by his grammar, which is probably suspiciously ‘better’ than an educated native’s, not by his vocabulary, which may well be wider, but by his unacceptable or improbable collocations.” (P. Newmark. *Approaches to Translations*, 1981: 180)

3) “It has been wisely said that the adjective is the enemy of the noun. If we make a habit

of saying 'the true facts are there,' we shall come under suspicion when we profess to tell merely 'the facts.' If a *crisis* is always *acute* and *an emergency always grave*, what is left for those words to do by themselves? If *active* constantly accompanies consideration, we shall think we are being fobbed off when we are promised bare consideration. If a decision is always qualified by *definite*, a decision by itself becomes a poor filleted thing. If conditions are customarily described as *prerequisite* or *essential*, we shall doubt whether a condition without an adjective is really a condition at all. An *unfulfilled vacancy* may leave us wondering whether a mere vacancy is really vacant. If a part is always an *integral part* or a *component part* there is nothing left for a mere part except to be as a spare part." (E. Gowe. *The Complete Plain Words*, 1979: 81-82)

4) "… if it [the science of translation] decides in favour of a theoretical approach, it runs too great a risk of becoming methodically sterile and producing findings which have only limited relevance to a practically oriented science of translation." (Wolfram Wilas, *The Science of Translation: Problems and Methods*, 1982: 14)

5) "Assumptions and propositions about translation normally arise only from practice and should not be offered without examples of originals and their translations. As with much literature à thèse, the examples are often more interesting than the thesis itself."（P. Newmark. Approaches to translations, 1981:19)

[作者简介]程镇球，外交部资深翻译家，《新时代汉英大词典》主编，曾参与党和国家许多重要文献、报告的翻译工作。

（《中国翻译》1991 年第 3 期）

第二节 程镇球：政治文章的翻译要讲政治

政治文章的翻译要讲政治

程镇球

翻译要忠实于原著，做到一个“信”字，这是大家都认同的。早在 17 世纪，英国诗人 Andsew Marvell (1621—1678) 就说过：

He is translation's thief that addth more,
As much as he that taketh from the store of the first author.

(大意是：谁要是在翻译中对原著有所增添或有所减损，他就如同窃贼。)

但是在翻译不同文体的文章时，掌握忠实的尺度是大不一样的。翻译《红楼梦》的英国汉学家大卫·霍克思（David Hawkes）在评论美国诗人庞德 (Ezra Pound) 译的中国诗时说道：

"Perhaps, since Chinese poetry must lose so much in translation (everything but the base sense, and sometimes a good deal of that), it can, with advantage, have something added."

(大意是：翻译中国诗词不得不丢掉许多东西，连意义有时也丢失不少，或许在翻成英文时加点东西进去也不无裨益。)

这当然不是一般意义上所谓的"信"了。

在政治文章的翻译中，我们掌握忠实的标准就要严格得多，这是因为政治文章涉及国家大政方针、基本政策等，稍一疏忽，后果严重。首先，我们必须紧扣原文，不得任意增删。例如在香港回归之前我们常说的一句话：中国政府"决定于一九九七年七月一日**对香港恢复行使主权**"(粗黑部分系作者所加)。准确的英文译法是"The Government of the People's Republic of China has decided to *resume the exercise of sovereignty* over Hong Kong with effect from July 1，1997."。在1984年发表的中英政府关于香港问题的联合声明英译本中就是这样写的，但是1990年和1991年人代会上《政府工作报告》的英译文均未译出"行使"两字，到1992年才改正过来。也许有的译者认为译成 resume the sovereignty over Hong Kong 就足够的了，何必加上 exercise，使译文显得累赘呢？其实，这里"行使"两字恰恰是最关键的词。香港是清政府于鸦片战争失败后割让给英国的。清政府于1842年8月29日被迫签订的《南京条约》(又称《江宁条约》)是近代史上中国被迫签订的第一个不平等条约。新中国成立之初，中国政府即刻宣告不承认所有强加于中国人民头上的一切不平等条约。不承认《南京条约》也就是不承认割让香港的合法性。香港的主权仍然属于中国，不过由于英国事实上的霸占，我们无法行使我们的主权，直到1997年7月1日。因此，"恢复行使主权"中的"行使"两字在英译中是绝对不可以省去的。

政治翻译不能任意删字，当然也不能任意加字，或者离开原文自由发挥。下面举个例子来说明。1987年6月12日邓小平在与南斯拉夫领导人谈话时，针对广东有人提出搞特区，说道："我说名字叫经济特区，搞政治特区就不好了。……当时我们党内还有人采取怀疑的态度，香港舆论界不管是反对我们的还是赞成我们的，也都有人持怀疑的态度，不相信我们是正确的。"(《邓小平文选》)第三卷，239，以下均简称《文选》)英文译成："But I said they should be called special economic zones not special political zones, because we didn't want anything of that sort... At the time, a number of people of different political persuasions, from Hong Kong journalists to Party members, were skeptical about that policy." (Deng Xiaoping, *Fundamental Issues in Present-day China*, 1987: 90，以下简称 *Fundamental Issues*)。"搞政治特区就不好了"完全可以译为："not special political zone, which would not be right (or advisable)"。译成 because one didn't want anything of that sort，严格讲来不是翻译，而是释义 (paraphrasing)，不过还未出格。后一句英文相当简洁，但与中文原意大相径庭，把"不论是反对我们的还是赞成我们的"译成 people of different political persuasions，已经过

于“自由”。这句话本来只指香港舆论界，现在连党员也包括进去了，党内哪来各种政治信仰不同的党员呢？我们主张扣紧原文，不要任意增删，目的就是要忠实于原文，在政治文献的翻译中，首先要在政治上忠实于原文。1994 年出版了《邓小平文选》全书的英译本，以上这句话的英译文改为了：“At the time, some people in the Party had doubts about that policy, and some of the people in Hong Kong whether they were for us or against us, were skeptical too and thought it was incorrect.” (*Selected Works of Deng Xiaoping*, Vol. Ⅲ 1994: 236)。

紧扣原文的同时，原文的词序也需加以注意，不要轻易颠倒，避免犯政治性错误。例如 1982 年 9 月 24 日邓小平与英国首相撒切尔夫人谈话时指出 (该谈话于 1993 年 9 月在《人民日报》上公开发表):“我担心的是今后十五年过渡时期如何过渡好，担心在这个时期中会出现很大的混乱，而且这些混乱是人为的。这当中不光有外国人，也有中国人，而主要是英国人。”(《文选》第三卷，14) 起初的英译文是“I am worried there may be major disturbances in this period, man-made disturbances. These would be created not just by foreigners, chiefly Britons, but also by Chinese.”。本来原文的意思是很清楚的：制造混乱的人中间有中国人，有外国人，而这些人里面主要是英国人。而这里的英译把顺序颠倒过来，重点移到后面，制造混乱的人变成主要是中国人了。英译者可能认为英国人也是外国人，把英国人提前和外国人放在一起处理，文字上要简洁得多，好像也符合逻辑，结果词序一打乱，意思就变了。英译文在发表后曾引起读者强烈反应。这种以词害意的做法在政治文献的翻译中是绝对不容许的。1994 年出版的《邓小平文选》第三卷英译本中改正了这个错误，译文如下：“I am concerned that there may be major disturbances in this period, man-made disturbances. These could be created not just by foreigners but also by Chinese, but chiefly Britons.” (*Selected Works of Deng Xiaoping*, Vol. III, 1994: 25)。但是修改后的译文与原文还有些出入，不够清楚，似可改为：“…These could be created by Chinese as well as foreigners, but chiefly by Britons.”。

紧扣原文的同时，一些“小零件”也不应放过。例如，汉语里没有冠词，译成英语，用不用冠词也大有讲究。例如 1967 年阿以战争中以色列占领了阿拉伯国家的大片领土，联合国安理会于同年通过第 242 号决议案，要求以色列撤出其占领的阿拉伯领土：“call for Isreal' s withdrawal from ‘territories occupied in the recent conflict' in return for the right to live in peace within secure and recognized boundaries”，即所谓“以土地换和平”。阿拉伯国家要求以色列撤出所有被占领土，指出决议的法文本、西文本中在 territories 前应加上 the，但是安理会的决议英文本故意含糊其词，未使用 the。英国《经济学家》周刊就指出在撤军范围上是可以讨价还价的：“There can, and should, be geographical flexibility — Resolution 242 studiously omitted the definite article before ‘territories'” (*Economist*, 27 July 1991, p.13)。由此可见，一个定冠词意义非同小可。从上述联合国决议来看，有 the 就指一切被占领土，没有 the 就可以不包括全部在内。

其次，政治文章的翻译要仔细衡量用词的政治含义与影响，例如“华侨”“海外侨胞”等词的译法就需要斟酌。1992 年 9 月 30 日党领导人李先念在国庆招待会讲话中指出“早日实现祖国统一，是全国各族人民包括台湾同胞、港澳同胞和海外侨胞的共同心愿。”英文译成：“It is the common wish of all Chinese, including the compatriots in Taiwan, Hong Kong and Macao and overseas Chinese, to see an early reunification of the motherland.”。

把“海外侨胞”译成 overseas Chinese 是欠妥的，因为 overseas Chinese 的含义比较广，相当于海外华人（包括侨居海外的中国人和华裔外国人），他们中间 90% 的人已经加入居住国的国籍，这些人的“祖国”严格地讲已经不能说是中国了。特别是号召他们发扬爱国主义精神，这个国是指哪一国呢？华侨问题在某些东南亚国家比较敏感，翻译不当，会引起误解和不必要的疑虑。《人民日报》1992 年 3 月 13 日第六版报道钱其琛在柬埔寨答记者问时明确指出：“中国的一贯政策是不赞成双重国籍。……持中国护照的华人是华侨。”很明显，“海外侨胞”应该译成 overseas Chinese nationals，或者 Chinese nationals (or citizens) residing abroad。1979 年 6 月 15 日邓小平在中国人民政治协商会议第五届全国委员会第二次会议开幕词中提道：“台湾同胞、港澳同胞和国外侨胞心向祖国，爱国主义觉悟不断提高，……。”(《文选》第二卷，186) 英文译文是：“The thoughts of our compatriots in Taiwan, Xianggang (Hong Kong) and Aomen (Macao) and of Chinese nationals overseas turn with longing to the motherland, and their sense of patriotism has grown constantly stronger.”(*Selected Works of Deng Xiaoping*, 1975–1982: 193)。这里“国外侨胞”译成 Chinese nationals overseas 是正确的，但是请注意，“华侨”与“海外华人”的区别不是人人都清楚的。直到最近，还有的领导同志说：“我们有几千万爱国同胞在海外。”

在强调翻译要注意的政治含义和影响方面还可以举出不少例子。例如 1984 年 10 月 3 日邓小平在会见港澳同胞国庆观礼团时，针对他们担心我们政策会变的心理，强调指出：“我们中央政府、中共中央即使在过去的动乱时代，在国际上说话也是算数的。”(邓小平《建设有中国特色的社会主义》增订本，1987：63)，以下简称《建设》) 英译文是：“Moreover, our Central Government and the Central Committee of the Communist Party always live up to their international obligations, and that was true even during the years of turbulence.” (Deng Xiaoping, *Fundamental Issues*，1987：65)。原来的英译文是：”Among other things, our Central Government and the Central Committee of the Chinese Communist Party mean what they say on international affairs, which was true even in the years of turbulence.”。有人提出香港问题不属于国际事务（international affairs）范畴，而且译文给人一种国际上讲话算数、国内讲话可能不一定算数的感觉，因此把 mean what they say on international affairs 改为 mean what they say to the international community，可是这样改并没有解决问题，接着改为 always live up to their international obligations。obligations 改为 commitments 可能更好些。现在看来，整句译文还有改进的余地。

再次，从事政治文章翻译的同志要有政策头脑和政治敏感。我们可以举一些例子来说明。1983年6月26日邓小平与美国新泽西州西东大学教授杨力宇谈话时指出："祖国统一后，台湾特别行政区可以有自己的独立性，可以实行同大陆不同的制度。"(《建设》, 18)

这里"独立性"当然不能译成independence。所谓独立性，就是指谈话后面列举的各项权力：司法独立，终审权不须到北京；台湾可以有自己的军队，大陆不派人驻台，不仅军队不去，行政人员也不去；台湾的党、政、军等系统都由台湾自己来管等等。这句话的英译文是："After unification with the motherland, the Taiwan special administrative region will assume a unique character and may practise a social system different from that of the mainland." (*Fundamental Issues*, pp. 19-20) "独立性"译成unique character是可以的，因为我们的对台政策确实是独特的，史无前例的。不过，"独立性"也可以考虑译成will have a distinctive character of its own，文字上可能更顺当些，也不损原意。

1994年6月15日《中国日报》(*China Daily*)第一版头条报道了江泽民主席在教育工作会议上的讲话，内称："...Jiang stressed the importance of shifting the focus from economic construction to relying on scientific and technological progress and improving the skills of workers."。难道"一个中心"(以经济建设为中心)要变了？这可是一条特大的新闻。查一查当时的《人民日报》，原来中文是这样说的："具有决定意义的一条，就是把经济建设转到依靠科技进步和提高劳动者素质的轨道上来"。可见要转的是把经济建设主要依靠增加投资等转到依靠科技进步和提高劳动者素质的方面上来。其实，稍有政治敏感度的译者都会发现问题，中央以经济建设为中心的方针决不会这样随随便便改变。《中国日报》有可能是转载新华社的译文，但是即使如此，报纸的编辑也有责任重读一遍，在政治上把关。

又如《关于建国以来党的若干历史问题的决议》第30节第2段有关独立自主、自力更生的论述中指出："我们在任何时候都需要争取外援，特别需要学习外国一切对我们有益的先进事物"。英译文是："It is always necessary for us to try to win foreign aid and, in particular, to learn all that is advanced and beneficial from other country."。这里try to win foreign aid中的try to加得好，如果不加try to就可能给人误解，以为我们非获得外援不可。中文是"争取"，争取到争取不到不完全取决于我们，争取不到外援我们照样要建设。我们的基本立足点是独立自主、自力更生，依靠本国的力量和人民群众的努力。

翻译的政治敏感还表现在对于政治形势变化的反应敏锐上。1980年1月16日邓小平在中共中央召集的干部会议上强调要有一个安定团结的政治局面时指出："'四大'，即大鸣、大放、大字报、大辩论……这个'四大'的做法，作为一个整体来看，从来没有产生积极的作用。"(《文选》第二卷，257)英译文是："The 'si da,' that is, speaking out freely, airing one' s views fully, writing big-character posters and holding great debates...But when we sum up our historical experience, we have to recognize that, taken as a whole, these practices have never played a positive role." (*Selected Works of Deng Xiaoping*, pp. 241-242)。这是沿用"四大"的过去的译法。当时是肯定"四大"的，但是现在要重新评价，过去的译法就不合适了。你

否定"四大"，外国人看到或听到原译就会问："What's wrong with speaking out freely and airing one' s views fully?"。1981年《关于建国以来党的若干历史问题的决议》第26节第5段宣布："取消了不利于发扬社会主义民主的所谓'大鸣、大放、大字报、大辩论'"。"四大"英译就有了改动："The so-called right to 'speak out, air views and hold debates in a big way and write big-character posters,' which actually obstructs the promotion of socialist democracy, was deleted from the constitution."。这种译法也并非完全新译，因为在《毛泽东选集》第五卷的英译中已出现过："感谢右派，'大'字是他们发明的。我在今年二月二十七日的讲话中，并没有讲什么大鸣、大放、大辩论，没有这个'大'字。"英译文是："We are indebted to the Rightists for inventing the expression 'in a big way.' In my talk of February 27 this year I didn't use this expression 'in a big way.'" (*Selected Works of Mao Tsetung*, Vo1.V, 1977: 502)。

政治敏感还要求翻译反应迅速，尤其在口译方面。例如有一次中央负责同志接见外国记者时谈到"六四"政治风波时，引用了一句中国成语："吃一堑，长一智"。译员译成"A fall into the pit, a gain in your wit"，这个译法没有问题。但是该记者说译文太文了，一般外国读者不好理解，能不能改得通俗明白一点儿，如 learn from past mistakes。这一说法，在有的情况下未尝不可，但用在"六四"上就很不妥了，无异是说我们犯了错误。要改只能改成 learn from our experience 为宜。

政治文章的翻译要注意掌握分寸，用词轻重要恰如其分。例如1987年4月26日邓小平会见捷克斯洛伐克总理什特劳加尔时在谈话中指出："在我们同东欧各国各党的关系这个问题上，我们有相当的责任"。英译文是："So far as our relations with the countries and Parties of Eastern Europe are concerned, we are largely responsible for the problems that occurred." (*Fundamental Issues*, p. 174) "相当的"译成 largely，用词显然欠妥，把与东欧各国、各党关系恶化的责任主要归咎于中国了。应该把 largely 去掉，改用下面一类译法为好："We should take considerable (or a good portion of) responsibility for the interruption of our relations with (or for the problems that arose), etc."。

1984年7月31日邓小平会见英国外交大臣杰弗里·豪时着重指出："解决台湾、香港问题可以有两种方式，一种是非和平方式，一种是和平方式。非和平方式，或者说用武力解决问题，总是不好的。"原来的英译文是："There are two ways available: non-peaceful and peaceful. The non-peaceful means, the use of armed force, is not desirable under any circumstances."。"总是"译成 under any circumstances，基本上把非和平方式排除在外了，这是严重的误译。后来，把 under any circumstances 改为 for either case (*Fundamental Issues*, 59)，但"总是"的意思仍未译出，语气不对，而且把"不好的"译成 not desirable 也不够贴切。我们认为"总是不好的"译成 is not a happy one in any case，可能较为恰当。

1984年10月6日邓小平接见参加中外经济合作问题讨论会全体中外代表时指出："经验证明，关起门来搞建设是不能成功的，中国的发展离不开世界。"(《邓选》第三卷，78) 初译时英文为："Our experience shows that China cannot rebuild itself with its door closed to the outside world and that it cannot develop without the help of other countries."。"中国的发展离不开世界"在英文里变成"没有别国的帮助中国就不可能发展"了，这不仅文字上离原文太远，而且与下文"自力更生"的论点相冲突。用词不问轻重，随意离原文发挥，这在政治文章翻译中是最忌讳的。后来译文改为："Our experience shows that China cannot rebuild itself behind closed doors and that it cannot develop in isolation from the rest of the world." (*Selected Works of Deng Xiaoping*, Vo1.11I，p.86)。

政治翻译中还有一个用词太轻的问题。最为突出的一个例子是经常见诸报章的"伤害中国人民的感情"一语。通常译成 hurt the feelings of the Chinese people。hurt sb' s feelings 指的是不顾情面，使人感到不快。这在英文里分量是很轻的，不符合原文的意思。把 hurt 改成 lacerate，feelings 前加 national 可能好些，但还没有解决问题。"感情"两字恐怕不能从字面上来理解。也许有时这句话改译成 wound the national dignity of the Chinese people 可能更合原意。

政治文章的翻译还要推敲用词的主观性和客观性。例如我们曾经说过："中国实行开放政策，中国的一些武器要进入国际军火市场。我们不能保证这些武器不流入某些国家。"这里"要进入"和"会进入"是一个意思。"会"是客观的，不管主观愿望如何，都会发生；而"要"有两层意思：主观上要想这样和客观上要发生。这句话里的"要"指客观上必然会发生的，因为实行开放政策，就难以控制武器的流向。"不能"也有主客观之分：可以是客观上难以保证，也可以是主观上不打算保证。这里的"不能"也是指客观上的意义。正确的译文应该是："China is pursuing an open policy. Some Chinese weapons are bound to reach the international arms market. We don't think it possible to guarantee that those weapons will not find its way into certain countries."。"要"最好不译成 will，更不能译成 must，"不能"不可译成 cannot。

除了主观与客观的区别之外，还有一个用词语气的主动和被动的问题。《北京周报》1992 年 11 月 2 日 (Vol.35, No.44) 的一期中"Highlights of the Week"一栏第四条"Fruitless Trip by the Hong Kong Governor"中有这样一句话："Lu Ping, the Chinese official in charge of Hong Kong affairs, threatened to replace Hong Kong's government when it (the Chinese government) takes over the colony in 1997 if the governor presses ahead with his plan."。这里的 plan 当然是指香港末代总督彭定康违背《中英联合声明》搞他的所谓政改，但鲁平会用这种口气讲话吗？这种话很像一些英国和亲英报纸的语调。事实上，香港末代总督和其他一些人不甘心退出历史舞台，结束殖民统治，千方百计找麻烦，在香港回归过程中设置障碍，我们是被迫作出反应的，不是主动在进行什么"威胁"。《北京周报》那句话如果是根据中文翻译的，应该仔细查一查原文是怎么说的；如果是记者直接用英文写的，很可能是受到外报外刊的影响，这一点值得我们从事对外宣传工作同志的警惕。我们认为，上面那句话的译文应该修改，例如改为："Lu Ping, the Chinese official in charge of Hong Kong affairs, said that China would be forced (or would have no option but) to replace Hong Kong's government when it (the Chinese government) takes over the colony in 1997 should the governor press ahead with his plan."

提到彭定康，顺便讲一讲"千古罪人"的译法。有人把它译成 the criminal of millennium、the criminal for a thousand years，或 the criminal of all time。这些译法的共同缺点是把"罪人"译成 criminal，而我们讲的"罪人"并不属于法律的范畴。也有人避开罪犯，采用意译的办法，如 one who stands condemned through the ages、person who is held up to infamy through the ages、one who goes down in history as a man of infamy、a man nailed to the eternal pillory。这些译法的共同缺点是不够简洁。比较明白易懂而又简短的译法有 a man of eternal infamy(or guilt)、the villain of all time。我个人倒比较欣赏彭定康自己的译法 the eternal villain。

以上讲了不少关于政治文章的翻译要突出政治的话。是不是因为中国是社会主义国家，所以特别注意政治倾向，强调政治含义呢？其实，世界上所有国家在政治上都毫不含糊，因为政治涉及国家的根本利益。比如，同样是从事武装活动，西方国家把亲西方的人叫作"自由战士"（freedom fighters），而把反西方的人叫作"恐怖分子"（terrorists）或"极端分子"（extremists）。北约不顾国际法的基本准则，野蛮地轰炸中国驻南斯拉夫大使馆，造成重大人员伤亡与财产损失，中国人民理所当然地表示愤怒，举行游行示威。西方报刊称之为"中国在煽动'民族主义情绪'"（feeling of nationalism），而他们自己国家出现相同的行动，却称之为"爱国主义"（patriotism）。在用词方面，西方也十分讲究内涵和分寸。例如在 20 世纪 90 年代初海湾战争时，世界舆论要求美国与伊拉克再次接触，挽救和平。当时美国国务卿贝克（James Baker）表示双方可以进行"讨论"（discussion），但不能进行"谈判"（but not negotiation）。"讨论"是讨论如何执行安理会的决议，"谈判"就有互相让步（give and take）的含义。

政治文章上用词严格，最说明问题的例子是苏联垮台后在东德、西德统一上的措辞。美国前国务卿基辛格（Henry Kissinger）用了 unification，而贝克用的是 reunification。美国报章杂志最初用法也不一致。德国和法国对此均比较敏感。德国总理科尔（Helmut Kohl）最初用的是 reunification，但后来一直用 unity，有意避开 reunification 的说法。法国也只用 German unity。美国专栏作家萨菲尔（William Safire）1990 年 3 月 19 日在《先驱论坛报》上撰文写道："统一（只包括东德和西德），而重新统一（就要加上西里西亚②、东普鲁士③、苏台德区④，想起来了，还要加上可爱的阿尔萨斯－洛林③）["Unification (just East and West Germany) and reunification (throw in Silesia, East Prussia, the Sudetenland and now that we think of it, Sweet Alsace-Lorraine)"]。难道这种区别仅是咬文嚼字、无关痛痒吗？请看当时德国极右分子的言论："东德实际上是中德"（eastern Germany is really middle Germany），"还要恢复更多东边的土地"（lost territories further east to be reclaimed）。

最后，我们想特别强调一下西方传媒对第三世界的渗透，在无形中对中国传媒界的影响。在前面提到的《北京周报》报道鲁平关于香港的谈话就是一例，这种例子并不少见。例如北约在向南斯拉夫发动进攻之前，多次施加压力，迫使南斯拉夫接受他们关于科索沃的所谓和平方案。《中国日报》(*China Daily*) 1999 年 3 月 19 日头版上的消息是这样说的："The international community was expected to give Jugoslavia until Wednesday to accept a peace proposal on Kosovo after the breakdown of negotiations in Paris, diplomatic sources said yesterday."。原文显然是转载西方通讯社的电讯，把"北约"与 international community 等同起来，好像国际社会完全站在北约一边，这和中国人民和中国政府的立场背道而驰。明明是北约向南斯拉夫提出最后通牒，却称之为"和平建议"(peace proposal)。又如以美国为首的北约绕过联合国安理会，对南斯拉夫狂轰滥炸，伤害无辜的平民百姓，完全是违背国际法的侵略行径，可是西方报刊和电台均称之为 Strike Against Jugoslavia，用中性词汇掩盖其霸权主义的侵略行径。但是奇怪的是，中国英文报章杂志也跟着称之为 Strike Against Jugoslavia，难道我们对西方传媒的渗透不应该敲响警钟，提高警惕吗？！

注释

① David Hawkes, *Classical, Modern and Humane*, Chinese University Press in Hong Kong, 1959: 233-234.

② 现分属波兰、捷克、斯洛伐克

③ 现分属波兰与乌克兰

④ 现属捷克

（《中国翻译》2003 年第 3 期）

第三节 王弄笙：外事汉英翻译的几点体会

外事汉英翻译的几点体会

王弄笙

汉英翻译的主要目的是使英文读者了解中文著作。译者应仔细琢磨原作语言，透过表层框架，探明语言的深层含义。对原作语言的理解越彻底，译作越能深刻、准确地反映原作的精神实质。要做到这一点，首先要找出汉英翻译的主要问题（或矛盾），然后加以解决。我认为原文作者与译者之间在经历、知识、对事物的理解和表达能力上的矛盾是原文和译文两种语言之间的矛盾。汉英两种语言有许多差异，有社会、历史、经济和文化等方面的不同背景。当然它们之间也有共同点，对相同之处翻译时可以用对应词互相转换，对不同之处可以用翻译技巧加以解决。此外，应当扩大背景知识，熟悉和研究原文中所涉及的主题和专业，还要广泛阅读、精读优秀的英语文章，多听以英语为母语国家的人的讲话，看看他们对某一个词句、某一个问题在某一种特定场合如何表达，当我们碰到类似情况时就可以拿来为我所用。

我从事汉英翻译 30 多年，仍然经常碰到许多难以解决的问题。现就我的实践经验，谈几点粗浅的体会：

一、从事翻译工作，尤其是外事翻译工作，首先要有政治敏感。对于重要的有政治含义的词句，特别是涉及方针政策的词句，必须掌握好分寸。例如：

（1）在《中英关于香港问题的联合声明》中第三条第（六）款“香港特别行政区将保持自由港和独立关税地区的地位”。

The Hong Kong Special Administrative Region will retain the status of a free port and a separate customs territory.

“独立关税地区”初译时直接用对应词译成 an independent customs territory，这是错误的，因为容易被误解为香港特别行政区是一个独立于中国的政治实体，而实际上中国政府于 1997 年 7 月 1 日对香港恢复行使主权，香港特别行政区直辖于中华人民共和国中央人民政府。本段只是强调香港将保持自由港和独立关税地区的地位。我们后来译成 a separate customs territory 则清楚地表达了原文的意思。

（2）“中国的经济是一个大问题。”

China's economy is an important (a major) question.

这句话的本意是说中国的经济是一个很重要、范围很广的问题，如果翻译不假思索，每个字都以对应的英文词译出来，译成：“China's economy is a big problem.”，那就出了毛病，好像中国的经济出了问题。

（3）领土主权涉及国家的重大利益，因此翻译时要特别注意。譬如“中国台北”应译为 Taipei, China 或 Chinese Taipei，而不能译为 Taipei (China)，因为这样译有可能被解释为台北代表了“一个中国”，有“两个中国”之嫌。“中国大陆”应译为 mainland of China 或 China's mainland，而不能译为 mainland China，否则就变成了“大陆中国”。

（4）以色列军队应从其占领的领土上撤出去。

The Israeli forces should withdraw from the territories occupied by them.

英译文中 territories 之前的冠词 the 必须译出，因为它意味着以色列必须从其占领的全部领土中撤出去。不加冠词 the 则意味着只从部分领土中撤出去。

二、汉英翻译要求“信、达、雅”，其中以“信”为最重要，没有“信”，“达、雅”则无从谈起。要能够以最清晰明快的英文准确地表达原文的精神实质，就既要反对离开原文意思，片面追求译文流畅的自由主义倾向，又要反对拘泥于原文字句、“对号入座”，片面强调所谓“忠实”的机械主义倾向。形式和内容发生矛盾时，应重精神实质，而不是表面形式。

（5）就职时必须依法宣誓拥护……基本法，效忠香港特别行政区……

... When assuming office, … must, in accordance with law, *swear* to uphold the Basic Law of… and *swear allegiance* to the Hong Kong Special Administrative Region.

译文中有两个 swear，给人以重复的感觉，因此曾考虑用 pledge allegiance 来代替。但这样就表达不出要“宣誓效忠”的意思。所以为了忠实于原文，就只能牺牲文字美。

（6）因为这是为国家为人民办最好的事，能取得人民的支持。

This is because we have the support of the people, for we are working *in the best interests of the state and the people.*

“办最好的事”，并非指具体去 do the best things，况且英文也不这样讲。翻译这句话时应当跳出字面的约束，探明深层的含义。现译文是“为国家和人民的最高利益工作”，当然也就清楚地表达出“办最好的事”了。

（7）使中央委员会领导年轻化

Bring younger comrades to the leading posts of the Central Committee.

初译为 make the Central Committee members younger，从表面上看，一字对一字，好像很“忠实”于原文。但稍微一琢磨，就会发现它不合乎逻辑，因为不可能使原有的成员变得年轻，所谓年轻化是指把更年轻一些的人选到中央委员会。现译文处理灵活，反映了原意。

（8）改革和开放也使民族精神获得了新的解放。

The reform and opening up policy has also further liberated *the nation ideologically*. 或者 …emancipated *the minds of the people.*

初译机械地把“民族精神”译成 national spirit 这样就曲解了原文。national spirit 代表民族的精神，譬如勤劳、勇敢是一个民族的精神。这句话的原意是使得我们的民族在精神上和思想上获得新的解放。

（9）告诉已经生育和迟早要生育的孩子……

to tell their *children of today and tomorrow*

初译为 to tell the children who were already born and those who are to be born, 这个译法听起来很滑稽，而 children of today and tomorrow 则把“今天的孩子们和子孙后代”的意思都表达得十分清楚，而且有一定的文采。

（10）如果苏联能够帮助越南从柬埔寨撤军

...if the Soviet Union can *(do something to) contribute to* the withdraw of Vietnamese troops from Cambodia...

初译为 if the Soviet Union can help Vietnam withdraw Vietnamese troops from Cambodia, “帮助”译成 help 说明没有吃透原意。这句话的原意并不是说在越南撤军时，苏联应帮越南什么忙，而是指苏联应当有所作为，促使越南撤军。现译则把苏联应为越南撤军作出自己的贡献的意思讲清楚了。

（11）中国人口的 80% 在农村，如果不解决这 80% 的人的生活问题，社会就不会是安定的。

…80% of China's population live in the rural areas. There will be no social stability unless their *daily needs are met*.

"生活问题"怎样译比较准确？不能生硬地译 problem of livelihood，这样太抽象。译成 living conditions 又可能被误解为"生活条件"。这里"解决生活问题"就是指"满足生活的需要"。daily needs 包含了衣食住行等各方面，甚至精神文明方面的需要，面可宽可窄，所以现译文比较贴切。

三、某些带有中国特色的语汇很难在英文中找到对应的词或词组。译者应根据实际情况创造一些新的说法。

（12）"加强同发展中国家的团结与合作是中国外交政策的基本立足点。

To strengthen its unity and cooperation with other developing countries is a *basic principle underlying* China's foreign policy.

"基本立足点"曾经译成 a basic point of departure（基本出发点）和 a cornerstone（奠基石），但这两种译法都不够贴切，而 a basic principle underlying… 则比较确切地表达了"立足"的原意。

（13）不搞改革，不坚持开放政策，我们制定的战略目标就不可能实现。这是一个关，这个关必须过。

We cannot reach our strategic goal unless we carry out reforms and adhere to the open policy. This is a *key process* we must go through.

中文里经常谈到"过关"，"关"究竟怎么译，要看具体情况而定。在这句话里，"关"不是指 pass、juncture 或 checkpoint，也不是指 ordeal 或 barrier，而是指必须经过的一个重要的过程。

（14）可以鼓励、劝说台湾首先跟我们搞"三通"：通商、通航、通邮。

They can encourage and persuade Taiwan first to have "*three exchanges*" with us, namely, the exchange of mails, trade, and air and shipping services.

"三通"是个概括的说法，严格说来 trade 本身就是双向的，译成 exchange of trade 是不恰当的。况且 exchange 的意思是"交换、交流"，"通"字的含义不明显。"三通"的新的译法是"three links"：link of trade, travel and post，这样就把"通"字连在一起的味道译出来了。

（15）五讲四美三热爱

the movement of "five stresses, four points of beauty and three aspects of love" (stress on decorum, manners, hygiene, discipline and morals; beauty of the mind, language, behavior and the environment; love of the motherland, socialism and the Communist Party)

原来曾译为 five stresses, four beauties and three loves, 如果后面不加解释性的翻译，不了解中国情况的外国人会怎样理解呢？很可能理解为"四个美人、三个情人"。现译文避免了产生这种误解，但也不是十分理想的译法。

四、要做好汉英翻译，必须不断积累英语词汇和表达方式，以便根据不同的情况从中选择准确的译法。

（16）增强经济

galvanize, boost, invigorate, enliven, stimulate the economy

一切向钱看

money worship

mercenary mentality

money-mad

money maniac

成不了气候

cannot prevail

cannot get anywhere

cannot have their way

cannot hold sway

不能向人民交代

It would be difficult for us to account for it to the people.

We will not be able to justify ourselves to the people.

We can't present the case to the people.

We can't face our own people.

社会分配不公

income disparities

unfair distribution of social wealth

unfairness as shown by income disparities

（17）过去实行“闭关自守”政策，结果搞得“民穷财困”。

...pursued the policy of "self-seclusion", resulting in "the destitution of its people and exhaustion of its financial resources."

“民穷财困”的最初译文是：...its people were reduced to destitution and its financial resources were exhausted, 这个译文意思虽然对，但比较啰唆，不符合原文风格。中文只有四个字，因此英译文也应简练。

（18）人非圣贤，孰能无过。过而能改，善莫大焉。

To err is human and to mend is a supreme merit.

原文是文言文，如果按照白话文译成“No one can claim infallibility as none is saint; so long as he corrects his mistakes, his merit is great.”, 就太啰唆，显然不合文章的风格了。

（19）在香港特别行政区基本法中有这样一条：“禁止任何叛国、分裂国家、煽动叛乱……及窃取国家机密的行为”。

初译文为 to prohibit any act of treason, acts to spit the country, incite rebellion,…and steal state secrets, 意思虽对，但文字松散，不像法律条文。最后定稿为 to prohibit *any act of treason, secession, sedition and hem of state secrets*，这样文字严谨，适合条文的风格。

（20）除旧布新

初译为：“Get rid of the old and bring in the new. ”。这样的译法联想不妙，老人看了不会高兴。改译为：“Bid farewell to the old and usher in the new.”。

五、为了准确表达原作意思，有时译文需要加字或减字。

（21）苏联内部对中国政策究竟怎么样，我们还要观察。

The Soviet authorities have to decide *among themselves* what China policy to pursue, and so we still have to wait and see.

初译为“What China policies are to be pursued after all *within the Soviet Union*, we still have to wait and see.”。

“苏联内部”并非指“苏联国内”，而是指苏联的领导层必须决定对中国采取什么样的政策。因此现在译文加字是完全必要的。

（22）对于旧中国政府……批准的……议定书，中华人民共和国政府决定不予承认。

The Government of PRC has decided *not to recognize as binding on China* the… Protocol… ratified by the defunct government of China.

议定书是客观存在的，中国政府只是不承认它对中国有效力，因此不能译为 not to recognize the protocol。

（23）分清职责

define the duties incumbent on *each person or post*

“分清职责”的意思在中文里十分清楚，即指每个人的职责或岗位责任。但英译文如果只译 define the duties 则不清楚是什么样的 duties，而加字之后的译文就十分明确了。

（24）香港特别行政区的区旗是五星花蕊的紫荆花红旗。

The regional flag of the Hong Kong Special Administrative Region is a red flag with a bauhinia *highlighted* by five star-tippet stamens.

加上 highlighted 之后，衬托了紫荆花的风貌，文字上也比较顺。

（25）各国共同努力

multinational effort

在英译文中已包含了“共同”的意思，因此可以不必译出对应词。

（26）我们确定搞两个开放：一个是对内开放，一个是对外开放。

We have *decided on* an open policy in two respects: namely, to open up both externally and internally.

“搞”字在英译文中不必译出，因为它的含义已十分清楚。

六、对于有些固定的习惯用法和专有名词，我们应当沿用其特定的译文，而不应当改变译法。

（27）国际法主体

subject of international law 不能译成 main body of international laws

国家主权平等原则

principle of sovereign equality 不是 principle of state sovereign equality

不首先使用核武器

the non-first use of nuclear weapons 而不是 not to be the first to us nuclear weapons

七、汉英翻译的困难之一就是如何避免出现 Chinglish，使译文不晦涩，读起来像地道的英文。如何攻破这一难关？我认为主要有以下两种办法：

（一）在翻译实践中有意识地记录常用语和“老大难”的译例，找出其难点。在大量阅读英文原作，尤其是关于中国的文章、书刊时，要用心注意外国人对同一问题如何表达，进行比较研究，“择优录取”贴切的译法。

现在举最简单的例子：

（28）“提高人民的生活水平”是翻译中经常遇到的一句话。通常我们译为 to raise or improve the living standards of the people，当然这样译也不错，但在英文刊物和外国人的讲话中，很少用 living standards。他们有各种不同的说法，我们都可以借用，譬如：

a. to improve (or: better) the lives of the people

b. to improve (or: uplift) the quality of their lives

c. to improve the texture of the life of the people

（29）“差额选举”原译为：

a. the practice of nominating a larger number of candidates than the number of posts to be filled

b. election with more candidates than posts

这两种译法都是解释性的，比汉语的表达方法累赘多了。外国人用 competitive election 或 selective election，我们不妨采用，但为了带点中国特色，最好选用 multi-candidate election，这样可以和“等额选举”single-candidate election 对称。

（30）由于超生不报户口的“黑孩子”怎样译？外刊称之为 off the-book babies，这是指没有在户口簿上登记的孩子。

（31）我们经常碰到“关系网”“走后门”等词，外刊中有如下的用法：

关系网 build *a broad network of personal connections*

有关系（后台硬）的人 *a well-connected group of men*

拉关系走后门获取物资和服务 build *connections or cement backdoor sources for* goods and services

凭借个人关系来经营

operate on *networks of personal connections*

走后门和官倒

backdoor deals and official black-marketing

（32）“编内”和“编外” *in-staff and off-staff*

fall into the “off-staff” category

Anyone who is not up to the requirements should be categorized off-staff.

to be taken back to in-staff

an off-staff worker

（33）“计划外怀孕”

pregnancy outside plan 外国读者不易懂。外刊描写为 *unscheduled* pregnancy。

（34）“不应给农民发白条”

should not issue *IOUs* to farmers

“白条”是地方官员收购下农民的粮食或物资暂时付不了钱而开具的证明条，持此条兑换现金，实际上是一种拖欠形式。英文里“我欠你的债”，叫 I owe you，它的谐音是 IOU，与我们的“白条”类似。因此，“白条”的英译文完全可以借用此字。

（35）改革使权力层层下放

Reforms increasingly *passed* authority *down the line*.

“层层”译成 at every level 很难表达“一层一层往下放”的意思，现在的用法十分生动地把“层层下放”的意思译出来了。

（36）“互相借鉴对方的经验”通常译为 to learn from each other's experience；外国人用 *profitably share* our experience，英文味道更足一些。

（37）要回家同亲人团聚

want to be home with their families，表达简洁而亲切。

（38）使中日友好事业延续到 21 世纪及今后世世代代

carry the cause of China-Japan friendship *into* the 21st century and *beyond*

into 和 beyond 两个字把“延续到”和“今后世世代代”清楚地表达了出来。

（39）我每时每刻都在关心人质的命运

I *carry the fate of the hostages with me* every single day.

这个表达方式使人一目了然，关心人质的心情跃然纸上。

（40）几天的工夫，由于抢购，货架上的货就空了。

Within days, panic buying emptied store shelves.

这个表达方式生动简洁。如果译为“In a matter of a few days, the store shelves have become empty because of panic buying.”，文字啰唆姑且不谈，货物被一扫而空的抢购动态画面就看不见了。

（二）在阅读英译汉文章时，注意对我们有用的片语和句型，然后再查阅英文原作是怎么说的，也就是利用 back (or: reverse) translation 的办法来为汉英翻译服务。以下几个例子都是英→汉→英，我们不妨来逐个分析一下：

（41）These principles have nourished the soul of our nation.

这些原则一直是我们民族的精神支柱。

如果我们脱离开原来的英文，把“精神支柱”再译成英文，我们应当选择什么词？“精神支柱”的对应词是 spiritual pillar，但这两个字一个是抽象的概念，一个是具体的，搭配不当，而且是 Chinglish。采用原英文表达方式，“给民族的灵魂提供营养”，也就把“精神支柱”的内涵意思译出来了。

（42）了解彼此生活的情况，建立人与人之间友谊的纽带

“生活的情况”怎么译？英文的习惯不说 situation of our life，而译为 living conditions 则可能被误解为“生活的条件”。这里实际上是指“怎样生活和生活过得如何”。现在我们再来看看原英文是怎样表达的：

to share the texture of our daily lives, to forge the human bonds of friendship, 这里 texture 一字用得十分恰当，含义广而深，符合中文的“情况”之意，通过反译把该字学到手，以后再碰到类似的情况就可以应用自如了。

（43）中国正在发生日新月异的变化。

照字面译成英文即为“China is changing with each passing day.”, 这个译文比较平淡，只讲了中国在变化，但褒贬不清楚。采用英文原文“China crackles with the dynamics of change.”，则把中国充满活力、经历日新月异变化的韵味译出来了。

（44）互相尊重的精神是我们今天文化合作的基础。

照字面译为 The spirit of mutual respect is the basis of our cultural cooperation, 听起来是中文式的英文。采用英文原文 The framework of mutual respect sustains our own cultural cooperation today，不仅英文味道十足而且较好地表达了中文的意思。sustains 有“支撑”的意思，它代替了 the basis of，但比 basis 更有力量。

前面我通过部分实例来叙述我在汉英翻译工作中的几点体会，可能说明不了多少问题，但也许可以起到抛砖引玉的作用。

[作者简介] 王弄笙，外交部外语专家。北京外国语学院毕业，曾留学英国，曾任外交部翻译室主任、中国驻巴布亚新几内亚和萨摩亚大使，多年从事政治和外事翻译。

（《中国翻译》2000 年第 2 期）

第四节 王弄笙：汉英翻译中的 CHINGLISH

汉英翻译中的 CHINGLISH

王弄笙

严复的“信、达、雅”三个字精辟地概括了翻译的标准，这个标准要求译文既能忠实准确地表达原意，又能通顺流畅、文辞优美、可读性强。但在实践中达到这个标准，却不是一件容易的事。

汉英翻译中有两种倾向：一种是一味追求译文流畅、文辞优美，忽略乃至偏离了原意；另一种是过于拘泥原文字句，机械地从字面上“对号入座”，译文不顺而且难懂。这两种倾向都不符合“信、达、雅”标准。在外事翻译中，后一种倾向更为常见。造成这一问题既有主观原因，如怕译文出政治差错，认为直译比较保险，因而不敢越雷池一步；也有客观的因素，政治、外交翻译政策性强，不仅要求内容准确、文字严密，而且时间性强，给翻译的时间有限，译者经常处于完成任务的匆忙之中，难以从容地进行推敲润色，因而译文常常迁就中文，顾不得精益求精。在我 40 年的翻译工作中，在限定时间内出手的译文常常留下一些永久的遗憾。

当然，我们的翻译工作一直在进步、在发展，尤其是改革开放以来的 20 年时间里，解决了大量出现的新问题、新词汇、新提法，在外交和对外宣传工作中发挥了巨大作用。但我们工作中存在的问题也不容忽视，特别是译文质量方面的问题。

提高译文质量需要多方面的努力，我感到今后最需要也是最难解决的问题之一就是如何克服“中式英文”，即 Chinglish 问题。

Chinglish 是我上面所说后一种倾向的一个表现，它的存在导致某些译文生硬晦涩，使讲英语的读者敬而远之，影响了对外宣传的效果。这不能不引起我们的注意。

对 Chinglish，我们需要作一些理论上的探讨，但我认为更主要的是如何从实践中去求得解决。解决了这个问题，就可能使我们的译文更完美，更接近于“信、达、雅”这个标准。当然，这不是一朝一夕所能解决的，需要我们持续不懈地去努力。

由于中国与英语国家的历史背景、政治、经济、社会、文化以及价值观等不同，汉译英容易产生中式英文，就像英译汉容易出现欧式中文一样。因此，要求译者不仅精通汉语和英语，而且熟悉英语国家人们的生活背景、思维方式和语言习惯，时刻关注英语发展动态，多听外电，多读英文原著和原文，逐渐克服 Chinglish，使英译文读起来比较地道。

现就有关 Chinglish 几个问题谈几点看法，与前辈和同行探讨。

I. 产生 Chinglish 的主要原因及其表现形式

一、带有中国特色的词汇不断出现。改革开放以来，产生了不少新词汇、新提法，它们都是中国特有的，在英文里没有或一时找不到相应的译法，即使译出来也需要一定的磨合的过程。译文往往是解释性的，解释不了就字对字译出，因而容易出现 Chinglish。例如：

（1）“三讲”（讲学习、讲政治、讲正气）

初译：emphasize the need to study, to have political awareness and to be honest and upright

改译：emphasis on three things: study, politics and integrity

初译是解释性的，显然没有原文简洁。改译简单明了，但也没完全摆脱中式英文的味道，另外 politics 一字有时含贬意。

（2）“经济法制化” manage economic affairs according to law 或 put economic operation on a legal basis or within a legal framework

“科研成果产业化” apply scientific research results to industrial production

“国民经济信息化” build an information-based national economy

“社会知识化” build a knowledge-driven society

“国际关系民主化” Democracy should be practised in international relations.

汉语中经常出现“化”字，有的可直译，譬如“经济全球化”，现译成 economic globalization。但不能一律简单译成“ize”，譬如把上句译成 International relations should be democratized，意思就走样了。

上述例句均为解释性的译文，免不了中式英文的味道。

二、搭配不当。由于受到汉语字面的影响，翻译中往往不是犯语法错误，而是更深层次的搭配不当的问题。例如：

（3）我们将……在新的世纪里不断谱写建设有中国特色的社会主义的新篇章。

We will go on achieving fresh successes in building socialism with Chinese characteristics in the new century.

“谱写新篇章”在有的上下文可以译成 write a new chapter，例如“在中泰友好交往的历史中，谱写了新的篇章。”可译为：“We have written a new chapter in the annals of Sino-Thai friendship.”而在例句（3）中就不能这样译，因为 write a chapter 与 building socialism 是不能搭配在一起的。

（4）若干一般常见的搭配不当的例句：

“来信写道”译为 the letter writes 属搭配不当，也是拟人化，应为 the letter reads

“取得成就” make achievements 应为 score 或 attain achievements

“革命接班人” successors of the revolution 应为 revolutionary successors

“革命事业接班人” successors to the revolutionary cause 应为 successors in the revolutionary cause

有的词句尽管搭配不当，但因长期使用而被英语国家接受，可谓约定俗成，例如：

“把中国建设成为” build china into 属 Chinglish，应译为 turn China into。

但在克林顿欢迎江主席的讲话中就用了 build San Francisco into a thriving cosmopolitan city，可见英语也在吸收外来语，也在不断发展。

三、重复和累赘。汉语和英语对名词、动词、形容词和副词的用法不同，所以对重复强调的用法也不一样。汉语中经常出现重复使用名词的现象，而英语则较多地用代词、短语或省略来表达。例如：

（5）为了开好本次大会，邮联大会中国组委会全力以赴做了大量的准备工作。中国政府和北京市政府均对本次大会的筹备给予了大力支持。很多国家政府和邮政主管部门也为中国筹备本次大会提供了有益的帮助。在此，我谨向所有支持本次大会筹备工作的国家、部门和朋友们表示最衷心的感谢！

初译：The Chinese organizing Committee of the Postal Union Congress has gone all out to make preparations in order to make the Congress a success. The Central Government and the Beijing Municipal Government of China have rendered unfailing support to the preparatory work of the Congress. The Governments and competent postal departments of many countries have furnished kind assistance to China's preparatory work for the Congress. Here I'd like to express my most sincere thanks to all countries, departments and friends that have given us support to the preparatory work for the Congress.

在这句话中，“大会”出现了五次，初译在英文中也出现五次。“筹备”一词在汉语中出现三次，在英译文中也出现三次。译文句子非常累赘，有 Chinglish 的味道。

改译：The COC has gone all out and done a lot of preparatory work for the Postal Union Congress to make it a success. Both the Central Government and the Beijing Municipal Government of China have rendered unfailing support to its preparations. The Governments and competent postal departments of many countries have provided China with kind help in the work. Here I wish to express my most sincere thanks to all the countries, departments and friends that have given us support in this regard.

改译后，“大会”和“筹备”都只出现过一次，句子简练一些。

（6）为了推动中美关系的发展，中国需要进一步了解美国，美国也需要进一步了解中国。

初译：To promote the development of China-U.S. relations, China needs to know the U.S. better and the U.S. also needs to know China better.

改译：To promote China-U.S. relations, China needs to know the U.S. better and vice versa.

改后译文避免了重复，英文较顺。

（7）依法治国……建立社会主义的法治国家

初译：govern the country by law... and build the socialist country ruled by law, 这种表达累赘且费解。

改译：exercise the rule of law... and turn China into a socialist country with an adequate legal system，这样避免出现两个 country，层次比较清楚。

四、过多使用修饰词。汉语中经常用很强的副词修饰动词和形容词，用形容词修饰名词，以加重语气。而译成英语时需要斟酌，不能一字一字地照译，否则往往导致强调过头，适得其反，削弱了原文的力量。例如：

（8）我们要继续坚定不移地坚持以经济建设为中心。

我们要继续坚定不移地推进改革开放。

我们要继续坚定不移地保持社会稳定。

我们要继续坚定不移地贯彻执行独立自主的和平外交政策。

a. We will continue to unswervingly focus on economic development.

We will continue to unswervingly press ahead with reform and opening-up.

We will continue to unswervingly maintain social stability.

We will continue to unswervingly carry out the independent foreign policy of peace.

b. We will steadfastly focus on economic development, resolutely press ahead with reform and opening-up, persistently maintain social stability and unswervingly pursue the independent foreign policy of peace.

c. We will unswervingly focus on economic development, press ahead with reform and opening-up, maintain social stability and pursue the independent foreign policy of peace.

四个“坚定不移地”全译成 unswervingly，这样的英译文不仅不能加重语气，反而弱化了表达效果并显得累赘。如果译成不同的副词也不可取，给人以副词堆砌的感觉，只用一个副词修饰四个动词应该就可以了。再如：“彻底粉碎” completely smash，smash 本意就是 break completely，已经包含了“彻底”的意思，加上 completely 语气反而弱化。

“完全征服” completely conquer，conquer 不可能是 partly。

“极为可耻” extremely shameless，shameless 已是最高级。

“伟大的历史性转变” “This is a great historic change.” 在英语里，historic 已经包含了 great 的意思。

五、不适当的省略。有时汉语简洁，但译成英文必须补缺。

（9）农业搞好了，农民能自给，五亿人口就稳定了。

初译：If agriculture is in good shape and the peasants self-supporting, then the 500 million people will feel secure.

改译：If agriculture is in good shape and the peasants are self-supporting,…

前半句主语和动词都是单数，后半句主语是多数，因而必须据此加一复数动词而不能省略。

（10）人的意志想要避免，也不可能。

It cannot be avoided even if people want to 必须加 avoid it。

前半句 avoided 是被动，而后半句 avoid 是主动，因而不能省略。

六、拟人法。这种现象在汉语中经常出现，而在译成英语时，往往因受汉语字面影响而使译文有 Chinglish 的味道。

（11）中国社会主义建设的航船将乘风破浪地驶向现代化的光辉彼岸。

a. The ship of China's socialist construction will brave the wind and waves and sail to the glorious destination of modernization.

ship 没有生命，而搞 modernization 的主语应当是人。

b. China will stride forward in building socialism, like a ship braving the wind and the waves, towards the glorious destination of modernization.

b 例译文并不理想，但克服了拟人化，比 a 略有改进。

（12）世纪之交，中国外交空前活跃。

不能译成：At the turn of the century, China's diplomacy is most active.

因为 diplomacy 是没有生命的，active 的主语应当是人。现译“The turn of the century finds China most active on the diplomatic arena.”就解决了拟人化的问题。

（13）创新是一个民族进步的灵魂。

初译：...Innovation is the soul of a nation's progress.

改译：...Innovation sustains the progress of a nation.

soul 是有生命的，而 innovation 则没有，两者在一起是拟人化，改译纠正了这一点。

七、没有注意词类转换。汉译英有时不能完全按照原文是什么词类就译成什么词类，而需要根据情况对词类进行调整和转换。

（14）我们之间关系的发展使我们不仅成为亲密的朋友而且成为兄弟。

a. The development of our relations has made us not only close friends but also brothers.

b. Our relations have so grown that they bind us not only as close friends but also as brothers.

例句 b 吃透了原文的精神，转换了词类，使用了英语的表达方法，英语味道比 a 句要强。

（15）轻纺工业产品的花色品种增多，质量继续有所提高。

a. The designs and variety of light industrial and textile products have increased and their quality has continued to improve.

翻译时词类完全按照中文，有 Chinglish 的味道。

b. Light industry and textile products are now available in better designs and quality and in richer variety.

例句 b 比例句 a 有明显的改进。

（16）中国的富强和发展不会对任何国家构成威胁。

a. The strength, prosperity and development of China will pose no threat to any countries.

b. A strong, prosperous and developed China will pose no threat to any countries.

例句 a 是字对字翻译，例句 b 比较自然。

II. 如何避免 Chinglish，使译文读起来像地道的英文

一、首先要吃透中文的精神，摆脱中文字面的束缚，从英语读者的角度出发，按照英语习惯对句子进行重组，以清晰的文字表达原文的意思。

（17）维护世界和平是大有希望的。

a. To maintain world peace is very hopeful.

b. There are great hopes for the maintenance of world peace.

c. The prospect for world peace is very bright.

d. The prospects for world peace are very encouraging indeed.

前两句基本是字对字翻译，后两句英文比较通顺。

（18）同时，也从一个角度反映了他们心怀祖国、放眼世界的精神面貌和文化生活。

初译：In addition, their pictures reflect, from a certain angle, their mental outlook of having the whole country in mind and the whole world in view as well as their cultural life.

改译：In addition, their pictures reflect, from a certain angle, their mental outlook, their love for the motherland and wide-ranging interest in the world as well as their cultural life.

初译句子用了套语，比较臃肿，不好懂，改译后比较通顺易懂。

二、在工作中有意识地记录常用语和“老大难”的译例。多听外电、大量阅读英文原著原文，尤其是关于中国的文章，看看外国人对同一个词、同一个事物以及成语如何表达，进行比较研究后“择优录取”较贴切的用法，为我所用（但在借用这些词汇和表达方法时，一定要注意其政治倾向和不同的上下文）。例如：

（19）“新世纪即将到来之际”，外报、外电中有很多说法，搜集起来，用时就方便了。

as the new century approaches

on the verge of the new century

at the dawn of the new century

at the threshold of the new century

as the new century is just round the corner

（20）……增长百分之几十，有的成倍增长

increase by double-digit percentages or in some cases several-fold

如果有具体数字，譬如增长了 7.4%，翻译不会有任何困难。但“百分之几十”则不好表达，既然外报有这种表达法，而且与中文也恰好吻合，我们拿来用就是了。

（21）bring out the best in people，“人尽其才”通常译为 put people’s talents to the best use，而现英文句型更生动地表达了“充分发挥人的能力”的意思。

(Tickets, priced from…to…,) are far out of the reach of the ordinary workers“望尘莫及”

If…, all the other problems would melt away“迎刃而解”

a special one-time case“下不为例”

visitors who overstayed their permits“客人住宿证明过期”

downsizing for efficiency or cut payroll to increase efficiency“减员增效”

上述这些英文说法用的都是小字、短字、简单字，都比较形象，均可为我所用。

三、阅读英译汉文章时，注意搜集常用的词、短语、句子，查阅英语原文是如何表达，利用 reverse or back translation 的办法，不断积累地道的英语词汇和句型，也就是：英→汉→英。

（22）“我最近常常想到你和贵国”“You and your country have been much in my thoughts recently.”，这个用法比 have often thought of you 地道。

（23）“你目睹了中国和世界在本世纪走过的非凡历程”“You have witnessed the sweep of a remarkable century, both in China and abroad.”。这里 sweep 即是“历程”，它比 course 更为形象，而且有“走过”的动作。

（24）“大力继承这些遗产并发扬光大”… are dramatically building on this legacy 比 inheriting and carrying forward this legacy 简练贴切。

（25）“经济改革改变了中国的面貌和人民的日常生活”“Economic reform… has transformed China’s landscape and its people’s daily lives.”。landscape 的用法可以效仿。

（26）“美籍华人独特的文化和……勤奋观念加强了我们社会的凝聚力。”“Chinese Americans’ unique culture and values of… hard work have strengthened the fabric of our society.”。fabric 的用法值得学习。

（27）“每个国家都得根据自己的传统寻找发展方案。”“Each country has to look for development approaches within its own traditions.”。within 可以译成“根据”，那么在类似情况下，“根据”也可译成 within。

（28）“在零售和烹调行业方面，家办企业的买卖完全超过了国家办的。”“In the retail and catering sectors, household operations have completely outmarketed the state.”。household operations 和 outmarket 都可拿过来为我所用。

四、天下无难事，只怕有心人。培养对语言的浓厚兴趣，随时随地学习以英语为母语的人在不同场合对不同事物的表达方式，从中吸收对我有用的。

（29）我们在许多不同的场合都用“辛苦了”一词，而英语国家的人则随着情况的变化而变换说法。譬如，客人刚抵达时，主人可以说：“Did you have a good trip?”；某人辛勤工作后，就可以表扬他：“Thank you for your hard work.”或“You’ ve been working hard!”。

但这次江主席在检阅部队时说，“同志们辛苦了！”（还有“同志们好！”）怎样翻译，我没有把握。至于“同志们好！”显然不能译成 Hello 或 How are you 之类。是否可以译成：Salute 也许需要问问外国朋友。

再如：客人们抵达后，外国主人问道，“Would you like to make yourself comfortable?”。我想，这正是我们平时所说“想方便一下么？”

（30）会谈时英方人员说，“We have to consult the opinions of a wide cross-section of opinion.”，这正是我们所说的“我们必须广泛听取各界人士的意见”。

（31）“凭票入场”外国人用“Admission is by ticket only.”，我们可以举一反三，将“凭柬上一号观礼台”译成“Admission by card only.” or “Please present this card.” Venue: Reviewing Stand No.1。

总之，各种各样的英文材料，广告、路标、宣传品等等都可作为学习材料。

最后一点，要跟上飞速发展的时代，不断学习新出现的词汇和知识。仅举几个例子：

Quickionary	扫描器字典
Telephovision	电视电话
Illiberal Democracy	反自由的民主
A not-for profit group	非营利集团
Megatrends Asia	《亚洲大趋势》
Quantum Fund	量子基金
Hedge Fund	对冲基金

以上我只是着重谈了中式英文的产生原因以及如何避免和减少这种现象。有些例子也不尽恰当，某些改译的译文也不甚理想，仅供大家探讨，不妥之处欢迎批评指正。况且我提出的一些办法只能治标不治本。如果要从根本上来解决，还需要提高译者的综合素质，尤其是语言素质和修养，不仅汉语要好，英语尤要精通，而且知识面要广。一般说来，译者英语的造诣越深，其译文中的 Chinglish 就越少。

（《中国翻译》2000 年第 2 期）

第五节 刘士聪：写好英语句子——永远的基本功

写好英语句子——永远的基本功

刘士聪

1963 年 7 月 4 日，美国总统 John Kennedy 提名授予 E. B. White “Presidential Medal of Freedom”。这是和平时期美国授予平民百姓的最高荣誉，奖励那些对提高美国生活品质有重要贡献的人，“who contribute significantly to the quality of American life.”。

同年 12 月，President Johnson 为 E. B. White 颁发这个奖项，颁奖词说他是“An essayist whose concise comment on men and places has revealed to yet another age the vigor of the English sentence.”（from *E. B. White Reader*）

做汉英翻译，写好英语句子是一个基本的要求，也是一个很高的追求。英语句子一方面结构严密，一方面又变化无穷。严谨规范的句法形式，相对稳定的动词搭配和灵活多样的表达方式，使英语句子呈现万千的景象。好的英语作家写起句子来，真是如鱼得水，如鹤乘云，“从心所欲，不逾矩”。他们用简单的词语构筑多变的句子，表达复杂的概念。在这“简单”、“多变”和“复杂”之中，渗透着英语的丰韵和风姿。

学习翻译英语句子大概要经过三个阶段：句法阶段、语义结构阶段、审美阶段。在句法阶段，学好语法规则和句法关系。在语义结构阶段，培养对英语的“语感”，学习翻译符合英语表达习惯的句子，这需要较长的时间。在审美阶段，除了句法和语义结构方面的训练以外，主观上的审美修养起着很大作用。这牵扯到译者对具有艺术感染力的句子的判断和感悟，培养翻译具有艺术感染力的句子的能力，进而形成有个性的语言风格。

本文译者仍在第一、二阶段里摸索，仍在努力使翻译的句子正确，符合英语习惯，希望读起来尽可能像英语。这是今后很长时间里的奋斗目标。庆幸的是，本章译者认识到了这是学习汉英翻译的途径。下面所举译例，有的与此相关，有的也许牵强，只想说明这个道理。

① 关于“荼蘼”的翻译

“荼蘼”是一种花，其名称写法不一。《现代汉语词典》（修订本）里没有“荼蘼”这一词条，而有“荼縻”，其解释是，“落叶小灌木，攀缘茎，茎上有钩状的刺，羽状复叶，小叶椭圆形，花白色，有香气。供观赏。也作酴醾。”《辞源》里有 [荼蘼] 条，其解释是，[荼蘼] 即酴醾。由此看来，“荼蘼”、“酴醾”和“荼縻”是指同一种花。为方便，这里以“荼蘼”作为通用之名。

“荼蘼”偶尔出现在古诗里。《辞源》在解释“荼蘼”时引了苏轼诗句，“酴醾不争春，寂寞开最晚”。《红楼梦》第六十三回《寿怡红群芳开夜宴 死金丹独艳理亲丧》，宝玉和众姑娘玩“占花名儿”游戏，麝月掣得一签，上有一枝荼蘼花，题着“韶华胜极”四字，并有一句诗：“开到荼蘼花事了”。蔡义江在《红楼韵语》（中华书局，2004）里说，此诗句出自宋代王淇《春暮游小园》：“一从梅粉褪残妆，涂抹新红上海棠。开到荼蘼花事了，丝丝天棘出莓蔷。”

“开到荼蘼花事了”一句，霍克斯译作“After sweet rose there is no more blooming”；杨宪益和戴乃迭译作“When the rose blooms, spring flowers fade”。一是将“荼蘼”译作 sweet rose，一是将其译作 rose，两个译文都用了 rose，各有自己的考虑，这里不作讨论。如何翻译作为标题的《荼蘼》，很费一些踌躇。吴光华主编的《汉英大辞典》（1993）给“荼蘼”和“酴醾”的英译文都是 roseleaf raspberry，并附有拉丁文，这可能是植物学的分类名称，用作一篇散文的标题似乎缺少诗意。

再从文章的上下文看，文章《荼蘼》里的荼蘼花与《辞源》里的“荼蘼”（酴醾）和《现代汉语词典》（修订本）里的所描述的“荼蘼”（酴醾）是同一种花无疑，但文章里却说“他手里拿着一枝荼蘼，且行且嗅。荼蘼本不是香花，他嗅着，不过是一种无聊举动便了”，这又与《现代汉语词典》所描述的“有香气”的特征不一致。

考虑到以上种种因素，在没有找到更合适的译法之前，暂且用音译方式处理，“A *tumi* flower”，听起来不错，在行文里使用起来也方便。

② 原文：我常得着男子送给我底东西，总没有当它们做宝贝看。

译文：From time to time I would receive something from boy students but I did not attach much sentimental value to them.

这里的“总没有当它们做宝贝看”，意思是，“我”对此并不很敏感，没有因此而动感情。这反衬了下面的“我底朋友师松却不如此”，意思是，师松对这类事情很敏感，动了感情。开头的这句话没有直译，而将其译成“I did not attach much sentimental value to them”，是考虑到后面发生的事情，考虑到文章“情调”的一致，即“Shisong attached too much sentimental value to the *tumi* flower she received from Zongzhi”。

③ 原文：荼蘼本不是香花，他嗅着，不过是一种无聊举动便了。

译文：As *tumi* flowers have no scent, he did it out of habit, I guessed.

这里“无聊举动”里的“无聊”和一般意义上的无聊不同，是说那是很自然的习惯动作，手里有了花，不论香不香，会习惯性地嗅一嗅。因此，就作了这样的处理。

④ 原文：就速速伸手去接

译文：She hastened to take it…

“速速”在这里是一个重要副词，需要将其含义译出来，用了动词 hastened。

⑤ 原文：我不是从宗之手里递给你，交你照管底吗？

译文：Don't you know when Zongzhi left me in your hands he meant for you to take care of me?

这样译只是为了更自然，比“Didn't Zongzhi leave me… ”更顺口。

⑥ 原文：呀，宗之底眼、鼻、口、齿、手、足、动作，没有一件不在花心跳跃着，没有一件不在她眼前底花枝显现出来！

译文：She was excited with the illusion that its stamens began to vibrate with Zongzhi's eyes, lips, teeth, hands, feet and every gesture, dancing on each and every petal of the flower.

这里的“呀”表示女主人公激动的心情，翻译时没有用感叹词，而用了 excited。眼、鼻等在花心的跳跃是女主人公的幻觉，因此用了 illusion，并用动词 vibrate 和分词 dancing 表示“跳跃”和“显现”。这样译句子形式简洁，符合英语用法，意思清楚，也生动。

⑦ 原文：这真是……！

译文：How incredible…!

“这真是……”后面是什么，作者没有说出来。根据上下文，可能是“令人难以置信”或“不可思议”之类，所以译成“How incredible…!”

⑧ 原文：怎么一朵小小的荼蘼就可使她着了魔？

译文：Why should she have become infatuated with such a tiny flower?

“着了魔”的意思可用不同的词来表示，但 infatuated 很合适，《牛津高级英语词典》（第六版）解释该词为 having a very strong feeling of love or attraction for sb./sth. so that you cannot think clearly and in a sensible way，这个意思符合女主人公的情况。

⑨ 原文：你敢保她不把那花当做你所赐给爱底标识，就纳入她底怀中，用心里无限的情思把它围绕得非常严密吗？

译文：Who can doubt that she accepted the flower as a symbol of love from you and then began to cherish it with all her feelings from the bottom of her heart?

这里的译文对原文做了一些梳理，意思没有走样。有时需要做类似的处理。

⑩ 原文：皱一皱他那副冷静底脸庞

译文：with a fleeting frown on his well-composed face

with a fleeting frown 和 with a frown 意思有出入，区别在于是“皱一皱”，还是一直皱着眉头。

引自 *Holy Bible* (New Revised Standard Version), The New Testament, Luke: 48

[作者简介] 刘士聪，南开大学英语教授；《英语世界》顾问。2009 年，刘士聪教授因其在英汉互译实践方面做出的突出贡献，荣获中国翻译协会颁发的“资深翻译家”荣誉称号和表彰证书。

（《中国翻译》2006 年第 1 期，2018 年 4 月刘士聪教授修订）

第六节 刘士聪、高微：关于“学地道英语”

关于“学地道英语”

刘士聪　高微

最近，北京外国语大学英语系危东亚教授谈到“学地道英语”的问题，他说：“所谓地道英语就是英语特有的表达方式。从这个角度看，地道英语并不是什么玄远的东西，在我们日常接触的英语里就有，在许多课文里就有，在不少录音里就有，就等我们去发现，去学习。”

他讲得很对，讲得很好。别人也谈到过学地道英语的问题，但如何学地道英语，确实值得深入研究。“学地道英语，不仅仅是学生的事，也是老师的事，也是英语修养很好的人的事。在我们国家，有这么多人在学习英语，应该出很多出类拔萃的英语人才。他们应该讲得好，写得好，译得好，好到令英美人认可、甚至羡慕的程度。人们也许会问，在我们这个环境里学英语，这是可能的吗？人们所关心的是语言环境和学习条件。现在的语言环境和学习条件，比起从前（比如五、六十年代）好多了。现在实行开放政策，图书资料、音像资料，应有尽有；英语广播、英语电影，经常可以听到看到；与外教外商谈话交流的机会也很多；更另人鼓舞的是，现在鼓励学生努力学习，不惜花钱、添置设备、创造条件，让学生学好，学好了还给奖学金。在过去条件比较拘谨的情况下出了一大批优秀英语（也包括其他语种）人才，现在完全有条件出更多、更优秀的人才。

在我们这个以汉语为母语的语言环境里，能否学习地道英语？应该肯定地说，能够。只要下够了工夫，又讲究学习方法，完全能够的。

讲到学习方法，人们都主张多听、多说、多读、多写，在这几“多”当中，“多读”尤其重要，特别是英语已经有了一定的基础，再提高一步，主要是靠多读。读书对学英语的中国人很重要。即使是以英语为母语的人们，不读书也写不出好文章。既然读书对提高英语实践能力很重要，如何读书，也就成了一个十分重要的问题。

首先，需弄清什么是地道英语，读书时可多加注意。严格地说，地道英语应该是现当代英语民族中受过良好教育、有较高文化修养的人们所讲、所写并为他们所认同、所接受、所欣赏的英语。对于学习英语的中国人，要想使自己的英语能让英、美人认同、接受、欣赏，不是很容易的事，但也不是不可能的事。这需要花很长时间的工夫，涉及多方面能力的培养，其中最主要的是通过读书逐步熟悉英语思维方式和学习地道的英语表达方式。这在句子范围内，主要是指字词、习语和句式；在句子范围以上，主要是指句子之间或在语段之内的衔接。

一、句式

若论与思维方式直接相关的表达方式以及句与句之间的衔接方式，英语与汉语有很多相似和对应之处，这种现象在英美人写的英语作品里不难发现；但由于其特有的思维方式而产生的“特有的表达方式”，则需作重点研究。我们所讲、所写的英语与英语本族人所讲、所写的英语之间的差异也主要表现在这方面。

Robert Graves 在他的 *The Reader over Your Shoulde*r 一书中作了很好的分析。他说，“‘呆板’英语和外国语言很相似，外国人很机械，因而也很正确地使用它，但以英语为母语的人总是倾向于使用灵活英语。‘呆板’英语就像阿拉伯口语一样很容易学，但灵活英语则像学者使用的阿拉伯语，没有一个智者会声称他已经掌握了。”(“Fixed” English compares well enough with other languages, but is often more mechanically, and therefore more correctly employed by foreigners than by those whose mother tongue it is and who are always inclined to slip back into free English. “Fixed” English is an easy language to learn, like colloquial Arabic; but of free English, as of scholarly Arabic, no wise person will ever claim final mastery.) 他所说的“灵活”英语就是我们依据自己所习惯的思维方式所构造的句子，字词是英语的，思维方式和句法是汉语的。这种英语虽然语法总是很正确，但是机械（mechanical）、呆板（rigid）、僵硬（stiff），没有灵气，缺乏美感。这在学生的作文和翻译练习里多得很，这种

现象之所以存在而且难以克服，就是因为对使用英语的本族人“特有的表达方式”不够敏感，因而也就缺少模仿的意识。例如：

例 1 *It is impossible* to begin to understand the structure of Oxford or Cambridge *unless* one first understands the nature and function of the Colleges, *which* have no resemblance whatever with the institutions which are also called “colleges” in American universities. (“Oxford and Cambridge: World-famous Universities”)

这句话说了两层意思：不首先弄清楚这些学院的性质和功能是不可能懂得牛津或剑桥结构；这些学院和美国大学里也称作学院的机构不同。我们凭直觉知道这是基于英语思维写出来的英语句子，从句子组织上看，“It is impossible to… unless”是常见的英语句式；后面跟着两个从句，一个是以 which 引起的非限定性定语从句，它又包含着另一个也是以 which 引起的限定性定语从句。先说句子的核心内容，再说从句，再用后置的限定从句说明前面的从句里需要说明的成分。我们讲汉语的人在表达同样内容时思维方式是不同的，因而语序也随之不同。读书时对于这种现象多留意，在写作和翻译时便于模仿。

例 2 The dominating position of the national daily morning papers is due to the *smallness* of the country, *with every* large town in England and Wales *able to be reached* by train in less than five hours from London. (“Voracious Newspaper Readers”)

这句话值得注意的是它的简洁，作者用一个短语 due to the smallness of the country 作表语，而没有用表示原因的从句 because the country is small。表达同样的意思，短语总比从句简明、轻巧，此外，smallness 不是常规用法，它是由形容词加 -ness 构成的名词，这种用法本身就很新颖；再有，with 短语和被动的不定式短语 able to be reached 也是构成句子简洁的有效办法。用简洁的句式把复杂的概念表达得如此清楚，这不能不说是英语的语言之美，也不能不说作者运用语言的巧妙、熟练。

例 3 Sportsmanship is the ability to practise a sport in obedience to its rules, while also showing generosity to one’s opponent and good temper in defeat. (“The English Reserve”)

这是一个关于体育道德（sportsmanship）的定义，作者借助三个介词短语说明“体育道德”所包含的三个重要内容：遵守体育规则；对对手表现宽容；失败时不失风度。英语介词短语的功能值得研究。

例 4 My Lord Mayor, My Lords, and Gentlemen: I am sure you will not be surprised to be told that the poor words at my command do not enable me to respond adequately to your most kind greeting, nor the too flattering words which have fallen from my friend, the Lord Mayor, and from my distinguished colleague, the Lord Chancellor. (Edward John Phelps)

这是美国驻英国大使爱德华·菲尔普斯于 1900 年离任时发表的告别演说中的第一句话，表现出作者的虚怀。这句话要说明的关键内容是 You will not be surprised，这个意思在英语里是开门见山先说出来，然后再说为什么；而汉语的习惯多是先说明情况再下结论。石幼珊的译文注意到了这一点，译得很恰当：

"市长先生、各位爵士、各位先生：诸位对我的亲切致意，还有我的朋友市长先生和我的尊敬同行大法官阁下刚才对我的过誉之词，对于这一切，要是我说自己拙于词令，无法用语言表达我的感激，*想必你们不会觉得奇怪*。"

如果按英语的顺序翻译这句话，汉语就别扭了。

例5　To such a task we can dedicate our lives and our fortunes, everything that we are and everything (that) we have, with the pride of those who know that the day has come when America is privileged to spend her blood and her might for the principles that gave her birth and happiness and the peace which she has treasured. (Woodrow Wilson)

这是美国第二十八届总统威尔逊要求国会对德宣战讲话中的一句话，全句 59 个字，却奇迹般地包含了七个不同功能的从句，一个套一个，环环相扣，把一层套一层的信息在一个十分紧凑的句子里说得清清楚楚，值得我们仔细研究。

例6　In mid-afternoon a curious darkening of the sky, and a lull in everything that had made life tick; and the way the boats suddenly swung the other way at their moorings with the coming of a breeze out of the new quarter, and the premonitory rumble. Then the kettle drum, then the snare, then the bass drum and cymbals, then crackling light against the dark, and the gods grinning and licking their chops in the hills. (E. B. White: "Once More to the Lake")

这一段文字描写午后下雨之前天气变化的景象，用的是两个不完全句，分别由几个短语组成，有名词短语和形容词短语。前一句叙述天气初变的情况，节奏较慢，这种慢节奏是由名词短语与 a lull in everything 及其从句和 the way 及其从句来实现的；在 the premonitory rumble 到来之后，是一系列雷电交加的变换情景，节奏很快，与上一句形成对照。这种写法是为了创造一种特殊的气氛，表现手法值得特别注意。

以上几个例子意在说明，英语本族好的作家所写的文字，对于我们总有值得借鉴的东西。对英语句式进行全面归纳和概括十分困难，因为社会现实的复杂性，以及由社会现实而产生的人的思想情感的微妙性，再加上这二者又处在不断变化之中，实践中的语言现象比理论家的总结要丰富得多，要复杂得多。如果再把每个人、每个作家都有他 / 她自己独特的表达方式和叙事风格考虑在内，语言的丰富性和复杂性是难以想象的。诚然，一个民族的思维方式有其可以归纳的特点，对其语言的表现方法也可以进行总结和分类，进行分析、综合，找出其带有规律性的东西，是文体学研究的重要内容。对于学习用英语写作和翻译的人来说，一方面要借鉴理论性的总结来提高自己的理性认识，但更应该在向活的语言学习中增加感性认识，并在实践中学习、模仿、提高，并逐步形成自己的语言风格。学习写作和翻译，一方面在原则上，即在特定语言的基本规律上"不逾矩"，一方面又能在运用上"从心所欲"，即有自己的语言特色（当然，一个人语言特色的形成还包括思想、情感和气质等因素），否则，学习写作和翻译的人都按照别人归纳出来的若干句型去写、去译，文章难免会有千篇一律之嫌，失去了个性，丧失了风格。怀特说过，"初学者……应该坚决摆脱人们相信的那些表示风格的手段——都是一些造作、花活和粉饰。风格是通过平淡、朴素、有序和真诚表现出来的。”(The beginner ...should begin by turning resolutely away from all devices that are popularly believed to indicate style—all mannerisms, tricks, adornments. The approach to style is by way of plainness, simplicity, orderliness, sincerity.)

我国清代著名爱国者、向西方学习的先驱容闳 (1828—1912) 在《西学东渐记》(*My Life in China and America*) 一书中提到他在马萨诸塞州孟松学校留学时的校长查尔斯·哈孟德时说:“他培养学生在古典和当代文学中爱美的情趣，并具有以此来激励学生的本领。在我们每日的诵读课上，他特别强调指出句子及其结构之美，比强调语法规则、语气和时态更甚。” (He had the faculty of inspiring his pupils with the love of the beautiful, both in ancient and modern literature. In our daily recitations, he laid a greater stress on pointing out the beauties of a sentence and its construction, than he did on grammatical rules, moods and tenses.)

我们作为学英语的学生，研究各种特有的英语句式和结构，研究英语句子之美，并在实践中学习写好句子，是学习地道英语的重要一步。

二、句子的衔接

学习地道英语先是学习写好句子，然后把具有相关内容的句子有机地衔接起来，组成一个语段,这是学习地道英语的又一个重要步骤。句子的衔接有很多手段,举以下几种为例:

1. 依赖文章的内在逻辑

关于写文章，毛泽东说过这样的话:“看一篇文章好不好，不一定看文章各段落之间文字上的联系如何，主要是看文章的内在联系如何。如果内在联系得紧，那么倒不一定追求形式上联系”(《今晚报》, 99 / 7 / 1)。

句与句之间的连接也是一样。依赖文章的内在联系将多个句子在更大的范围内组成一个有机体，这在我们的古汉语里比较多见。如范仲淹的《岳阳楼记》开头几句就是这样:

例 1　庆历四年春,滕子京谪守巴陵郡。越明年,政通人和,百废俱兴。乃重修岳阳楼,增其旧制，刻唐贤、今人诗赋于其上，属予作文以记之。

作者用三句话，说了三个“属予作文以记之”的重要背景内容，句与句之间没有必要使用连接词或副词，全靠文章内容的联系自然衔接起来的。

在英语作品里,这种情况也很普遍。十九世纪英国作家 Robert Bridges 有一篇散文叫“A School Portrait”，文章的第一段共四句话，句与句之间未用一个连接词:

例 2　I had not visited Eton for many years, when one day passing from the Fellows' Library into the Gallery I caught sight of the portrait of my school-friend Digby Dolben hanging just without the door among our most distinguished contemporaries. I was wholly arrested, and as I stood gazing on it, my companion asked me if I knew who it was. I was thinking that, beyond a few whom I could name, I must be almost the only person who would know. Far memories of my boyhood were crowding freshly upon me:…

这四句话中每一句都是前一句的自然发展。作者访问伊顿公学时无意间看见老同学的肖像于是被吸引住了，同伴问那是谁，他认为他几乎是认识他的唯一的人，接着便是一系列往事的回忆。这种本身就有逻辑性的内容以及有条有理的叙述方式无须使用连接词，用了反而有多余之嫌。这样写的结果就是一个行文既清晰又简洁的段落，使读者的注意力集中在一个核心内容上。

2. 使用连接词和副词

在多数情况下，句与句的衔接是靠连接词和副词。

例 3

A) This portrait-gallery of old Etonians is very select… But how came Dolben there?

B) English food has a bad reputation abroad. This is most probably because foreigners in England are often obliged to eat in the more "popular" type of restaurant. Here it is necessary to prepare food rapidly in large quantities, and the taste of the food inevitably suffers, though its quality, from the point of view of nourishment, is quite satisfactory. Still, it is rather dull and not always attractively presented. Moreover, the Englishman eating in a cheap or medium price restaurant is usually in a hurry at least at lunch and a meal eaten in a leisurely manner in pleasant surroundings is always far more enjoyable than a meal taken hastily in a business-like atmosphere. In general, it is possible to get an adequate meal at a reasonable price; in fact, such a meal may be less expensive than similar food abroad. For those with money to spare, there are restaurants that compare favourably with the best in any country. (*British Scenes*—"English Food")

作者在这里使用了多种手段把句子连接成一个有机的段落，其中有指示代词（this），副词（here、still、moreover），介词短语（in general、for those with money to spare）等，这是一个比较典型的运用语言衔接手段将句子组成语段的例子。

3. 使用代词

人称代词和指示代词的使用不仅是为了避免重复，也是句与句之间的连接手段。下面一段话有五个短句，第一句里的 Britain's National Anthem，分别在后面的四句话里三次被代词 It 所代替，一次被物主代词 Its 所代替，这样就构成了一个前后连贯、内容集中的段落。

例 4　Mystery and romance surround Britain's National Anthem. It was never written or composed as such. It grew out of the people. It is first mentioned in the 16th century. But its text (first in Latin) has frequently been changed and added to. (*British Scenes*—"God Save the Queen")

4. 在一个语段里重复使用一个重要词汇可以使句子衔接紧密，产生行文的连贯性。例如下面一段里，在 have precedence over、take precedence over 和 enjoys precedence 中重复使用了 precedence 一词，这就把几个句子自然而然地连成一个有机的整体。

例 5　The sons of the sovereign have precedence over daughters. The daughters take precedence over daughters of the sovereign's brother. In both cases seniority enjoys precedence.

(*British Scenes*—"The Queen: Personification of the State")

5. 前后照应

有时采取修辞手段使一个语段里的前后意思互相照应，也可以产生句与句之间的连贯效果。下面两个句子之间虽然没用连接词，但第二句里的 from this bird's eye view 是和第一句里的 fly…in a helicopter 相照应，两个句子浑然一体。

例 6　If you could *fly low over London, in a helicopter,* for example, you would see below you the winding course of the River Thames, flowing from west to east and dividing London into the two parts known as the north bank and the south bank. The division between "the City" and the "West End" would be less obvious *from this bird's eye view*. (*British Scenes*—"London")

以上是连接句子的几种主要方式，在阅读中注意观察，还能发现一些别的连接方式。

三、用词

优秀的英美作家用词总是恰如其分（the right word in the right place）。对于学英语的外国人来说，做到用词恰当，包括恰当的搭配，是一件十分困难的事情。美国语言学家奈达曾经说："一般人可以在 4—5 年内很好地掌握一种语言的句法，但如果有谁——特别是在进入成年以后开始学习外语——能在二十年之内掌握一种外语的习惯搭配，那是很难得的。" (The average person can quite well master the syntactic structure of a language in four or five years, but it is the rare individual who masters the semotactic structure of a foreign language in less than twenty years, especially if he begins this process after he has become an adult. (*The Theory and Practice of Translation*, 158—159)

可见，正确使用词汇和搭配不是小事情，尤其是英、美人用起来得心应手、我们不太容易掌握的那些简单词汇和搭配，例如下面各句里斜体字所标明的部分：

例 1　It should be noted that everyone has to pay these contributions, whether or not he has *occasion* to use the benefits he is entitled to. (*British Scenes*)

我们常见的 occasion 作 a particular time or situation 解，如 "Soon it (British National Anthem) was sung on all patriotic occasions."。而这个例句里的 occasion 作 "机会" 解，这时，我们常常会用 opportunity 或 chance。

例 2　小姨独自用块旧布缠了一柄 "刷子"，将里外墙壁刷了一遍。（梁晓声：《黑纽扣》）

She *fashioned* a brush with old strips of cloth, and used it to wash all the walls.

（"The Black Button," translated by Liu Shicong & Christine Ferreira）

同样，fashion 是常见名词，作为动词很新颖，意思是 to make in a certain way。因此，这句话的译文使用 fashion 是很好选择。习语的使用不在多少，而在恰当。下面的例句都是很好的习语：

例 3　In the final test, the success of our race will be *in proportion* to the service that it renders to the world. (Booker T. Washington's words)

in proportion to 可作 "相称" 或 "成比例" 讲，这句话可译为 "我们的种族成功与否取决于它对世界所做的贡献”。

例 4　There is no censorship of the press in Britain, though all newspapers are responsible for what they publish, and can be sued for libel for publishing articles that *go beyond the bounds of decency*. (*British Scenes*)

To go beyond the bounds of decency，这个习语的核心词是 decency,《牛津高阶英汉双语词典》说，这个词的意思是，“honest, polite behaviour that follows accepted moral standards and shows respect for others”，这个意思用一个汉语词汇难以表达完整。它可以用在不同的语境下，是一个很好的搭配。

总的来说，一篇英文韵味很浓的文章在句式和句与句的衔接上符合英语民族的思维方式和语序，在字词和习语的使用上恰如其分，只有这样才能准确地表达作者的思想和情感。这是从学习语言的角度说，如果进而讨论文章的说服力和感染力，还要涉及修辞和整篇文章的组织等问题，可由专家们另作专门的论述。现在还是回到我们的题目上来，作为学英语的中国人，若能从字词、习语、句子以及句子的连接几个方面去努力，经过长时间的观察、研究和实践，学习地道英语并不是不可能的。

这个道理是容易讲通的，而能不能学好，关键在实践（说、读、写、译）。正如我国魏晋时代文学理论家陆机在《文赋》中的一句话：“恒患意不称物，文不逮意，盖非知之难，能之难也。”

（《天津外国语学院学报》2000 年第 1 期，2018 年 4 月刘士聪教授修订）

[作者简介] 刘士聪，南开大学英语教授；高微，天津科技大学外国语学院教授

主要参考文献

1. 程镇球．翻译论文集．北京：外语教学与研究出版社，2002.
2. 程镇球．汉英翻译问题——在全国中译英学术研讨会上的发言 //《中国翻译》编辑部．中译英技巧文集．北京：中国对外翻译出版公司，1992.
3. 段连城．呼吁：请译界同仁都来关心对外宣传 //《中国翻译》编辑部．中译英技巧文集．北京：中国对外翻译出版公司，1992.
4. 冯树鉴．名词化短语的特点与翻译．外语与外语教学，1992（4）：35-40.
5. 过家鼎．联合国的翻译工作．中国翻译，2004（1）：52-54.
6. 姜倩，何刚强．翻译概论．上海：上海外语教育出版社，2008.
7. 孔慧怡．重写翻译史．香港：香港中文大学翻译研究中心，2005.
8. 孔慧怡．99 全国暑期英汉翻译高级讲习班学员资料调查．中国翻译，2000（2）：60-62.
9. 李钢．和而不同——历史文化视阈下的《论语》英译研究．博士论文．长沙：湖南师范大学，2012.
10. 李长栓．非文学翻译理论与实践．北京：中国对外翻译出版公司，2004.
11. 李学平．通过翻译学英语——150 实例使你迅速提高汉译英能力．天津：南开大学出版社，2012.
12. 刘宓庆．新编汉英对比与翻译．北京：中国对外翻译出版公司，2006.
13. 刘晓丹．法律语言的特点与法律翻译．牡丹江教育学院学报，2007（3）：40-41.
14. 卢小军．中美网站企业概况的文本对比与外宣英译．中国翻译，2012（1）：92-97.
15. 马会娟．汉译英翻译能力研究．北京：北京师范大学出版社，2013.
16. 马祖毅．中国翻译简史．北京：中国对外翻译出版公司，1998.
17. 马祖毅，任荣珍．汉籍外译史．武汉：湖北教育出版社，2003.
18. 马士奎．从母语译入外语：国外非母语翻译实践和理论考察．上海翻译，2012（3）：20-26。
19. 茅盾．为发展文学翻译事业和提高翻译质量而奋斗 //《翻译通讯》编辑部．翻译研究论文集（1949—1983）．北京：外语教学与研究出版社，1984.
20. 孟祥春．“我只能是我自己”——葛浩文访谈．上海翻译，2013（4）：46-49.

21. 平卡姆 . 中式英语之鉴 . 北京：外语教学与研究出版社，2009.
22. 钱钟书 . 林纾的翻译 . 中国翻译，1985（11）: 2-10.
23. 任学良 . 汉英比较语法 . 北京：中国社会科学出版社，1981.
24. 谭载喜 . 西方翻译简史 . 北京：商务印书馆，2000.
25. 施晓菁 . 引言 // 李长栓，施晓菁 . 理解与表达：汉英翻译案例讲评 . 北京：外文出版社，2012.
26. 李长栓，施晓菁 . 理解与表达：汉英翻译案例讲评 . 北京：外文出版社，2012.
27. 王克非 . 翻译文化史论 . 上海：上海外语教育出版社，1997.
28. 王建国，何自然 . 重过程，还是重结果——译者的母语对英译文本的影响 . 上海翻译，2014（2）: 7-12.
29. 谢天振等 . 中西翻译简史 . 北京：外语教学与研究出版社，2009.
30. 邢福义，汪国胜 . 现代汉语 . 武汉：华中师范大学出版社，2011.
31. 杨封宁 . 英汉语言比较与翻译 . 天津：天津大学出版社，2006.
32. 叶子南，施晓菁 . 汉英翻译指要——核心概念与技巧 . 北京：外语教学与研究出版社，2011.
33. 余华 . 许三观卖血记 . 收获，1995（1）.
34. 余华 . 在细雨中呼喊 . 北京：作家出版社，2008.
35. 余华 . 兄弟 . 北京：作家出版社，2008.
36. 赵兴民 . 联合国文件翻译 . 北京：外文出版社，2011.
37.《中国翻译》编辑部 . 中译英技巧文集 . 北京：中国对外翻译出版公司，1992.
38. 庄绎传 . 汉英翻译 500 例 . 北京：外语教学与研究出版社，1980.
39. Campbell, S. *Translation into the Second Language*. London: Longman, 1997.
40. Li, Thompson. 主语与主题：一种新的语言类型学 . 国外语言学，1984 :（2）.
41. Lise W. Machine Translation—Is It Working in Japan?. *Language International*, 9 (1):27-35.
42. Neubert A. Competence in Languages, and in Translation// C Schaffner, B Adab. *Developing Translation Competence*. Amsterdam: John Benjamins, 2000: 3-18.
43. Nida E. Science of Translation. *Language*, 1969 (3):483-498.
44. Pym A. Redefining Translation Competence in an Electronic Age: In Defense of a Minimalist Approach. *Meta*, 2003 (4): 481-497.
45. Yu Hua. *To Live*. trans. Michael Berry. New York: Anchor Books, 2003.
46. Yu Hua. *Chronicle of a Blood Merchant*. trans. Andrew F. Jones. New York: Anchor Books, 2004.
47. Yu Hua. *Cries in the Drizzle*. trans. Allan Barr. New York: Anchor Books, 2007.
48. Yu Hua. *Brothers*. trans. Eileen Cheng-yin Chow, Carlos Rojas. New York: Pantheon Books, 2009.

参考答案及参考译文

第二章　汉英翻译的过程

第一节　练习题

A special economic zone is a medium for introducing technology, management and knowledge. It is also a window for our foreign policy. Through the special economic zones we can import foreign technology, obtain knowledge and learn management, which is also a kind of knowledge. As the base for our open policy, these zones will not only benefit our economy and train people but enhance our nation's influence in the world. Public order in Shenzhen is reportedly better than before, and people who slipped off to Hong Kong have begun to return. One reason is that there are more job opportunities and people's incomes and living standards are rising, all of which proves that, in the final analysis, ethical progress is based on material progress.

第二节　练习题

We should not be too romantic in interpersonal relations. Human beings are funny in that they tend to first see merits in a new acquaintance. This is like dining in a restaurant. You will be favorably impressed with the first two courses. However, the more you have, the more sober you become until the dinner ends up with all the flaws exposed. Consequently, your joy would give way to anger; your praises to criticism or even fault-finding; and your nodding in agreement to shaking the head. What accounts for all this is that, in the first place, you are hungry when you start to eat. As the saying goes, hunger is the best sauce and vice versa. Secondly, you will feel fresh the first time you visit the restaurant, which can be called "The Alien Effect."

第三章　汉英翻译语篇实践

第一节　练习题

1. 澳门简介

Introduction to Macao

As a small fishing village, Macao was originally named as Hao Jing or Hao Jing Ao, because the port then was called "Ao." Macao and the surrounding areas were teeming with Hao (i.e. oyster). The inner wall of the oyster shell is as shiny as mirror, so Macao got the name of Hao Jing (oyster mirror), and the later generations changed it into a more elegant homophone. From this name, some aliases of Macao such as Hao Jiang, Hai Jing and Jing Hai were derived.

The name of Macao originated from the Goddess of the Sea, who was worshipped by Chinese fishermen. The descendants built a temple for the Goddess at the place where she came ashore.

When the Portuguese reached here in the mid-16th century, they asked the locals about the name of the location, but the locals had a misunderstanding that the Portuguese asked the name of the temple. The answer is "Ma Ge," and according to the pronunciation, the Portuguese transformed it into "MACAU," the Portuguese name of Macao. In the following 400 years, eastern and western cultures blended well in this city, and a large number of historic and cultural heritages were sustained, endowing Macao with distinct features.

Since December 20, 1999, Macao has become a special administrative region of the People's Republic of China. Under the "One Country, Two Systems" policy, Macao has been enjoying a high degree of autonomy as well as the rights of administration, legislation, independent justice and final adjudication. Macao's social and economic characteristics will be preserved and carried on.

With a small area, Macao is one of the most densely populated regions in the world, and has reached high income per capita compared with other Asian regions.

Location

The Macao Special Administrative Region (MSAR) is a part of China's territory. It is located in the Pearl River Delta at the southeast coast of China. Bordering on Guangdong Province, it is 60 km from Hong Kong and 145 km from Guangzhou.

Area

Due to land reclamation along its coastline, Macao has expanded its land area from 10.28 km^2 in the 19th century to 28.6 km^2 today, which is equal to one fortieth of Hong Kong and one twenty-third of Singapore. Macao consists of Macao Peninsula and the two islands of Taipa and Coloane. Macao Peninsula adjoins the Chinese mainland in the north, and three bridges (i.e. Nobre de Carvalho Bridge, Friendship Bridge (Ponte da Amizade) and Sai Van Bridge) in the south link the peninsula to Taipa, while the two islands are connected by the six-lane 2.2 km Taipa-Coloane Causeway.

Chinese and Western Cultures and Customs

Before the 19th century, Macao was one of the major ports of China as well as an important port in Asia for international trade. Along with the flourishing of trade, Macao attracted many people around the world; hence, a city where the people from Europe, Asia, Africa and America were mixed together came into being.

As the earliest, most frequent and most important place in China for having access to modern Western articles and culture, Macao was regarded as a bridgehead for China to contact Western culture. Meanwhile, the foreigners living in Macao, through various media, introduced to other countries the Chinese culture, ideologies and customs they had known in Macao—a gateway for foreign countries to learn about China.

A large number of China's pioneering undertakings were initiated in Macao, e.g. the first Western-style university (Colégio de Sao Paulo), the first Western-style hospital (St. Raphael's Hospital), the first Western-style printing house (Printing House Attached to Colégio de Sao Paulo), the first newspaper in foreign language (*A Abelha da China*).

During the past 400 years, various communities were established in the Historic Center of Macao with joint efforts of the Chinese and Portuguese, representing the architectural features of Chinese-style and Western-style buildings and the blending of different religions, cultures, habits and customs of the Chinese and Portuguese. The affectionate, unsophisticated and comprehensive community culture has become the most valuable characteristic of Macao.

World Heritage

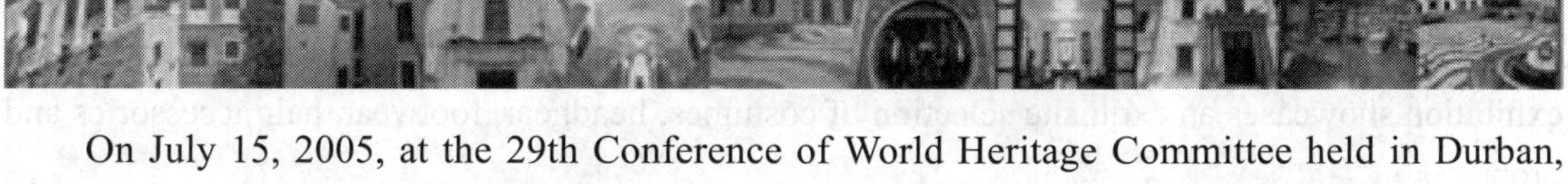

On July 15, 2005, at the 29th Conference of World Heritage Committee held in Durban, South Africa, "The Historic Center of Macao" was recognized and became China's 31st item of world heritages. In the selection of the Top Five Most Beautiful Ancient City Blocks of China by *Chinese National Geography Magazine*, Macao ranked the third place. In the Historic Center, there are 25 historic buildings, where Macao residents assemble and live. These sites are appealing to tourists.

The Historic Center of Macao includes the oldest Western architectural heritage in China today, and represents the combination of eastern and western architectural techniques. The Historic Center of Macao witnesses the development of Western religions and cultures in China and the Far East, and testifies the historic origin of China's folk religions spreading to the Western world.

The Historic Center of Macao is the reflection of diversified coexistence of Chinese and Western cultures, constituting the unique blend of cultural heritages existing in China's historic cities. The Historic Center of Macao presents an orderly integration of Chinese and Western communities, which have been indispensable to the habits, customs and traditions of the residents from different places since ancient times.

The Historic Center of Macao has the best preservation reflecting the exchange between Chinese and Western cultures in the over 400 years. It is China's oldest and biggest historic area with rich and centralized European and Chinese architectural heritages while European-style buildings take the dominating place. It not only witnesses the spreading of Western religions and cultures in China and the Far East, but displays the exchange, mutual supplementation and coexistence of Chinese and Western cultures in over 400 years.

For more details concerning the Historic Center of Macao, please enter this website: http://www.macauheritage.net/mherit/indexE.asp

2. 粤剧简介

Introduction to Cantonese Opera

Tracing its roots back almost 300 years, Cantonese Opera originated and got popularized in the provinces of Guangdong and Guangxi in China. As a comprehensive art form, it blends literature, history, music, dance, visual and martial arts. In addition to those elements, the art of the theater plays an important role: costumes, headgear, makeup, props, stage sets and lighting all serve to accentuate the characterization of the roles that are performed and create the right atmosphere for the different situations that are presented on stage.

With the aim of presenting the highlights of the theatrical arts of Cantonese Opera, this exhibition showcases an exquisite selection of costumes, headgear, footwear, hair accessories and props.

3. 香港机场世贸中心简介

Introduction to World Trade Center—Hong Kong International Airport (WTC-HKIA)

The World Trade Center—Hong Kong International Airport is the world-class, professional and fully-equipped business and conference centers and members' club.

The World Trade Center—Hongkong International Airport (WTC-HKIA), located in one of the world's premier international hubs, is in a uniquely accessible location. With a provision of comprehensive services such as ready-to-use offices, conferencing facilities, a trade information library, and the members' club (Airport World Trade Center (AWTC) Club) with fine dining facilities, this provides a one-stop and highly flexible working environment that every business traveler needs. You can enjoy our fully furnished offices by simply sitting down, plugging in, and becoming operational instantly. Our offices are available either for personal office use or for business meetings; even hourly leases can be tailor-made for you. After a taxing business meeting, you can adjourn to the AWTC Club for your dining pleasure, which serves award-wining Chinese cuisine. It is the perfect place to entertain clients and business partners. The WTC-HKIA is a Regular Member of the World Trade Centers Association consisting of over 300 WTCs representing more than 750,000 international businesses over 90 countries.

Website: www. wtchkia.com Email:info@wtchkia.com

4. 香港浸会大学年报摘译

Planting the Seeds of Knowledge

In September 2012, the Hong Kong Baptist University(HKBU) welcomed the historic double cohort of students under the "3+3+4" academic reform. The run-up to this milestone event involved meticulous preparation in term of ensuring that the University had the requisite teaching and learning facilities to cope with the expanded student body and the administrative infrastructure to simultaneously deliver two undergraduate programs. Despite the immense complexities and many challenges, HKBU's plan for the implementation of the "3+3+4" reform was smoothly rolled out.

To further enhance HKBU's whole person education ethos, the University designed a new four-year undergraduate curriculum. The new curriculum seeks to equip students with both breadth and depth of knowledge, featuring an effective General Education (GE) program, the opportunity for greater choice through free electives and more interdisciplinary exposure. In addition, an outcome-based approach to teaching and learning that emphasizes the University's seven graduate attributes was adopted across all programs. Most Faculties/Schools also moved to adopt broad-based admission giving students an overall understanding of their chosen discipline in the first year which would help them make an informed choice of major in the second year.

The GE program at HKBU has been purpose-built to provide students with the foundation of a well-rounded university education. In 2012–2013, 142 GE courses, including six interdisciplinary courses, were offered. From 2013–2014, the "GE Off Campus" project will be launched to encourage students to link GE with their personal and professional development through participation in thought-provoking activities such as appreciation of drama, art performance and experiential learning. With the sponsorship of the HKBU Century Club, the "General Education Outstanding Students Award Scheme" will also be launched to reward students who have excellent academic results in GE courses, active participation in GE activities and enthusiastic community service.

第二节 练习题

1.

Under the old economic operational mechanism, the effectiveness of resource utilization is seriously handicapped. An incomplete market, coupled with lethargic company performance, inevitably keeps resource utilization efficiency low, and ineffective supply of resources cannot be remedied with the economy's internal strength alone. In both scenarios, intervention in the economy can be effected only through noneconomic means. However, if economic operational mechanisms remain intact, problems will keep snowballing even if the government can reconcile the conflicts resulting from low resource utilization efficiency through noneconomic means. When the problems come to a head, the conflict between resource supply and demand will be fully exposed. An economy in disarray invariably forces firms to seek the way out through underground transactions in an attempt to protect their interests (as well as the interests of their workers). This may enable a few firms to somewhat improve their resource utilization efficiency, but for society as a whole, such efficiency will remain low and tend to be aggravated by such underground transactions. This is because the underground market may force firms to pay a high price if they want to turn such transactions to their favor, thereby steering resource allocation further from the right course.

2.

In 2009, China National Offshore Oil Corporation (CNOOC) overcame the adverse impacts of austere macroeconomic difficulties, typhoon and others on production and operation, and achieved the performance better than expectation. This company kept good development and healthy financial operation, and achieved the sales income of RMB 209.60 billion and total profits of RMB 52.40 billion. At the end of 2009, the total assets of this company reached RMB 518.30 billion, 20.4 percent up the same period of the previous year. CNOOC realized the synchronous growth of reserves and output and the synergistic development of upstream, midstream and downstream, further perfected the integrated industrial pattern of this company. This company's oil and gas output of upstream, output of fertilizer, methanol, ethylene, natural gas power and others increased greatly than the previous year.

By the end of 2009, CNOOC Ltd. under CNOOC had had total net proven reserves of 2.66 billion barrels of oil equivalent.

In 2009, CNOOC made total 15 new discoveries through self-run exploration in Chinese sea areas, and successfully evaluated 11 oil and gas structures; made two new discoveries through cooperative exploration, and successfully evaluated one oil and gas structure.

In 2009, CNOOC made new breakthrough in deep-water exploration, newly discovered natural gas in Liuhua 34-2 Gas Field, and successfully evaluated Liwan 3-1 Gas Field.

In addition, CNOOC obtained remarkable effects in the evaluation of Kenli 10-1 Structure; discovered multiple small oilfields around Wenchang Oilfield Cluster, as is promising to drive the overall development.

In 2009, CNOOC had more than 20 offshore oilfield projects under construction, and realized the punctual commencement of production in most newly constructed oil and gas fields and the advanced production of three new projects; successfully completed the annual production objective, achieved the net oil and gas output of 227.70 million barrels of oil equivalent, 17.2 percent up the same period of the previous year.

Abroad, CNOOC holds the equity of oil and gas blocks of Indonesia, Australia, Nigeria and other countries.

In order to further optimize the allocation of downstream resources of this company and propel the integrated strategy of upstream and downstream, CNOOC set up a refining and chemical division for the centralized management of oil refining, petrochemical, heavy oil utilization, petroleum and chemical products sales of this company.

In 2009, CNOOC Huizhou Oil Refinery Phase I Oil Refining Project with an annual production capacity of 12 million tons per year was put into production, ending the "no refining but exploitation only" history of CNOOC. CNOOC made outstanding achievements in heavy oil utilization and won the bid for Chang'an Street Reconstruction Project for the excellent quality of CNOOC 36-1 asphalt, and obtained more than 50 percent of asphalt sales volume; filled in domestic blank by newly-developed naphthenic base environment friendly highly-aromatic rubber oil, produced and sold 1,459 tons of rubber oil, and realized industrialized production of rubber oil. Original differential products reached large scale, thereof the annual production and sales volume of "50 asphalt" was up to 48,000 tons, 79 percent up than the previous year. CNOOC became the largest "50 asphalt" producer and supplier in China; the varieties of commercial asphalt increased from 6 to 10.

In 2009, CNOOC achieved the physical goods sales and trading volume of 19.24 million tons, and gained the sales income of RMB 70.70 billion, successfully breaking through the barrier of petroleum products market. By the end of 2009, CNOOC had had affiliates in 23 key domestic cities including Beijing, Shanghai, Tianjin, Guangzhou and Wuhan, overseas institutions in Hong Kong, total 208 gas stations with the reservoir capacity of 900,000 m^3 and 28 oil depots in North China.

On September 7, 2009, CNOOC reorganized Shandong Haihua Group Co., Ltd., and held 51 percent of its shares. Shandong Haihua Group Co., Ltd., founded in mid-1990s, was a large state-owned enterprise integrating coal chemical, salt chemical and petrochemical and mainly developing rising ocean chemical industries.

第三节 练习题

1.

We will unswervingly implement the principle of "One Country, Two Systems," under which the people of Hong Kong administer Hong Kong, and the people of Macao administer Macao, both with a high degree of autonomy, and fully support Hong Kong and Macao in maintaining long-term prosperity and stability. We will support Hong Kong in consolidating and elevating its position as an international financial, trade, and shipping center, developing industries with local advantages, and fostering new areas of economic growth. We will support Macao in developing its tourism and leisure industry and appropriately diversifying its economy. We will conscientiously implement the Outline of the Program for Reform and Development of the Pearl River Delta, vigorously promote the construction of the Hong Kong-Zhuhai-Macao Bridge and other major cross-boundary infrastructure projects as well as the development of Zhuhai's Hengqin Island, deepen cooperation between Guangdong and Hong Kong and Macao regions, and increase economic ties between the mainland and these two regions. The great motherland will remain a staunch supporter of Hong Kong and Macao forever. As long as the governments of Hong Kong and Macao special administrative regions and their people from all walks of life work together, accommodate and help each other, and jointly safeguard overall prosperity, stability, and development, Hong Kong and Macao will enjoy a brighter future.

Last year relations between the two sides of the Taiwan Straits made important progress from a historic new starting point, and a positive trend toward peaceful development emerged. Cross-Straits exchanges and cooperation constantly deepened, and complete, direct, two-way mail, transport and trade links were established. We took important steps to normalize cross-Straits economic relations, and economic cooperation between the two sides gradually became institutionalized. The constant improvement and development of cross-Straits relations brought real benefits to our compatriots on both sides. In the new year, we will continue to adhere to the principle of developing cross-Straits relations and promoting peaceful reunification of the motherland, firmly embrace the theme of peaceful development of cross-Straits relations and constantly create new conditions for it. We will strengthen economic, trade, and financial contacts between the two sides; deepen industrial cooperation; support the development of Taiwan-funded enterprises on the mainland; and safeguard the lawful rights and interests of our Taiwan compatriots. We will encourage qualified mainland enterprises to invest in Taiwan. We will support the economic zone in Fujian Province on the west coast of the Straits in playing its role in pioneering new approaches to exchanges and cooperation between the two sides. We will promote a win-win situation, set up an economic cooperation mechanism that reflects the characteristics of both sides by negotiating and signing an economic cooperation framework agreement (ECFA). We will expand cultural and educational exchanges, and work with Taiwan to promote Chinese culture. We will increase exchanges between people from all sectors of society on both sides, so that everyone can share in the fruits of the peaceful development of cross-Straits relations and more fully realize the importance of promoting peaceful development. We will uphold the principle that the mainland and Taiwan belong to one and the same China, strengthen the political foundation for the peaceful development of cross-Straits relations, and enhance mutual political trust between the two sides. We firmly believe that with the concerted efforts of the Chinese people, we will achieve the complete reunification of the motherland.

2.

The two sides reviewed the long-standing serious disputes between China and the United States. The Chinese side reaffirmed its position: the Taiwan question is the crucial question obstructing the normalization of relations between China and the United States; the Government of the People's Republic of China is the sole legal government of China; Taiwan is a province of China which has long been returned to the motherland; the liberation of Taiwan is China's internal affair in which no other country has the right to interfere; and all U.S. forces and military installations must be withdrawn from Taiwan. The Chinese Government firmly opposes any activities which aim at the creation of "one China, one Taiwan," "one China, two governments," "two Chinas," an "independent Taiwan" or advocate that "the status of Taiwan remains to be determined."

The U.S. side declared: The United States acknowledges that all Chinese on either side of the Taiwan Straits maintain there is but one China and that Taiwan is a part of China. The United States Government does not challenge that position. It reaffirms its interest in a peaceful settlement of the Taiwan question by the Chinese themselves. With this prospect in mind, it affirms the ultimate objective of the withdrawal of all U.S. forces and military installations from Taiwan. In the meantime, it will progressively reduce its forces and military installations on Taiwan as the tension in the area diminishes. The two sides agreed that it is desirable to broaden the understanding between the two peoples.

第四节　练习题

1.

Expert Committee for World Tourism Cities Federation

Draft Charter for Consideration and Amendments

Chapter One　General Provisions

Article One

Expert Committee for World Tourism Cities Federation (hereinafter referred to as Expert Committee or EC) aims to boost the scientific development of international tourism. Authorized by World Tourism Cities Federation (hereinafter referred to as the Federation), EC is designed to raise the academic and democratic level of the Federation with more suggestions from experts and scholars in the tourism field through scientific researches, personnel training, academic exchanges, etc.

Article Two

As the senior advisory body and think tank of the Federation, EC shall organize its activities with the authorization of the Federation.

Article Three

EC shall play its role with integrity, creativity and scientific rigor.

Chapter Two　Duties

Article Four

With the authorization of the Federation and research center, EC will:

1. Make suggestions and comments on development plans and policy papers on big issues of the Federation.
2. Strengthen communications between the Federation and government, enterprises, consultancies in member countries, as well as encouraging international cooperation and conferences both inside and outside the industry.
3. Track and study the hot issues on the development of international tourism and member cities, as well as making investigations, judgment and suggestions with the authorization of the Federation.
4. Host forums and academic salons to talk about major issues like tourism theories and practice, policies, laws and regulations, in order to make suggestions to member cities on their development.
5. Offer advice and help to member cities in their academic researches with the authorization of the Federation.
6. Make comments on some standards of the evaluation index system of the social development

level in member cities, and propose scientific advice before revising and reviewing them.

7. Offer the latest researches to electronic or printed publications of the Federation.
8. Undertake other work assigned by the Federation and the research center.

Chapter Three Structure and Members

Article Five

EC consists of 1 chairman, 2 vice-chairmen (one Chinese expert and one expatriate expert), several other members, and 1 academic secretary. The Chinese vice-chairman shall be responsible for the overall work of EC.

Article Six

EC has a Secretariat, which handles its day-to-day work, information communication and coordination work.

Chapter Four Selection of Staff Members

Article Seven

EC is made up of a group of prestigious, responsible scholars with high academic level, experts with rich experience of tourism, as well as the brightest mind in the field. They are recommended by universities, scientific institutions, the Federation and the tourism system. Those approved get appoint letters from the Federation and their profiles are posted on the official website of the Federation.

Article Eight

An EC member shall meet the following requirements:

1. Having integrity, ambition, and a good sense of responsibility, as well as acting in accordance with his professional ethics;
2. Having high qualification in terms of professional knowledge and social qualification in the tourism field;
3. Having extensive theoretical and practical expertise and wide experience in tourism, as well as judgment and analytical abilities;
4. Having a fit body and be able to complete the tasks undertaken;
5. Fulfilling other conditions of EC.

Article Nine

The first EC members shall be selected through consultations held by the initiators and experts of the committee before being employed directly by EC for a 5-year term. Upon expiration of a term, an expert could renew his or her term according to the need of EC on a voluntary basis.

Article Ten

The term of office of EC shall be five years, and it could be renewed.

Article Eleven

If an EC member is considered unsuitable for the post by his employer or by himself, he shall submit a written application to the Secretariat in order to stay on.

Article Twelve

EC members violating laws, regulations or this charter, or members with more than three unexcused absences from the activities of EC in a year, shall be fired by the Secretariat in written form.

Article Thirteen

The restructuring of EC is allowed with the permission of the Secretariat.

Chapter Five Membership Rights and Responsibilities

Article Fourteen Rights of EC Members:

EC members have the following rights:

1. To participate in activities held by EC, to have priority to access public documents like the annual report of the Federation, and information, materials, statistics provides by the research center;
2. To have free access to briefings, electronic journals, magazines published by the Federation and research center according to need;
3. To participate in academic conferences, exchanges at home and abroad, and publish papers as a EC member;
4. To get documents, materials, statistics and background information related to his or her work; to have priority to attend related academic conferences organized by the Federation or the research center;
5. To fully voice or reserve his or her opinions in consultation and evaluation;
6. To make advice for the Federation and EC;
7. Other rights vested by the Federation.

Article Fifteen Obligations of EC members:

EC members have the following obligations:

1. To abide by related laws and regulations, as well as regulations and stipulations by the EC;
2. To take an active part in consultation, judgment, academic seminars, and to finish his or her work on time;
3. To provide EC and the Federation with related information and updates, as well as suggestions;
4. To keep work rules and guard work secrets, without authorization. An EC member should not

leak statistics, documents related to Federation like research tendency, research results and annual reports;

5. Not to engage in commercial activities in the name of the Federation and EC without authorization of the Secretariat and the research center.

Chapter Six Management

Article Sixteen

The Federation shall finance EC on its operation, and the Secretariat shall offer to build working environment for EC and grant to its members.

Article Seventeen

The Annual General Meeting of EC shall deal with global tourism development strategy and tendency, comment on the development index of world tourism cities, hear the annual work report and plan of EC, and study on important issues of EC.

Article Eighteen

EC members could hold impromptu meetings if necessary.

Article Nineteen

EC shall preside over expert seminars occasionally to make investigations, share feedbacks and consultations on projects authorized by the Federation.

Article Twenty

EC shall offer consultation and suggestions by using a collective decision-making process.

Article Twenty One

EC members making great contribution to the development of the Federation and scientific researches on tourism will be invited to the Annual General Meeting after being nominated by the chairman and approved by the Secretariat and EC. Besides, he or she will be awarded, and his work unit will be informed of this.

Chapter Seven Supplementary Articles

Article Twenty-two

This charter was passed by all the members of EC, and it shall come into force the day it is issued by the World Tourism Cities Federation

Article Twenty-three

For the amendment of this charter, a two thirds majority of EC members is required.

Article Twenty-four

The power of interpretation of this charter shall be vested in the World Tourism Cities Federation.

第五节　练习题

1.

Traditional Department Stores: the "Disappearing Industry"?

According to statistics, the total transactions of China's e-commerce market hit RMB 7 trillion in 2011, with an annual increase of 46.4% compared to the previous year. The achievements of the e-commerce have posed a great challenge to the market share of traditional department store industry. Given no substantial change in demand for the short term, the fact that a growing number of people go online shopping means the corresponding customer loss for the department stores. Insiders said that the categories in the department store industry with considerable sale decline in recent years were precisely those convenient to purchase online, such as household electrical appliances, IT products, textiles, and even luxury goods.

At the same time, some traditional department stores also face the embarrassment of being reduced to the "fitting room" for e-commerce. Many people go to the stores to choose the style and size of clothes and other products, and then purchase them online, which gives birth to the so-called "number-copying clan" and "secret-photographing clan." With the expansion of online market, clothes, cosmetics, household products and other items have all been embraced into online shopping, where consumers select products at stores and buy online.

E-commerce's occupation of the market aside, intense competition within the industry, which has resulted from serious homogenization among traditional department stores, cannot be underestimated either. Besides, recent years have witnessed a surging wave of building shopping centers and malls by a large number of cities across the country, which adds to the difficulty in operating department stores given the already fierce competition. Almost all the department stores in the commercial blocks present quite similar sale contents, store design and product layout. According to a Ph.D. candidate, the shopping malls of different cities from Beijing to Fuzhou share much resemblance.

Under both internal and external pressure, will the traditional department stores become the next "disappearing industry"? Several experts interviewed have said that although the traditional department store industry is facing huge pressure from competition, it does stand a chance. By virtue of the integration of online and offline sale, differentiation competition and business mode innovation, the department store industry may successfully "counter-attack."

It is learnt that a considerable number of department stores have "gone online." Since 2012, many large department stores in Beijing have successively launched their online e-commerce platforms. The e-commerce of Tianjin Department Store is currently under implementation as well.

Meanwhile, department stores should follow the strategy of differentiated management and marketing in line with target customers. As a Ph.D. supervisor emphasized, although in recent years department stores faced increasingly severe business environment and intense competition from e-commerce and large commercial complexes, they lost only a portion of their customers. Department stores should further cultivate their current customer group, improve after-sale services and explore personalized service for customers.

In addition, traditional department stores should take advantage of the momentum of shopping center for transition. It is learnt that there is a correspondence law between the structure of retail industry and per capita GDP. The per capita GDP of $3,000–$5,000 corresponds to large-scale comprehensive supermarkets mainly, while per capita GDP of $5,000–$10,000 corresponds to shopping centers, franchised stores, specialty stores, and convenience stores. As China's per capita GDP has surpassed $5,000 in 2011, traditional department stores should seize the opportunity to transform themselves into shopping centers or other forms.

第六节　练习题

1.

It was in 1965 that nighttime began to stir in me a nameless dread. I am thinking how of that evening when a light rain drifted down. In my bed I lay, a child so little you could have set me there as easily as a toy. The dripping from the eaves simply called attention to the silence that surrounded me, and the steady onset of sleep was but a gradual forgetting of the rain's patter. As I glided peacefully into slumber, it was as though a secluded path had appeared before me, opening a passage between trees and shrubs. Then from far away there came the sound of a woman's anguished wails. When those hoarse cries erupted so suddenly in the still of the night, the boy that I was then shivered and quaked.

I can see myself now, a startled child, eyes wide with fear, the precise outline of my face obscured by the darkness. The woman's cries persisted. Anxiously, I expected to hear another voice, a voice that would respond to her wails, that could assuage her grief, but it never materialized. I realize how why I was gripped by such intense disquiet: it was because I waited in vain for that answering voice. Surely there is nothing more chilling than the sound of inconsolable cries on such a desolate night.

A second memory comes hot on the heels of the first: three or four white lambs trotting across the grass by the riverside, a daytime image, a way of easing the agitation evoked by the previous memory. But I find it hard to decide just where I was when this sight left its mark on me.

Several days may have passed before I seemed to hear a voice that answered the woman's cries. It was late afternoon. A storm had just passed, and dark clouds filled the sky like billows of smoke. I was sitting by the pond behind the house, and out of the damp landscape a man I did not recognize walked toward me. He was dressed completely in black and as he approached his dark clothes waved like a banner under the gloomy sky. When this image began to close in on me it brought to mind the unmistakable sound of the woman's cries. Even from far off in the distance the stranger fixed me with a piercing gaze, and he continued to stare at me as he drew nearer. Just as I was about to panic, he abruptly changed direction, mounted the path on the edge of the field, and gradually moved farther and farther away, his loose black clothes flapping loudly in the breeze. Now, when I look back on the past from an adult point of view, I always linger long on this particular moment, puzzling over why it was that I interpreted the rustling of his clothes as a response to the woman's cries in the evening drizzle.

第四章　汉英翻译的主要策略

第一节　练习题

1. China was among the first in the world to see the economic turnaround.
   rebound（recovery 与经济衰退关系更密，不符合中国的经济；slowdown、turnaround 更好）
2. up 9.8% and 8.5% respectively in real terms
3. affordable housing
4. maintain social order（social order 指的是社会等级，社会结构）
5. the Internet of Things
6. strengthen the common cultural bond 或 common cultural identity（Not: build a home of spirit shared by the whole Chinese nation）
7. the practice of democracy in international relations
8. He had a scratch yesterday and has gone to change dressing in the hospital.
   不是 He had a scratch yesterday and has gone to change medicine in the hospital.
9. proactive fiscal policy; make effective use of overseas resources
10. expire, pass away, end one's day, breathe one's last, pay the debt of nature, depart to the world of nature, kick the bucket, kick up one's heels
11. They preach taking from others, whereas we advocate giving to others.
12. In fact, middle age represents the prime of life, allowing no indolence, no self-indulgence.
    （Not: In fact, middle age represents the prime of life, allowing no indolence, no enjoyment.）
13. strong tea, thick soup, dense smoke
14. rob Peter to pay Paul
15. housing project for low-income residents
16. Eight Dos and Eight Don'ts
17. top priority

18. combat the global economic slump
19. issue IOU, crack down on counterfeit goods, punch machine, speak frankly, squealer, play one's trump card

第二节 练习题

1. solo concert
2. environment-friendly battery
3. democracy at the grassroots level
4. iron out differences
5. floorage floor space
6. give special favor
7.
   1) The Chinese people and the Chinese People's Liberation Army have defeated imperialist and hegemonist aggression, sabotage and armed provocations.
   2) This incident has seriously disrupted public order and normal life in Lhasa and the incident has also inflicted heavy losses of lives and property for the people in Lhasa.
   3) They left no stone unturned to undermine social stability in China, slandering and damaging the image of China, disturbing the State heads' visits to foreign countries and harming the safety of our nation's territory and sovereignty.
   4) The socialist system is the basic system of the People's Republic of China. Disruption of the socialist system by any organization or individual is prohibited.
   5) If the leaders of the United States choose to meet with the 14th Dalai Lama at this point of time, it would inevitably threaten the trust and cooperation between the two countries.
   6) The state ensures the rational use of natural resources and protects rare animals and plants. Appropriation or damaging of natural resources by any organization or individual by whatever means is prohibited.
   7) More and more Tibetans, me included, think the 14th Dalai Lama is not a pure religious leader. Under the cloak of religion, he is the head of a political group who has long been working to tear Tibet from the motherland and violate national unity.
8.
   1) a man of indomitable spirit
   2) He is a man full of adventure.
   3) Tom is a man of great enterprise.
   4) She had neither Clyde's force, nor, on the other hand, his resistance.
   5) He is adorable for his devotion to science.

6) A doctor certified to his insanity.
7) After his vacation he was in fine condition both physically and mentally.
8) After the car accident, she seemed to have fallen to pieces.

9. make a fortune
lose one's temper
dispatch a car
generate electricity
serve a ball
launch an attack
raise a question

10. Chinese cabbage (Not: white cabbage), password (Not: secret code), to fight a fire (Not: to save a fire) , puppy love (Not: early love), Buy one, get one for free. (Not: Buy one, present one.), acne (Not: youth spot), zoom lens (Not: long lens), instant noodles (Not: convenience noodles), contact lens (Not: invisible glasses)

11. artificial flower (Not: false flower), lip-synch (Not: false singing), counterfeit money (Not: false money), adulterated wine (Not: false wine), pseudo-news (Not: false news)

12. work wonders (Not: create wonders)
answer a telephone (Not: receive a telephone)
stimulate consumption (Not: pull consumption)
have one's opinion (Not: hear one's opinion)

13. They are the mainstay of our work today.
(Not: They are the important basis of our work today.)
We can safely predict.
(Not: We can completely predict.)
We must guard against rashness.

14. cocks crow
deer bellow
dogs bark
goats bleat
lions roar
tigers growl
wolves howl
horses neigh
elephants trumpet
cranes whoop

bears/bulls bellow
snakes hiss
frogs croak
magpies chatter
gooses cackle/ gaggle
nightingales jug
chicks cheep/ pip/ peep
mice squeak
asses/donkeys bray
sparrows twitter /chirp/ chirrup
cats miaow /mew/purr

15. I could read his mind.
He spotted her weak points.
16. non-freezing port /ice-free port
cold-food meal buffet
circulating capital /working capital
17. an infamous robber
a swindler
on the decline
18. impudent
improve the standards of living（Not: raise the level of the lives of the people）
19. museum, library, hotel, embassy, consulate, tea house, restaurant, barber's shop, gymnasium, exhibition hall, cultural center, art gallery, science and technology center, planerarium, photo studio

第三节　练习题

1. This thesis leaves much to be desired.
2. A measure of calm gave signs of returning after the flood subsided.
3. We can not ignore our neighbours; only at our peril can we ignore their distress.
4. Unemployment is widespread in some countries.
5. The employers there used violence.
6. Mary spoke with restraint in her face.
7. All peace-loving people demand the complete prohibition and thorough destruction of nuclear weapons.
8. A commitment to respect human rights that was not accompanied by international control

constituted a half measure.
9. The sight and sound of our jet planes filled me with special longing.
10. A great cloud rose from the ground and followed the trial of the great sun. At first it was a giant column, which soon took the shape of a supramundane mushroom. For a fleeting instant it took the form of the Statue of Liberty magnified many times.
11. Aggression took many forms: the unilateral denunciation of treaties and international commitments, interference in the internal affairs of other states, the use of threats against weaker neighbours, the imposition of unequal relationships, outright armed attack against the territories of other states and their dismemberment, the subjugation of colonial peoples and the denial of the right of self-determination and fundamental human rights.
12. In China's approach to relations with other countries, we find a welcome emphasis on principles of the equality of states and respect for the rights and views of small and middle powers.
13. Capitalist countries as a rule built up their heavy industry with funds obtained from abroad, whether by colonial plunder, or by exacting indemnities from vanquished nations, or else by foreign loans.
14. For that, use is generally made of correction motors which in the present state of the technique are complicated, very expensive and often do not give complete satisfaction.
15. They are striving for the ideal which is close to the heart of every Chinese and for which, in the past, many Chinese have laid down their lives.
16. A country that wishes to become a member of the WTO is to send its application before a working party is formed by the WTO for examination of the specific conditions of the country.
17. We know that a cat, whose eyes can take in many more rays of light than our eyes, can see clearly in the night.
18. We must just make the best of things as they come along.
19. Shaking with cold and anger, I climbed inside the train.
20. I have sometimes been led actually to change my mind as a result of this kind of imaginary dialogue.
21. Einstein's equations indicated that when a star several times larger than the Sun exhausts its nuclear fuel and collapses, its matter crushes together at its center with such force that it forms a singularity, an infinitely dense point with no dimensions and irresistible gravity.
22. Although experienced diplomats do not often share the popular skepticism about international law, there is a danger that the popular attitude may affect inexperienced officials and pressure groups within a state, and that the state may, as a result, be pushed into breaking

international law.

23. The election which has led to your being chosen to preside over this Assembly—a very wise choice indeed—is a tribute to your great country, which has contributed to the development of the history of free nations a tradition of peace that serves as an example for the legal community that we constitute, a country which has always commanded respect and admiration from all corners of the world.

第四节　练习题

1. Preserving the Past —High Street Bookshops Under Threat from E-commerce

Weed, a bookshop near Beijing Normal University, is closing down; Paper Tiger, a privately owned bookshop chain has also announced that it will be shutting down in the next three months; even Long Zhi Mei, the biggest advertising bookshop in China, has declared that it is going to close three of its bookshops at the end of the year.

High street bookshops are considered cultural landmarks and representative of urban culture in China and with them closing down one after another, their survival has once again become the focus of people's attention. How long can they hold out and what should they do in order to survive? Many people lament that China's high street bookshops, when faced with competition from low-cost online retailers such as Dangdang, JD, and Amazon, will collectively experience a winter of hardship. Some people even think that there is no longer a need for high street bookshops to exist.

Despite the increasingly difficult times experienced by high street bookshops, people still believe that they can never be replaced by online or virtual bookshops. "A city is never complete without its libraries, bookshops and newsstands. Although high street bookshops face competition from e-books and online bookshops, it doesn't mean they will disappear," said Professor Wan Yuguan, Head of Information Management Department of Peking University.

All Sages, a high street bookshop, has competed successfully with online bookshops. The secret to its survival in the electronic age lies in its choice of store location, product range and adoption of customer-based marketing strategy. Being close to Peking University, Tsinghua University and other prestigious Chinese universities and the Zhongguancun High-tech Park, the bookshop mainly sells books to university students, teachers and top white-collar workers in the IT and finance sectors. It even sells books online, complementing its high street activities, and this is a model that is being adopted by more and more bookshops. In addition, some bookshops have incorporated coffee shops, or have become "cultural salons." BELENCRE or "Between the Lines" is a fast developing bookshop that has adopted both models.

Most bookshops, however, are not so "lucky" and "visionary." The convenience of downloading and reading e-books, together with the substantial discounts offered by online bookshops mean that buying books online has become more and more popular among young people. The closure of a large number of high street bookshops reflects the current plight of private bookshops as a whole.

To date, there has been increasing support to save the high street bookshops, from the government as well as ordinary citizens. Insiders suggest that the Chinese government should establish a medium- and long-term plan for the development of high street bookshops. A short-term solution is to support their businesses through financial subsidies and government funding; in the long run, tax incentives and pricing regulations should be implemented to improve profitability and promote fair competition.

Although supportive government policies are essential for the survival and development of high street bookshops, it is more important for them to identify their own unique business models. As an important part of the national economy, the cultural industries will eventually improve along with the restructuring of the national economy. The protection of high street bookshops, representative of urban culture, is a sign of the healthy development of culture and its associated businesses.

2. Tips on Travelling to China the First Time

1) Which cities are preferable for tourists to visit on their first trip to China?

What you see depends how long you can stay in China. Generally speaking, tourists should first visit cities like Beijing, Shanghai and Xi'an.

Beijing is a political and cultural center that offers some scenic attractions: Badaling which is a part of the spectacular Great Wall; Gugong (Imperial Palace) where emperors of the Ming and Qing Dynasties lived; Yiheyuan (Summer Palace) which is an imperial garden of the Qing Dynasty; and Beihai, also an imperial garden used by successive emperors in the Yuan, Ming and Qing Dynasties. There is more to Beijing than buildings. Foods such as authentic Beijing roastduck and instant-boiled mutton have proved popular with tourists as well.

Shanghai, a shopping center for best buys, is the largest city in China. Tourists will be satisfied with what the city supplies, from various snacks and cakes to handicrafts and textiles. Neighboring Suzhou and Hangzhou, only a couple of hours away from Shanghai by train, are two garden cities, each considered by Chinese to be "paradise on earth."

Xi'an, the starting point of the ancient Silk Road, was capital intermittently for many dynasties in the Chinese history. The life-size terra cotta soldiers and horses of the Qin Dynasty (221 B.C.–206 B.C.), unearthed recently, are praised as the "Eighth Wonder of the World." Other interesting sites in the vicinity are Dayan Ta (Great Wild Goose Pagoda) and Gu Lou (Drum

Tower), both erected in the Tang Dynasty; and the Huaqing Hot Springs where visitors may bathe in the warm mineral water. This site used to be the private baths for Yang Guifei, the favorite concubine of the Tang Emperor. If you are of Chinese descent, you may pay tribute to the tomb of Huangdi (Yellow Emperor), the first Chinese emperor. In addition, tourists will enjoy the pleasing Tang music and dance, as well as the duplication of fancy Tang dishes available there.

2) When is the best time for the trip? Where are the best places available in winter?

China is a vast land with great contrasts in landscape and climate. Consequently, tourists may pay a visit anytime. Spring and autumn are supposed to be the best times to tour cities like Beijing, Shanghai and Xi'an.

If you dislike the cold, you can visit Kunming, "the Spring City", in South China, which is known for its year-round spring weather. A closer look takes you to the Stone Forest and the Dianchi Lake. You can also go to Xishuangbanna to enjoy subtropic scenery. Guilin in South China lies on the banks of the Lijiang River. Down-stream Yangshuo stands by. "Guilin has the most beautiful scenery in China, while Yangshuo is the most fascinating part of a Guilin tour," and so a tour of these cities will be a most rewarding experience for you. Harbin is particularly good for sightseeing in January and February. Those who have never seen any snow in Hong Kong or Macao may either view the ice festival or go skiing and skating in this world of snow.

3) What is well worth purchasing in China? Where are those things available?

China has won a worldwide reputation for handicrafts, silk, porcelain, carpets and textiles, all more reasonably priced and of greater variety than elsewhere in the world. Unique local creations are available in their own cities, such as Beijing's cloisonne and carpets, Shanghai's Chinese clothing and cotton textiles, Hangzhou's silk, Suzhou's antiques, and Xi'an's three-colored glazed pottery of the Tang Dynasty and terra cotta figures. If tourists are not able to reach these cities, most of these products can be purchased in the Friendship Stores in big cities like Beijing and Shanghai. These stores will also help you transport what you have bought. Some tourists who are keen on art may wish to buy antique objects we well as Chinese calligraphy and paintings. Be sure to get your receipts and an identification seal（a red wax seal）before you go through the Chinese customs.（何志范 译）

3. Chinese Banks Record Better First-half-year Performance

Chinese banks have again produced sparkling results, though they were unable to dispel concerns that their good fortune might yet turn to trouble because of non-performing loans and a slowing economy.

While western banks are slashing jobs as they struggle to get past the global financial crisis, their Chinese counterparts signalled that they would continue to expand aggressively at home and slowly build their global influence.

The story for much of the past year has been the divergence between Chinese banks' record results and the unshakeable doubts in the market that the bill for their past lending excesses has yet to come due.

China's four biggest lenders reported this week. The Agricultural Bank of China saw a 45 percent rise in first-half net profit. The Bank of China was the slowest, with a 28 percent increase. The Industrial and Commercial Bank of China, the world's biggest bank by market value, said profit was up 29 percent, while profits at the China Construction Bank, the country's second-largest lender, rose 31 percent. The banks' shares have been flattish on the week and down heavily on the year, as investors appeared to focus on the cracks in the foundations of the banks' success.

Worries continue to center on the surge in lending in China since late 2008, when Beijing used the banks—all of which are state-controlled—to lead a credit-fuelled stimulus for the economy. The risks of that approach have started to show in recent months as officials have tried to account for the loans given to local governments—about RMB 10,700 billion (USD 1,650 billion), according to the national audit office—and estimate how many might end up in default.

The banks used their first-half results to give the most thorough picture yet of the potential problem loans. Bank of China said it had given RMB 532 billion of loans to local government financing vehicles, 40 percent more than it had declared at the end of 2010, having reclassified a large number of corporate loans as government loans.

But the banks also tried to reassure about the health of these loans and their readiness for defaults. CCB said 84 percent of its loans to local governments were covered by cash flow and exceeded regulatory requirements. Guo Shuqing, CCB chairman, said he saw no need to raise more equity.

At the Bank of China, Li Lihui, the president, said provisions had been made for 217 percent of bad loans—also well above regulatory requirements.

However, May Yan, head of China banks research with Barclays Capital, said, "It's a trust issue in the reliability of the banks' due diligence and reporting. It looks like the impact [of the loans to governments] may not be big, but it is dubious how they estimate cash flow."

图书在版编目（CIP）数据

新编汉英翻译教程 / 武光军编著. —北京：中国人民大学出版社，2018. 6
大学高级英语系列教材　英语专业研究型系列教材
ISBN 978-7-300-25710-5

Ⅰ. ①新…　Ⅱ. ①武…　Ⅲ. ①英语-翻译-高等学校-教材　Ⅳ. ①H315.9

中国版本图书馆 CIP 数据核字（2018）第 068457 号

大学高级英语系列教材
英语专业研究型系列教材
总主编　武光军
新编汉英翻译教程
武光军　编　著
Xinbian Hanying Fanyi Jiaocheng

出版发行	中国人民大学出版社		
社　　址	北京中关村大街 31 号	邮政编码	100080
电　　话	010–62511242（总编室）		010–62511770（质管部）
	010–82501766（邮购部）		010–62514148（门市部）
	010–62515195（发行公司）		010–62515275（盗版举报）
网　　址	http:// www. crup. com. cn		
	http:// www. ttrnet. com（人大教研网）		
经　　销	新华书店		
印　　刷	北京鑫丰华彩印有限公司		
规　　格	185 mm × 240 mm　16 开本	版　　次	2018 年 6 月第 1 版
印　　张	16	印　　次	2018 年 6 月第 1 次印刷
字　　数	335 000	定　　价	36.00 元

中国人民大学出版社外语出版分社读者信息反馈表

尊敬的读者：

感谢您购买和使用中国人民大学出版社外语出版分社的 ____________ 一书，我们希望通过这张小小的反馈卡来获得您更多的建议和意见，以改进我们的工作，加强我们双方的沟通和联系。我们期待着能为更多的读者提供更多的好书。

请您填妥下表后，寄回或传真回复我们，对您的支持我们不胜感激！

1. 您是从何种途径得知本书的：

☐书店　　☐网上　　☐报纸杂志　　☐朋友推荐

2. 您为什么决定购买本书：

☐工作需要　　☐学习参考　　☐对本书主题感兴趣　　☐随便翻翻

3. 您对本书内容的评价是：

☐很好　　☐好　　☐一般　　☐差　　☐很差

4. 您在阅读本书的过程中有没有发现明显的专业及编校错误，如果有，它们是：

____

____

____

5. 您对哪些专业的图书信息比较感兴趣：

____

____

____

6. 如果方便，请提供您的个人信息，以便于我们和您联系（您的个人资料我们将严格保密）：

您供职的单位：______________________________

您教授的课程（教师填写）：______________________

您的通信地址：______________________________

您的电子邮箱：______________________________

请联系我们：贾乐凯　黄婷　程子殊　于真妮　鞠方安

电话：010-62515580，62512737，62513265，62515037，62515576

传真：010-62514961

E-mail：jialk@crup.com.cn　huangt@crup.com.cn　chengzsh@crup.com.cn
yuzn@crup.com.cn　jufa@crup.com.cn

通信地址：北京市海淀区中关村大街甲 59 号文化大厦 15 层　　邮编：100872

中国人民大学出版社外语出版分社